Imagining Lives

Imagining Lives

Autobiographical Fiction
of Yiddish Writers

Jan Schwarz

THE UNIVERSITY OF WISCONSIN PRESS

The University of Wisconsin Press
1930 Monroe Street
Madison, Wisconsin 53711

www.wisc.edu/wisconsinpress/

3 Henrietta Street
London WC2E 8LU, England

5   4   3   2   1

Printed in the United States of America

Library of Congress Cataloging-in-Publication Data
Schwarz, Jan, 1954–
    Imagining lives : autobiographical fiction of Yiddish writers /
    Jan Schwarz.
        p.   cm.
    Includes bibliographical references (p.) and index.
    ISBN 0-299-20960-1 (hardcover: alk. paper)
    1. Autobiographical fiction, Yiddish—History and criticism.
2. Yiddish literature—History and criticism.   3. Authors, Yiddish.
I. Title.
PJ5128.S39   2005
839´.13009—dc22   2004025718

This book was published with the generous support of the Koret
Foundation Jewish Studies Publications Program and the Chicago
YIVO Society.

For Rebecca

The individual mystery remains to tantalize the memoirist. Neither in environment nor in heredity can I find the exact instrument that fashioned me, the anonymous roller that pressed upon my life a certain intricate watermark, whose unique design becomes visible when the lamp of art is made to shine through life's foolscap.

Vladimir Nabokov, *Speak Memory: An Autobiography Revisited*

Contents

Acknowledgments

This book could not have been published without the generous subsidies provided by the Dorot Foundation of San Francisco and the YIVO Society of Chicago. I am very grateful to both organizations.

The Department of Germanic Languages and Literatures at the University of Illinois at Urbana-Champaign granted me release time from teaching during the fall semester of 2001. This enabled me to complete most of the manuscript. In particular, I would like to thank Professor Michael Polencia-Roth and Professor Karl-Heinz Schoeps, both of the University of Illinois, for their critical comments and support. I am grateful to Professors Paul Weichsel and Nils Jacobsen; their friendship became my anchor while I was serving as Assistant Professor at the University of Illinois.

The encouragement and inspiration of Professor David G. Roskies (Jewish Theological Seminary of America) introduced me to the field of Yiddish literature. He was particularly helpful as close reader of the doctoral dissertation at Columbia University (1997) on which this book is based. Professor Rakhmiel Peltz (Drexel University) guided me through the bread-and-butter of Yiddish scholarship with enthusiasm and high scholarly standards. I have also been privileged to work with the premier scholar of Yiddish literature in Israel, Professor Avrom Novershtern (Hebrew University). His encyclopedic knowledge of Yiddish literary history has been an invaluable help.

I am especially indebted to my dissertation advisor, Professor Dan Miron (Columbia University). He helped me to develop the concept for this book, while generously making available his wide knowledge of Yiddish literature in our many meetings over several years.

I would also like to thank Professors Janet Hadda (UCLA) and Seth Wolitz (University of Texas at Austin) for their unwavering support and, in particular, their incisive comments on the final drafts of the book.

As the Talmud teaches, I have learned much from my teachers and even more from my colleagues, but from my students I have learned most of all. My students in Yiddish language and literature at Gratz College (Philadelphia), the University of Illinois at Urbana-Champaign, the University of Illinois at Chicago, and at the University of Chicago and Northwestern University have taught me a great deal. They inspire me with their enthusiasm and inquisitive questions. In particular, I would like to thank Melissa Weininger, Ph.D. candidate in Jewish Literature, University of Chicago, for her compilation of the chronology of the writers' lives.

Of course, any errors contained in the book are mine alone.

The loving support of my wife, Rabbi Rebecca Lillian, sustained me throughout the writing of this book and the dissertation that preceded it. Her superb editorial skills allowed me to express my ideas in a foreign language. The book is dedicated to her with love.

Note on Transliteration

The transliteration of Yiddish follows the YIVO system, except for the personal names of some of the Jewish writers. In those cases, I have preferred to use the established English forms.

Imagining Lives

Introduction

In the absence of a living, struggling, singing, protesting Yiddish-speaking folk; in the absence of Yiddish schools, newspapers and political movements; in the absence of broad-based institutional support for the study of Yiddish—we, the scholars, can, if we so desire, recreate the landscapes of Yiddish by pursuing and mastering a rigorous mental curriculum.[1]

> David G. Roskies, "Yiddish Studies and the Jewish Search for a Usable Past"

Exile is strangely compelling to think about but terrible to experience. It is the unhealable rift forced between a human being and a native place, between the self and its true home: its essential sadness can never be surmounted. And while it is true that literature and history contain heroic, romantic, glorious, even triumphant episodes in an exile's life, these are no more than efforts meant to overcome the crippling sorrow of estrangement. The achievements of exile are permanently undermined by the loss of something left behind forever.[2]

> Edward W. Said, "Reflections on Exile"

This study examines the way in which Yiddish writers reconfigured the dominant autobiographical models in European and American literature by fusing them with Jewish content, sensibilities and literary modes. Among the many critical gaps in the field of Yiddish literature is the lack of a systematic study of the Yiddish literary autobiography. Ruth R. Wisse pointed out that "the field is still missing a good basic introduction to Yiddish literature and reliable critical biographies of almost all the major and minor writers. . . . Missing are studies in periodization, studies of literary groups, basic surveys of American Jewish literature, Russian Jewish literature, the Polish novel between the wars, the history of literary genres, and so forth. We don't have proper collected editions or bibliographies of most of the major writers, or the standard introductions that are basic for the orientation of every new student and class."[3]

The objective of this study is to fill one such critical lacuna by examining the Yiddish autobiography as an independent literary genre with its own artistic paradigms and history. Scholars of Yiddish literature noted long ago that the Yiddish literary autobiography exists as a separate genre consisting of works with a certain inter-textual continuity. However, they did not investigate this genre comprehensively and systematically. This study intends to do so by analyzing eight Yiddish literary autobiographies written by seven important Yiddish writers and published between 1894 and 1956. In addition to presenting close readings of these autobiographies and outlining the history of this literary genre, this study also seeks to highlight some general characteristics of twentieth-century Yiddish literature.

Writers as diverse as Sholem Yankev Abramovitsh, the "grandfather" of Yiddish literature, and Yankev Glatshteyn, co-founder in 1919 of the *inzikhistn*, a group of modernist poets in New York, initially viewed the autobiography as a problematic and inferior literary genre. Each turned to life-writing only in response to an urgent personal crisis. Such reticence to view the Yiddish autobiography as a legitimate literary genre is also reflected in the scant criticism on it. In fact, three of the works by Jonah Rosenfeld and Yankev Glatshteyn (whom I discuss in chapters 3 and 4), arguably the most original examples of Yiddish literary autobiographies in the twentieth century, were never examined beyond book reviews and a few critical articles. Even the autobiographical works of the classical trio—Abramovitsh, Sholem Aleichem, and I. L. Peretz (the subject of chapters 1 and 2)—and the two great masters of Yiddish prose after the Holocaust, Chaim Grade and Isaac Bashevis Singer (see chapter 5), have been analyzed only rarely as part of a literary genre. This study is the first systematic attempt to examine a body of Yiddish works that belong on the borderline between fiction and autobiography. These works' hybrid character enabled me to investigate questions of self, life history and literary art in Yiddish culture. In using Yiddish primary and secondary sources, I sought to reclaim a body of work doubly marginalized by being written in Yiddish and in a genre considered marginal in Yiddish literature.[4]

Critics have typically viewed Yiddish life-writing as artistically inferior to what they viewed as the canonical prose genres in Yiddish literature: the novel and the short story.[5] The notable exceptions, Glatshteyn's two Yash books, have been the object of recent interest after decades of critical neglect. The primary reason for this is the sophisticated modernist style of these works, which speaks to current critical sensibilities. As I discuss in chapter 4, however, it is emblematic that critical treatment of the Yash books essentially ignores their autobiographical character. In regard to the classical trio, critics have either viewed these writers' life-writing as the final examples of their novelistic art, artistically inferior to their earlier work (Abramovitsh and Sholem Aleichem), or as an important meta-poetic treatise of minor aesthetic and generic interest (Peretz). As a whole, the classical trio's life-writing has rarely been studied on its own as paradigmatic texts in the development of a distinct genre. The life-writing of Grade and Singer fare no better; little or no critical attention has been paid to how they rewrote the autobiographical paradigms created by the classical trio. More fruitful, I argue, is a critical approach that inquires into how the Yiddish autobiographers wrestled with European and American autobiographical models as they sought to describe their self-formation, life narrative and literary art.

The cultural, ideological and artistic paradigms that gave meaning to Yiddish literature during the flowering of Yiddish culture in the first half of the twentieth century hardly exist any more. Today, the Yiddish literary scholar is addressing an audience largely unfamiliar with the basic tenets of Yiddish culture. It is therefore left to scholars to provide the cultural vocabulary and critical perspectives in order to create meaning out of the often incomplete and disparate literary-historical material.[6] What propels the Yiddish scholar to do so is, in many ways, similar to what motivated Yiddish writers' turn to the autobiography. Like them, I was not interested in chronicling the minute details of time and place. Rather, I sought to map out the formal, narrative and stylistic methodologies through which the Yiddish autobiographers represented their life stories, in order to inscribe them in a meaningful cultural and historical context. Through the autobiographical journeys discussed in the chapters that follow, the century of the modern Jewish revolution (1882–1982) comes to life in the form of individual narratives woven into the matrix of the lost world of Eastern European Jewry.[7]

In David G. Roskies' words, "the absence of a living, struggling, singing, protesting Yiddish speaking folk" who used to read serialized fiction, life-writing and poetry in Yiddish newspapers and books must be the point of departure of any study of Yiddish literary history. Scholars of Yiddish literature are faced with the extra task of recreating a cultural landscape that no longer exists as part of a continuous, living literary tradition. Yiddish life-writing has become an icon of the lost world of Eastern European Jewry. Hopefully, this attempt to explore the richness of Yiddish life-writing as part of a once thriving Yiddish speaking folk's cultural self-expression—guiding it on its perplexing way from tradition to modernity—will provide today's reader with the tools to peel off the iconic veneer.[8]

The act of writing one's autobiography is often spurred by a growing consciousness of one's own mortality. Yiddish autobiography has the added feature of frequently addressing the possibility of collective mortality. The Yiddish autobiographer tells the story of his life as embedded in the broader context of a community and a culture lost to the forces of assimilation, emigration, war and the Holocaust. This link between individual and collective destiny is the most characteristic and compelling feature of the Yiddish autobiography. What prompted Yiddish writers' turn to life-writing as a viable artistic form was a combination of individual and collective ruptures. First of all, like literary autobiographers in other languages, Yiddish writers wanted to set the record straight by creating their own "official" version of their self-formation and artistic origins. However, except for Jonah Rosenfeld's *Eyner aleyn* (1940, All Alone) and I. B. Singer's extensive life-writing modeled more directly on the Rousseauian prototype, none of the other Yiddish life-writers were motivated by a similar quest for confessional self-justification. Instead, they subsumed their personal stories and selves in a Jewish collective way of life. As a rule, when Yiddish writers portrayed themselves they emphasized what they considered typical rather than uniquely individual. What propelled Yiddish life-writers was less the delineation of their inner selves in the Rousseauian mold than an attempt to return to an imagined time and place where self and collective were one. This strong desire to overcome what Yiddish writers experienced as an irreversible exile from their origins in the traditional Jewish *shtetl* situated their life-writing in the mainstream of Yiddish literature.

To help the reader maneuver through the conceptual thicket of the key terms used most frequently in connection with the topic of this book—confession, memoir, autobiography, autobiographical novel, autobiographical fiction and life-writing—I have used an instructive glossary. Compiler Donald J. Winslow points out that the term life-writing "has been used since the eighteenth century, although it has never been as widely current as biography and autobiography since these words came into the language."[9] The term autobiography was used for the first time in a British 1809 journal article.[10] Life-writing is the more inclusive term of the three; it includes autobiography, biography, autobiographical fiction, letters and diaries. There are at least three good reasons why the Anglo-Saxon rooted phrase, life-writing, is preferable to the Greek based word, autobiography.[11]

First, the term life-writing defines the area of inquiry in the broadest possible terms. This is especially useful in the introduction of a new area of research. Hopefully, this discussion of the Yiddish literary autobiography in prose will inspire others to investigate non-artistic memoirs, biographies, autobiographical poetry *(poeme)*[12] and epistolary writings. Secondly, life-writing corresponds to the Yiddish words *lebnsbashraybung* and *lebnsgeshikhte*. These words are frequently used as a generic subtitle in Yiddish autobiographies and in criticism originating in the German literary tradition (e.g., the subtitle of Sholem Aleichem's *Funem yarid*).[13] The writing of a life—*lebnsbashraybung*—is precisely what distinguishes Yiddish literary autobiographies from self-exploration and self-analysis. Thirdly, as pointed out by James Olney who introduced the area of autobiography studies in the U.S.: "For by whatever name we call the literature—autobiography, life-writing, or peri-autobiography—there exist a particularly intriguing kind of writing to be considered for which any one of the terms mentioned might be a fair enough designation, the crucial tactic, in my view, being not to insist on strict definitions and rigid lines of demarcation. I have always felt, and continue to feel, that it is best to think of what I am doing as exploratory in nature rather than definitive."[14] In a similar vein, this study is an exploratory and systematic examination of fictional forms of Yiddish life-writing in prose.

One of the most fundamental questions in criticism on life-writing is its use of fictional techniques in the construction of a life narrative. Two very different viewpoints characterize the range of criticism on this question.[15] Until the early 1970s most scholars approached it as a genre that reflects an extra-textual reality. As a result, life-writing was primarily viewed as a treasure trove of historical, cultural and social phenomena. Such a critical approach, which decodes life-writing as a repository of elements originating in an extra-textual reality, maintains that it is most frequently "nothing if not a referential art."[16] This view characterizes it as a nonfiction genre, a sub division of the biography ("self-biography") in which an autobiographer simply mirrors his life story.

A fundamentally different critical approach views life-writing as a literary genre that employs fictive techniques in the representation and creation of self and life story. Deconstructionists such as Paul de Man and Jacques Derrida have pointed out that all texts and, in fact, language itself is figurative because it unavoidably partakes in a fiction-making process. The way an autobiographer selects and creates the facts of his life and self is governed by the resources of the medium and the author's particular use of language. According to de Man, "Autobiography . . . is not a genre or a mode, but a figure of reading or of understanding that occurs to some degree, in all texts."[17] This mode is a universal textual feature and "the distinction between fiction and autobiography is not an either/or polarity but . . . it is un-decidable."[18]

In a historical context, Karl J. Weintraub argues that beginning around 1800, there emerged "the particular modern form of historical mindedness we call historism or historicism."[19] The autobiographer became an historian of the self, and the origin of the modern autobiography is conditioned by a historicist approach in which the present superimposes itself on the past. The term "autobiography" first appeared in 1809, signifying a fundamentally new way of thinking about the self and the increasing importance "of subjectivity as a normative and critical concept."[20] This new paradigm of the self belonged to the Romantic Era, the age of the personality. Most of what we call classical autobiographies was written in this period, which also gave rise to Herder and Goethe's grandiose idea of collating the "confessions of all ages" as an expression of the historical evolution of mankind.[21]

Prior to this period, the idea of the individual was linked, with a few exceptions, to a limited set of typified models of the self.[22] The individual was seen as representative of these cultural models, but did not exist independently of them. The idea of the ineffable individual was a product of the Emancipation and the Romantic Era which transformed the autobiographical act into an unparalleled quest echoed in Rousseau's famous introduction to his *Confessions* (1781): "I have resolved on an enterprise which has no precedent, and which once complete, will have no imitator. My purpose is to display to my kind a portrait in every way true to nature, and the man I shall portray will be myself."[23] Truthfulness became an unstated assumption of the modern autobiography. But the discrepancy between the autobiographer at the moment of writing and his protagonist, his former selves in the past, made the status of this truth highly ambiguous. Rousseau's phrase "the man I shall portray" defined the autobiographer as a divided self, a narrating "I" and a narrated "I" or "he." This quest for truthfulness, with the full awareness of its problematic and constructed character, has character-ized life-writing since Rousseau's *Confessions*.

Life-writing employs fictive discourse, making it impossible to make true distinctions between fiction and autobiography from narrative and stylistic points of view. Only the point that the author, narrator and pro-tagonist must be identical qualifies a text as an autobiography. This view has been convincingly elaborated by Philippe Lejeune in his the-ory about the centrality of the proper name. Lejeune suggests that the autobiographer establishes a contract with the reader, which is sealed by the proper name. By signing a text with his or her own name, which is also that of the narrator and the protagonist, the author establishes an "autobiographical pact" with the reader.[24]

Lejeune has since modified this approach, originating in a legal contractual mind set, by making the point that the reader is free to adopt modes of reading that are different from the one that the autobiographer inscribed in his text. Life-writing belongs to a referential system because it refers to phenomena beyond the text, the truth of which is confirmed by the use of the proper name. But it also belongs to a literary system in which the mimetic method can be employed for fictive purposes. Philippe Lejeune and Elizabeth Bruss are the most distinguished repre-sentatives of this pragmatic approach to life-writing, which analyzes the author's use of speech acts and grammatical signs (such as the proper name) as crucial for reading a text as autobiography.[25]

This basic assumption about the figured character of the "I" is shared by most critics of especially twentieth-century autobiographies, which "readily accept the proposition that fictions and the fiction-making pro-cess is a central constituent of the truth of any life as it is lived and of any art devoted to the presentation of that life."[26] The autobiography's undecided status is programmatically expressed in the title of Goethe's seminal *Dichtung und Wahrheit* (1809–1831, Poetry and Truth), and echoed in one of the first important works of criticism about the genre, Roy Pascal's *Design and Truth in Autobiography* (1960). As Goethe men-tions in his introduction "the half poetic and half historical treatment"[27] of his life story encapsulates the autobiography's status in the gray zone between poetry and truth. The autobiography never fully inhabits either of these two realms, but uses this ambiguity as it's most distinc-tive and creative potential.

In his *Confessions*, Rousseau redefined the Augustinian confession by turning his life story into a novel in which the quest for his "true" self replaced Augustine's quest for God. As a result, Rousseau severed his self from any other purpose or context than that of its own being as beginning and ending point. The obsessive way in which Rousseau explored and exposed his self so "the trivial becomes important, the shameful natural, and the puerile praiseworthy"[28] turned this quest into a paradigmatic new way of literary self-expression. As James Olney argues, Rousseau's *Confessions* inaugurated a new genre in European literature which combined confessional and novelistic modes: "In taking his self for his subject, in attempting to render his subjectivity in characters on a page (characters in a dual sense), and making his self-feeling the center and circumference of the act of life-writing, Rousseau merged autobiography with the novel and wrote what could well be seen—what, indeed Rousseau did see, but without using these words—as both the definitive and the ultimate Romantic text."[29]

Philippe Lejeune characterizes the autobiography as a parasitic genre grafted unto the novel: "Autobiography is, in literary history, a secondary phenomenon, dependent upon already accepted novelistic writing."[30] As a rule, the Yiddish autobiographer builds on his previous novelistic creations in fashioning the story of his life. In the case of poets and short story writers, they invented narrative forms inspired by modernist fragmentation and fusion of styles and forms (Peretz, Rosenfeld and Glatshteyn) and the short story vignette (Grade and I. B. Singer). Although, Yiddish life-writing to a large extent is modeled on the bildungsroman, "the peculiar nature of Jewish literary history"[31] sets Yiddish life-writing apart from the major examples of the genre in European and American literature.

Yiddish was closely intertwined with Hebrew in traditional Jewish life, and came to serve different artistic purposes than Hebrew. In contrast to Hebrew's scriptural status as the written language of the intellectual elite, Yiddish as *mame-loshn*, the mother tongue, became an excellent vehicle for imitating the colloquial speech, irony, satire and folkways of the Jewish community including women, children, the elderly and the lower classes. Benjamin Harshav points out that because of the varying functions of Yiddish and Hebrew, which Max Weinreich called "the internal Jewish bilingualism," the origins of the Yiddish novel in the nineteenth century were not based on the realist bourgeois novel:

The ambivalent qualities of Yiddish were a perfect vehicle for conveying simultaneously the rich and authentic naive world view of "simple people" and the deeper metaphysical and pan-historical insights of a "fallen aristocracy." That is why the really great work of Jewish novelists was not in their imitations of the much-admired Russian Realist novel, but was achieved when they reached back to the pre-Realist stage of European literature (Gogol and Cervantes), or to the parallel line of satire, grotesque, and *skaz* (monologues characterizing their own speakers), and developed an almost surrealist concatenation of argument as the backbone of their fiction. For these forms, rather than for the bourgeois social novel, unique and authentic internal material could be found; material based on the qualities of the conversational language and the associative style, filled with a mosaic of embedded stories, typical of the Jewish sermon tradition.[32]

Rousseau's *Confessions* and Goethe's *Dichtung und Wahrheit* and the specific origins of Yiddish fiction in the nineteenth century shaped the genre in unique ways. Yiddish life-writing exemplifies the genre's enormous potential for generic permutations and stylistic hybridity, which, in some cases, were realized independently of the realist novel and the bildungsroman. This point is eloquently summarized by Georg Misch, the founder of the academic study of life-writing, in his seminal *Geschichte der Autobiographie* (1907, *The History of Autobiography*): "Hardly any form is alien to [the autobiography]. Historical records of achievements, imaginary forensic addresses or rhetorical declamations, systematic or epigrammatic description of character, lyrical poetry, prayer, soliloquy, confessions, letters, literary portraiture, family chronicle and court memoirs, narrative whether purely factual or with a purpose, explanatory or fictional, novel and biography in their various styles, epic and even drama—all these forms have been utilized by autobiographers. If they were persons of originality they modified the existing types of literary composition or even invented new forms of their own."[33]

A survey of articles on Yiddish life-writing by Eastern European Jewish scholars such as Bal-Makhshoves (1910), Yankev Shatski (1925–1926), Nachman Mayzel (1940) and Shmuel Rozshanski (1984) presents a relatively uniform view of the genre. In general, these scholars describe Yiddish life-writing as different from similar genres in the major languages. Their critical vocabulary is almost identical: life-writing is a "truthful" (*vorhaftig*) and "quiet chronicle" (*protokolirn ruik*) of the prosaic lives of regular people (Bal-Makhshoves).[34] In a series of articles in the journal *Tsukunft* (1925–1926), the Jewish historian Yankev Shatski contrasts the characteristics of Jewish and non-Jewish memoirs: "Among us, you will not find what the Germans call *Denkwürdigkeiten*. That is memoirs of a quiet life; a life with nothing tragic or dramatic in it, but filled with events, both personal and collective, which have a great historical value. A German or a Russian clerk, intellectual, writer, or even a landowner has a feel for the quiet life, regardless of whether this way of life is disappearing or not. The non-Jewish life-writer does not require outside stimuli such as pogroms, revolutions, violent attacks, or the decline of a collective way of life."[35]

Although Shatski acknowledges that non-Jewish life-writing frequently depicts important and often tragic historical events, he emphasizes that the norm is the chronicle of the "quiet" life. The autobiographical impetus for Jewish life-writing, on the other hand, comes from historical disasters. In a survey of Yiddish memoirs (1940), the literary critic Nachman Mayzel summarizes his findings by stating that "memoirs always appear at the threshold of two periods, of two generations."[36] Mayzel points out that the decline of a historical period, or its complete obliteration, propels Jews to turn to life-writing. The sense of being the last witness to a civilization that has ceased to exist is a constant trope in criticism on Yiddish life-writing. In Yekhezkel Kotik's *Mayne zikhroynes* (1913), which is one of the prime examples in Yiddish of Shatski's idea of *Denkwürdigkeiten*, the memoirist emphasizes the cultural historical importance of his work as a portrait of a lost *shtetl* civilization: "I spent my youth in a small *shtetl* where Jews lived a poor but 'quiet,' and, if one may say, flavorful life. . . . This no longer exists today; the poetry of those former *shtetls* has been silenced too. The immigration to America has thinned them out, and the arduous life for Jews in Russia, which is filled with the black lead of anti-Semitism, has entirely ruined them. These gracious Jewish towns, which were weaker than the Jewish cities, were the first to die."[37] Shatski and Mayzel point out that Jewish life-writing give access to individual experiential realms which are not available in more conventional historical sources. The urgency of rescuing this material prompts these critics to become autobiographers themselves.[38] Their sensitivity to conditions of emigration and exile is encapsulated by Bal-Makhshoves: "the Jew is an eternal wanderer . . . which makes the life course of a regular Jew fantastic and 'highly interesting' as it is stated below the title of many novels."[39] Obviously, the imaginary potential of Jewish emigrant life spanning several continents and dramatic upheavals is an important part of the genre's literary appeal for a mass audience. Mayzel mentions that "during recent years, these half-belletristic depictions have become exciting reading material for the newspaper reader."[40]

It is important to keep in mind, that Yiddish fiction, life-writing and poetry, to a large extent, only existed for the Yiddish reader in the section of the Yiddish newspaper devoted to belles-lettres. All the works included in this study except Jonah Rosenfeld's *Eyner aleyn*, were originally serialized in major Yiddish newspapers *(Der yid, Der moment*, and *Forverts)*, or in the case of I. L. Peretz and Yankev Glatshteyn in small literary journals *(Di yidishe velt, Inzikh*, and *Der yidisher kemfer)*. In his article "The Sociology of Yiddish" (1981) Joshua Fishman summarizes the close relationship between the Yiddish press and modern Yiddish literature beginning with Abramovitsh's serialization of his novel *Dos kleyne mentshele* (The Little Man) in the journal *Kol mevaser* (1864): "The modern world of Yiddish books is to a large extent a by-product of the Yiddish press, for had not the latter subsidized the former (both in the sense of paying wages/honorariums to the authors, and being the first arena in which new books, in serialized fashion, saw the light of day) the books themselves would frequently not have appeared. However, for the lion's share of readers of the press, the books remained unseen and unknown and only the press itself remained to typify the world of Yiddish-in-print."[41] The Yiddish press played a crucial role by providing the author with a regular salary and a readership whose passion for "highly entertaining novels" determined the style, content and novelistic character of the Yiddish literary autobiography. Shmuel Rozshanski (1984) pointed out that the "modern Jewish revolution" provided the dramatic life-experiences that made "memoirs . . . the spinal cord [*ruknbeyn*] of Yiddish belles-lettres and masked autobiographies—its marrow [*markh*]."[42]

What all of these critics of Yiddish life-writing have in common is a deeply felt sense of the uniquely tragic character of Jewish history. Frequently these critics succumb to what the historian Salo W. Baron's called "the lachrymose view" of Jewish history. While it is important to view Yiddish life-writing as a result of the catastrophic historical destiny of twentieth-century Eastern European Jewry, its similarities with life-writing of other oppressed groups (African-American, gay and lesbian, etc.) must also be stressed. Yiddish life-writing provides a fascinating case study of a persecuted people's experiences conceived during its most dramatic upheavals in modern times. Thus, Yiddish life-writing is highly relevant as a paradigm that might elucidate how other oppressed groups use life-writing as a response to their collective history.

In a review of Leo W. Schwarz's anthology *Memoirs of My People Through a Thousand Years* (1940) Yankev Shatski summarized his theory of Jewish life-writing: "Jewish memoirs appear as a rule at the end of a period, when the communal forms of Jewish life have significantly changed. During the so called 'golden' periods of Jewish life (Spain,

Poland) Jews did not write memoirs; however, when the period
ended—in most cases caused by catastrophic events—the past became
an object for a longing after the 'lost paradise' and achieved a complete
or partly resurrection *(tikn)* in the personal form of writing that is called
memoirs. But even in those cases the purely personal is mostly not more
than a parable with a moral, and in no way an individual confession
(vide) of a human life as we see it among non-Jews."[43] Shatski's main
thesis is that Jewish memoirs were rarely modeled on the confessional
format because of the Jewish tendency to focus on communal, rather
than individual facets of life. This study elaborates on Shatski's thesis
by examining how Yiddish life-writing combined confessional and fictional modalities. Its main premise is that a cluster of artistic, ideological and life-historical features must be considered in order to explain
Yiddish life-writing's ambivalence toward confessional self-expression.

The self-revealing style which has been so much in vogue in
American and European life-writing since Rousseau's *Confessions* was
rarely adopted in Yiddish life-writing.[44] Peretz's introduction to *Mayne
zikhroynes* (1913–1914, *My Memoirs*) established an autobiographical
norm based on an understanding of literature as high art. He viewed it
as a secular replacement of religious observance, with the same air of
dignity and spiritual elevation. Peretz sought to create a new standard
for Yiddish literature which would set it apart both from its utilitarian
and didactic tendencies and *shund* (trashy literature). Consequently,
Peretz rejected the self-indulgent exposure of intimate facts which he
designated *opfal* (trash). Just as a *soyfer* (a scribe of sacred texts) im-
merses himself in a *mikve* (ritual bath) before writing a Torah scroll, the
Yiddish writer should purify himself in a symbolic *mikve* before sitting
down to write.[45]

The ethos of secular *yidishkeyt* (Jewishness) situated Yiddish literature
in the context of a cultural revival in which the writer became a cultural
leader with prophetic aspirations. As a culture hero he was not only
supposed to lead the way to a new *yidishkeyt* ideal; he had to embody it.
Intimate matters such as sexuality and marital life, crucial aspects of
the Rousseauian autobiography, were depicted modestly or avoided
altogether, so as not to stain the idealistic image of the Yiddish writer.

The second part of Shatski's thesis, that Jewish memoirs originated
at the end of a historical period in response to catastrophe is, as mentioned, a recurrent trope in criticism on Yiddish life-writing. As I demonstrate in chapter 1, this point is supported by the fact that the inception of Yiddish life-writing with Abramovitsh's *Shloyme reb khayims*

(1894, 1900) in the early 1890s was a response to the cataclysm of the 1881–1882 pogroms in Russia. Increased Jewish urbanization, secularization, and mass emigration (primarily to the U.S.) were among the consequences of this upheaval. Indeed, Abramovitsh uses Mendele moykher sforim's introduction to explain that the increasing disintegration of Eastern European Jewish society in the 1880s and early 1890s is his primary reason for turning to life-writing. A similar dynamic between particular historical moments and the turn to life-writing can be seen in the two works by Yankev Glatshteyn written 1934–1940 in New York. These two autobiographical novels describe the narrator's turn to life-writing as a response to Hitler's rise to power in 1933. Even more compelling as support for this thesis are the many Yiddish memoirs published after the Holocaust in response to the nearly complete destruction of Eastern European Jewry. The sheer quantity of these works often appearing in multi–volume editions, indicate that their authors sought to create an artistic replica "of a world that is no more," the title of I. J. Singer's posthumous autobiography from 1946 (see chapter 5). Shatski's thesis needs to be expanded and refined, however, by including biographical, artistic and generic perspectives.

The tripartite structure of this study is based on chronological and geographical criteria. The three parts represent the three historical phases of modern Yiddish literature: its inception with the classical trio (1860s–1914), the inter-war period (1919–1939) and the post-Holocaust years (after 1945). Three generations of Yiddish writers are represented, all of whom were born in Eastern European between 1836 and 1910 and whose works depict the main Jewish areas of Russia and Eastern Europe—Lithuania, Poland and the Ukraine. The life-writing of Grade is set in Vilna, the capital of Jewish Lithuania (Lite); Peretz's and Glatshteyn's works are situated in, respectively, Zamosz and in the vicinity of Lublin (both in Poland); and the Ukrainian cities of Odessa, Kiev and the *shtetl* Voronke provide the settings for Abramovitsh, Scholem Aleichem and Jonah Rosenfeld's works.

Yiddish writers in New York used regional localities and differences as an important backdrop for their life-writing.[46] Glatshteyn portrayed a distinctive Polish-Jewish experience in his Yash books; its central fictive character, Steinman was modeled on Peretz. Rosenfeld recreated turn of the century Odessa as a vibrant Jewish city of artisans, workers and prostitutes. Singer's extensive life-writing, particularly his autobiography, *Mayn tatns bezdn shtub* (1956) was set in the poorest section of Jewish Warsaw, Krochmalna Street. Grade recreated Vilna through his loving portrait of his mother, a stall-keeper at the Jewish market in Vilna. Each writer wrote about his childhood and youth in a traditional Jewish family in the *shtetl* or city from a vast cultural distance in time and place. The best example of this is Abramovitsh's introduction to *Shloyme reb khayims* which contemplates his distance in Odessa from his origins in the Lithuanian shtetl, Kapuli.

The most original use of distance as narrative device is exhibited in Glatshteyn's two Yash novels which depict his nine-week trip from New York to Lublin in 1934. The recollection of this trip is interspersed with fragments of memory and dream sequences that elaborate on exile and homecoming in determining the course of his life and his artistic self. Similarly, Grade and Singer's works contrast their families' stationary lives in Warsaw and Vilna with the autobiographer's departure and alienation from his origins. Situated in major metropolitan centers such as Warsaw, Odessa, and New York, Yiddish writers made the road from tradition to modernity their central theme. Their lives' progression from the *shtetl*, rooted in a feudal social order and collective religious ethos, to an individualistic capitalist society is questioned and even, in some instances, circumvented in Yiddish life-writing.

My selection of works is governed by what I found to be the most representative and artistically superior examples of the Yiddish literary autobiography in the three periods. My choice of the classical trio for the first section is indisputable, as it would be in any literary history of Yiddish narrative prose. The only other important work of Yiddish life-writing from this period is Yekhezkel Kotik's *Mayne zikhroynes*, which inspired Scholem Aleichem to complete his own autobiography *Funem yarid* (1913–1916, *From the Fair*). Kotik's work falls outside the conceptual framework of this study, however, as I exclusively examine literary autobiographies of professional writers. Kotik's work belongs to that vast group of Yiddish memoirs of non-professional writers that were published in increasing numbers until the late 1970s, especially in the U.S. and Israel. They exemplify the kind of life-writing that Shatski, Mayzel and Bal-Makhshoves praised for its "naive" direct style and importance as a primary source for Jewish cultural history.[47] Most Holocaust memoirs belong to this category. They were, as a rule, intended as testimonies and eyewitness accounts meant for the prosecution of perpetrators, and as an outlet for the need to bear witness to unspeakable crimes. In addition to memoirs of political leaders and devoted party members, cultural leaders, actors, painters and other artists, an important subgroup of Yiddish life-writing focuses on the writer's encounters with other literati. Some of these works have a certain artistic merit and are important as sources for Yiddish literary history. Finally, there is a rich Yiddish poetic genre of life-writing, the *poeme* or long narrative poem, which requires a separate study.

Two works from the inter-war period stand out for their artistic quality: Esther Kreitman's *Der sheydim-tants* (1936, Demon Dance) and David Bergelson's *Bam Dnieper* (1932, At the Dnieper). Kreitman's work was written in London in the early 1930s; Bergelson's during his wanderings between Berlin, the U.S. and Copenhagen before he settled permanently in the Soviet Union in 1934. Kreitman's work is the first example of the multifaceted life-writing in the Singer family, followed by her younger brothers, I. J. Singer and I. B. Singer's autobiographies in 1946 and 1955. Bergelson's work is a significant contribution to the genre for its highly original style, reminiscent of his novels and short stories. Artistically, it is one of the most convincing narratives about the origins of the communist artist in Yiddish literature. The story of disinheritance as the black sheep of the family for reasons of gender (Kreytman) and family constellation (Bergelson's protagonist Penek is the unwanted child of elderly parents) point to interesting similarities between the two works. They are not included here because this study's focus is on the U.S. as the main center of Yiddish life-writing after the classical trio.

Crossing the ocean to start a new life in the U.S. furnished Yiddish writers with the distance and perspective they needed in order to look back, and to refashion a new sense of self in the new world. The American multi-cultural "salad bowl" enabled Yiddish writers to draw on models for immigrant and ethnic life-writing in English which paralleled their own autobiographical quest. Yankev Glatshteyn's two Yash books and Jonah Rosenfeld's *Eyner aleyn* are the most original examples of this turn to life-writing in American Yiddish literature in the inter-war period. In inter-war Poland, in contrast, the more stable Yiddish speaking community favored literature that focused on social themes in a collective context. One of the most conspicuous exceptions was an anomaly in the history of Yiddish life-writing: the autobiography contest for Jewish youth in Poland sponsored by YIVO in 1934 and later in 1938–1939, which met with an overwhelming response. The autobiographies were written by young people age 16 to 22 and a selection has recently been published in English translation.[48]

The Holocaust drastically curtailed any significant contribution to Yiddish life-writing except for the memoirs of survivors written in the Americas, the Soviet Union, and Israel from the mid-1940s. The U.S.

became the main center of Yiddish literature; not until the early 1960s
did Soviet Yiddish culture slightly recover from Stalin's purges of the
major Soviet Yiddish writers 1948–1952. Y. Y. Trunk, I. B. Singer and
Grade's works are representative of the voluminous output of literary
autobiographies in the U.S. in the post-Holocaust period. By contrasting I. B. Singer and Grade, the greatest Yiddish prose writers after 1945,
I was able to highlight the artistically most creative rewriting of the two
paradigms of Yiddish life-writing originating in the Polish-Jewish environment (Peretz, Glatshteyn) and in the Lithuanian-Jewish (Abramovitsh). The prolific output of Yiddish life-writing published in Israel,
South-America, Canada, South Africa, France and the Soviet Union in
the post-Holocaust period requires studies of their own.

Yiddish women writers excelled primarily as poets. While they also
wrote some distinguished prose works (particularly short prose), only
a few literary autobiographies were among them.[49] Those most artistically compelling were modeled on Glikl Hamel's *Zikhroynes (The Life of
Glückel of Hameln)* written 1689–1719 in Germany and France and published for the first time in 1896. However, not until the German-Jewish
social reformer and feminist Bertha Pappenheim translated the work
into German in 1912 did Glikl Hamel's *Zikhroynes* become known outside scholarly circles. In 1913, the Yiddish literary scholar Shmuel Niger
bemoaned the fact that Glikl Hamel's *Zikhroynes* had been inaccessible
to the Yiddish reading public for so long.[50] Similarly, the Soviet Yiddish
literary scholar Max Erik stated that "Glikl's [*Zikhroynes*] . . . were for
centuries hidden and did not have an influence on its own generation;
the work is perhaps more important as a grand memorial of the Yiddish
literary renaissance."[51] In this sense, Glikl's *Zikhroynes*, which the Jewish literary historian Israel Zinberg characterized as "an artistic work of
broad scope and significance," influenced Yiddish life-writing.[52] The re-
discovery of Glikl's *Zikhroynes* by Yiddish scholars Max Weinreich, Max
Erik, and Israel Zinberg in the 1920s were part of their attempt to create
a historical foundation and ancestry for the Yiddish literary renaissance. As demonstrated by Khone Shmeruk, these scholars' critical
invention of "old Yiddish literature" through historical surveys and
anthologies of pre-modern Yiddish texts provided material and inspiration for Yiddish writers Itsik Manger and I. B. Singer in the 1930s.[53]
These writers appropriated styles, forms and narratives belonging to
"Old Yiddish literature" addressed to "women and ordinary men" in
the seventeenth and eighteenth centuries in the form of romance
novels, ethical wills and treatises, *tkhines* (women's prayers) and the

Tsenerene (the extremely popular Yiddish adaptation of the bible with commentaries).[54]

Similarly, a few women writing in Yiddish reclaimed their own distinctly female ancestry through the example of Glikl's *Zikhroynes* in such works as Bella Chagall's *Brenendike likht* (1945, *Burning Light*) and *Di ershte bagegenish* (1947, *First Encounter*), and Hinde Bergner's *In di lange vinternekht* (1946, Long Winter Night). All of these works were written far from major Yiddish centers: Paris in the 1930s (Chagall) and Redim, Poland, at the outbreak of World War II (Bergner). Chagall, the wife of artist Marc Chagall, and Bergner, the mother of Yiddish writer Melekh Ravitsh and grandmother of artist Yosl Bergner, were not professional writers. The three memoirs, their authors' only written work, were published posthumously.

The Montreal Yiddish writer Chava Rosenfarb pointed out in a 1992 article that in giving literary form to her incarceration in the Lodz Ghetto 1941–1944 she had to subsume her individual female experiences in a collective portrait of a doomed Jewish community: "my concern about the Yiddish woman writer's specific condition tends to fade into insignificance in light of the situation facing Yiddish post-Holocaust in general. What affects me the most is the continual sense of isolation that I feel as a survivor—an isolation enhanced by my being a Yiddish writer. I feel myself to be like an anachronism wandering about a page of history on which I don't belong. If writing is a lonely profession, the Yiddish writer's loneliness has an additional dimension. His readership has perished. His language has gone up with the smoke of the crematoria. He or she creates in a vacuum, almost without a readership, out of fidelity to a vanished language—as to prove that Nazism did not succeed in extinguishing that language's last breath, and that it is still alive."[55]

Yiddish life-writing can be viewed as an attempt to delineate and highlight the female realm—the mother figure and the female voice—that are embodied in the traditional image of Yiddish as *mame-loshn* (mother language). By contrast, Hebrew literature traditionally functioned as the scriptural and legal language of holiness *(loshn koydesh)* for men. From its beginnings in the 1860s, Yiddish literature expressed its writers' ambivalence about creating art in a low-status language associated with the kitchen, the street, the workplace, and, rarely, the study-house. Yiddish writers turned the gendered context of traditional Jewish society on its head by creating a Yiddish artistic idiom that was able to express the inner life of ordinary Jews, including women, children, the old and the lower classes. As a result, the gap between Yiddish writers' status as cosmopolitan cultural leaders and their origins among *di proste yidn* (ordinary Jews) became an important theme of their life-writing.

As David G. Roskies argues in *A Bridge of Longing: The Lost Art of Yiddish Storytelling* (1995), the paradigm of rebellion and "negotiated return" encapsulates the artistic careers of the most important twentieth-century Yiddish writers. The poet Yankev Glatshteyn provides a typical example of "a negotiated return" in Yiddish literature. As one of the leading modernist poets *(di inzikhistn)* in New York who, inspired by James Joyce and T. S. Eliot, revolutionized the poetic idiom in the 1920s and 1930s, Glatshteyn changed artistic direction following a 1934 visit to his dying mother in Lublin, Poland. This return to his native country exposed him directly to rising European anti-Semitism. The result of this experience was a much more in-depth immersion in Jewish sources and commitment to Jewish continuity and survival reflected in his two autobiographical novels *Ven yash iz geforn* (1938, *Homeward Bound*) and *Ven yash iz gekumen* (1940, *Homecoming by Twilight*).

Glatshteyn's 1938 poem "A gute nakht, velt" (Good Night, World), one of the most famous American Yiddish poems ever written, encapsulates the Yiddish writer's return. Here are the poem's first and last stanzas:

> Good night, wide world,
> great stinking world.
> Not you, but I slam the gate.
> With the long gabardine,
> with my fiery yellow patch,
> with proud stride
> at my own command—
> I am going back to the ghetto.
>
> . . . .
>
> I'm going back to our cramped space.
> From Wagner's pagan-music to chants of sacred humming.
> I kiss you, disheveled Jewish life.
> Within me weeps the joy of returning.
>
> A gute nakht, breyte velt,
> groyse, shtinkendike velt.
> Nisht du, nor ikh farhak dem toyer.
> Mit dem langn khalat,
> mit der fayerdiker, geler lat,
> mit dem stoltsn trot,

oyf mayn eygenem gebot—
gey ikh tsurik in geto.

. . . .

Ikh gey tsurik tsu dalet ames.
Fun vagner's gets-muzik, tsu nign brumen.
Ikh kush dikh, farkoltn yidish lebn.
S'veynt in mir di freyd fun kumen.[56]

That Glatshteyn turned his back on the Western Enlightenment with such angry contempt is highly emblematic of the changed circumstances of American Yiddish literature in the 1930s. After the Holocaust, Glatshteyn "continued to filter experience through the prism of the self"[57] without relinquishing his modernist credo by deepening his artistic mastery of Yiddish. However, the joy of returning, the final words of Glatshteyn's poem, is not only a significant literary response to rising anti-Semitism but a master trope that crystallizes the modern Jewish experience. Secular and religious Zionism, Bundism, neo-orthodoxy, and Jewish messianic movements (such as Lubavitscher Hasidim) suggested varied political, cultural and religious solutions that would "normalize" modern Jewish life. These movements advocated respectively a return to *eretz yis'rael* (the land of Israel); to Yiddish culture as the embodiment of the folk spirit integrated in a socialist international; and to a renewed faith in God and the coming of the Messiah. Today a Jew can make a geographical "homecoming" to the Land of Israel, which is inscribed in Israeli law as "The Law of Return"; and a *bal-tshuve* can "return" to a life governed by the observance of *halakha* (Jewish law). Only the Bundist patronage of a Yiddish cultural network as the backbone of a socialist and national reawakening of the Jewish people has been rendered obsolete by the Holocaust. The joy of returning is a main theme of Yiddish life-writing as well as a significant part of Yiddish literature. As Roskies succinctly frames it, "Yiddish is not merely a literature of exile. It is most decidedly and unambiguously a literature of homecoming as well."[58]

Although this study emphasizes return as a result of the introspective and retrospective character of life-writing, that is but one side of the coin. Before turning to autobiography later in life, Yiddish writers had been through a shorter or longer "rebellion" that resulted in the creation of some of the best fiction and poetry in Yiddish literature. Although I briefly touch on these writers earlier works, it is their return or homecoming in the literary imagination that has been my primary concern. It appears, though, that Yiddish literature displays a stronger tendency to mourn, chronicle and retrieve a world that was brought to a brutal end than other literatures.[59]

Yiddish literature is a prism of the modern Jewish experience. It records and creates "rebellious," often radical, ways out of the traditional world—assimilation, emigration, socialism—propelled by the dream of Jewish "normalization," simultaneously exhibits a heightened awareness of the transient character of the human condition. The latter is primarily due to the twentieth-century Jewish experience of repeatedly being targeted for ethnic cleansing and genocidal assaults on European soil. There is, however, a danger in glorifying the destroyed world of Eastern European Jewry by stressing only those works, genres, and styles that most compellingly express a nostalgic turn to the past. Particularly in the U.S., Jewish writers (in Yiddish and English) tend to romanticize Yiddish culture, to view it only as a relic from a vanished world. Literary scholar Joseph Sherman elaborates on this point: "Indeed, the determination of those Yiddish writers still left alive after the Holocaust was now to memorialize the vanished world of the *shtetl,* to foreground beauties, pieties, and traditions now effaced from existence. The attempt to 'normalize' Jewish life in eastern Europe through Yiddish fiction was wiped away by the ultimate illustration that Jewish life in Eastern Europe had always been 'abnormal.' Its ultimate "abnormality" was, appallingly, the Nazi genocide; after it, there would no longer be any Jewish life in Eastern Europe to "normalize" any longer."[60]

The best antidote to this romanticized view of Yiddish literature, with the acute awareness of the tragically altered circumstances of Yiddish literary studies, is a careful analysis of Yiddish sources in their original historical and cultural contexts. Yiddish life-writing provides a fascinating gateway into twentieth-century Eastern European and American Jewish experiences because of the original ways in which it interweaves fiction and fact, history and literature, the individual and the collective. Moreover, Yiddish life-writing is highly relevant for the study of other minority groups' life-writing, because it presents a microcosm of the universal human condition of oppression, exile and longing for a-world-that-is-no-more.

Part I

The Classical Trio

1

Setting the Stage

Telling the truth or not telling it, and how much, is a lesser problem
than the one of shifting perspectives, for you see your life differently at
different stages, like climbing a mountain while the landscape changes
with every turn in the path. Had I written this when I was thirty, it
would have been a pretty combative document. In my forties, a wail of
despair and guilt: oh my God, how could I have done this or that?
Now I look at that child, that girl, that young woman, with a more and
more detached curiosity. Old people may be observed peering into
their pasts, *Why?*—they are asking themselves. *How did that happen*? I
try to see my past selves as someone else might, and then put myself
back inside one of them, and am at once submerged in a hot struggle
of emotion, justified by thoughts and ideas I now judge wrong.

    Doris Lessing, *Under My Skin: Volume One of My Autobiography to 1949*[1]

Old, saturated with troubles, with a heart plagued and wounded by
flying arrows in the struggle of life, tormented by bitter, heavy sufferings, I returned to my little world from bygone days.

    Sh. Y. Abramovitsh, *Shloyme reb khayims*[2]

Sholem Yankev Abramovitsh's *Shloyme reb khayims* (Shloyme, the Son of
Khayim) and Peretz's *Mayne zikhroynes* established two alternate paradigms that became highly influential in the development of Yiddish
life-writing in the twentieth century. Before *Shloyme reb khayims*, Yiddish writers had written their autobiographies in Hebrew, presented
small self-portraits in Yiddish or Hebrew, or employed autobiographical form and style for fictive purposes in novels such as Abramovitsh's
Dos kleyne mentshele (1864, The Little Man) and Y. Y. Linetski's *Dos poylishe yingl* (1867, The Polish Lad).[3] There were several reasons for the
relatively late appearance of the first Yiddish autobiography, preceded

by the first modern Hebrew autobiographies, M. A. Gintsburg's *Aviezer* (1864) and M. L. Lilyenblum's *Hat'ot ne'urim* (1876, Sins of Youth).[4] Alan Mintz points out that the Hebrew writers turned to life-writing as a result of the spiritual and religious vacuum left by the break up of the traditional religious belief system. These works were structured as "apostasy" narratives about the excruciating experience of the loss of faith and being "banished from their fathers' table."[5] The Hebrew auto-biographer expressed his experience of confronting his isolated self after severing all ties to traditional Judaism by using a Rousseauian confessional mode that had been introduced to Jewish readers by Solomon Maimon in his *Lebensgeschichte* (1786).[6] The Hebrew autobiographies of Lilyenblum and Gintsburg combined two narrative and generic modes: "The intertwining of these two, the autobiographical mode and the apostasy narrative, is an example of how a particular literary form can be suited to the exigencies of historical experience."[7]

The artistic and ideological context of nineteenth-century Yiddish literature was fundamentally different from that of Hebrew literature. Until the late 1880s, Yiddish literature was primarily written as a vehicle for the *maskilim*'s philosophy of enlightenment. The entertaining, didactic novels in the Yiddish vernacular were addressed to the ordinary Jewish reader without sufficient knowledge of Hebrew or non-Jewish languages (German, Russian and Polish). As a result, nineteenth-century Yiddish literature had a potential mass audience, unlike Hebrew literature, which until the 1880s was addressed to a relatively small number of *maskilim*.[8] Even some of the best Yiddish writers in the nineteenth-century considered Yiddish literature aesthetically inferior to Hebrew literature. They viewed Yiddish literature in purely instrumental terms as a means with which to communicate their *haskalah* philosophy to the less educated strata of Eastern European Jewry ("women and unlearned men"). As a result, nineteenth-century Yiddish literature developed in a critical vacuum, and was generally neglected by the Jewish intelligentsia until the appearance of the first two collections of Yiddish literature and criticism in Sholem Aleichem's *Di yidishe folks-bibliotek* (1888, The Jewish Folk Library) and Y. L. Peretz's *Di yidishe bib-liotek* (1891, The Jewish Library).[9]

The Mendele figure in Abramovitsh's work exemplified the best of nineteenth-century Yiddish literature, which excelled in dramatic, satirical, and folkloristic forms displaying the insufficiencies of traditional Jewish society through subversive artistic means. Donning a fictive mask in the Mendele figure, Abramovitsh gained direct access to a traditional *shtetl* reality from which he had long been estranged both intellectually and culturally. Through Mendele's fictive perspective he could depict the traditional *shtetl* as both insider and outsider. This artistic play with a disguised fictional identity was not conducive to autobiographical self-depiction in the Rousseauian mode. A certain personal sincerity was required by the modern autobiographical quest, the very opposite of the traditional bookseller Mendele's subtle verbal plays and literary games of hide-and-seek. Dan Miron points out that the cultural and ideological gap between "the Jew" and "the writer," prompted him to develop new artistic forms and styles which would characterize the best of nineteenth-century Yiddish literature:

To become the good Yiddish writer (perhaps one should say the "ideal" Yiddish writer), Berditshevski [Hebrew and Yiddish writer, 1865–1921] insists, "One must know how to put every idea in the Jew's own mouth: how to let him understand it as if he himself said it and in the way he himself would have explained it." Certainly this is one of the more pregnant remarks ever made on nineteenth-century Yiddish literature in general and on its beginnings in particular. What it amounts to is the suggestion that, for his work to achieve the status of art, a Yiddish writer has to conceal his direct identity and to master technique of self-alienation or even of self-elimination in his writing. For that, the writer has to be endowed with a gift for histrionic disguise and with a sure sense of the proper limitations of feigned innocence. Making "the Jew" talk naturally and fluently and yet express at the same time "ideas" that might be quite remote from his own, the Yiddish writer is required to be a master of dramatic irony.[10]

This artistic discourse that emphasized "self-alienation or even . . . self-elimination," histrionic disguise and dramatic irony was antithetical to the Rousseauian quest for truthfulness in regard to self-depiction and life narrative. Only later in his literary career did Abramovitsh turn to a more conventional third person novel in *Dos vintshfingerl* (1888, The Magic Ring), which brought the Yiddish novel closer to the historical and mimetic approach required by the modern autobiography.

The Yiddish literary autobiographies *Shloyme reb khayims* and *Funem yarid* were realist novels narrated in the third person by the fictional characters Mendele and Sholem Aleichem, who, in spite of their very different fictional statuses, created a distance from Abramovitsh's and Sholem Rabinovitsh's life stories and selves. In contrast, Peretz's autobiography *Mayne zikhroynes*, written at the end of his life in 1913–1914, established a different autobiographical paradigm that became prooftext for the artistically most innovative Yiddish life-writing in the twentieth century. Peretz's paradigm was influenced by neo-Romantic and symbolist literary models, which not only fundamentally changed the Yiddish literary conventions of didactic satire, but also replaced fictional pseudonyms (such as Mendele Moykher Sforim and Sholem Aleichem) with an unmediated first person singular narrative "I." Peretz's autobiography was not based on the Rousseauian model—as were the Hebrew autobiographies from the 1860s to the turn of the century[11]—but on the early nineteenth-century autobiographies by Wordsworth and Goethe.[12] Life-writing was conceived as a genre about the origin of the artist in childhood, providing a set of meta-poetic keys to the writer's oeuvre. This neo-Romantic approach focused on the writer's artistic and philosophical testament rather than on the confession of his "real" life experiences.

This emphasis on life-writing's fictional character was already evident in *Shloyme reb khayims* and *Funem yarid*. The bildungsroman and artist novel provided the artistic models for the unfolding of Abramovitsh's and Sholem Aleichem's childhood narratives. Peretz's fragmentary assemblage of reminiscences was similarly modelled on the *haskalah* novel about the growing consciousness of the child protagonist in the traditional *shtetl*, leading him towards enlightenment and outward mobility. Significantly, however, Peretz reversed this typical *haskalah* plot by letting his protagonist refrain from breaking away from his parents in order to start a new enlightened life in the city. *Shloyme reb khayims* and *Mayne zikhroynes* emphasized two very different aspects of the autobiographical act: the former documented the historical and ethnographic environment that shaped the origin and development of Shloyme's artistic identity. The self was depicted as part and parcel of a collective way of life. Even the personal crisis that prompted Reb Shloyme to write his autobiography (depicted in Mendele's introductory monologue) was typified as representative of the modern intellectual man, cut off from his childhood past, sexuality, and natural environment. This focus on the collective aspects led to a diverse Yiddish memoir literature that sought to recreate a lost world as accurately as possible. In these works, the self became a one-dimensional entity, an eye-witness to a collective drama from bygone days.[13]

Yiddish life-writing modeled on Peretz's *Mayne zikhroynes* emphasized the self as a fictional construct. Some of the most original twentieth-century Yiddish autobiographers not only recreated authentic images of times and places from bygone days, but they also took on a self-reflective perspective. This turned the autobiographical act into a quest for self-orientation in the midst of existential crisis triggered by traumatic events such as the death of a parent, mid-life crisis, migration, psychological abuse and the Holocaust. In order to express this quest, Yiddish writers such as Yankev Glatshteyn and Jonah Rosenfeld created new literary forms and styles that presented a complex self in the process of becoming. This dynamic, evolving self required a different kind of autobiographical discourse than the one mapped out by Abramovitsh in *Shloyme reb khayims*.

The three autobiographies of the classical trio were left unfinished, either because of the writer's death (Sholem Aleichem and Peretz) or inability to complete the task (Abramovitsh). Abramovitsh wrote an incomplete second part of *Shloyme reb khayims*, which was serialized in the Warsaw Yiddish newspaper *Der moment* (1914). It continued the chronological sequence from part one by depicting the protagonist's *yeshive* years, leading up to his creative "rebirth" at seventeen in the beginning of part one. *Funem yarid* was cut short by the death of Sholem Aleichem in 1916. The writer had started writing his autobiography in 1908 and projected it as a multi–volume work.[14] The final chapter of Peretz's *Mayne zikhroynes* was originally intended to be the first chapter in a second part, but, with his sudden death in 1915, this chapter became the last one in an unfinished work. None of the classical Yiddish writers took their autobiographies beyond their late teens or early twenties; each is essentially a portrait of the artist as child and adolescent.[15]

In spite of its occasionally positive, even nostalgic depiction of the traditional *shtetl*, *Shloyme reb khayims* continued a nineteenth-century Enlightenment critique of Jewish life in the Pale of Settlement from Abramovitsh's earlier novels. The work's confessional aspect was highlighted in Mendele Moykher Sforim's long introduction to the work ("Ptikhta"). Its main part, a bildungsroman, expressed Abramovitsh's interest in providing an anthropological picture of his childhood and adolescence in the 1840s and early 1850s. Abramovitsh distanced himself satirically from the new individualistic, neo-Romantic trends in Yiddish literature in Mendele's "Ptikhta." Abramovitsh did not see the exploration of the individual psyche as an end in itself; rather, he viewed the individual as encapsulating the ethnographic patterns of the Jewish collective. By doing so Abramovitsh was faithful to his literary credo in *Sketches to My Biography* (1888), in which he viewed literature as primarily a vehicle for enlightenment.[16]

Abramovitsh returned to writing in Hebrew in 1886 following several years of creative paralysis. He had been unable to write due to a severe depression caused by the death of his daughter Roshl at the age of

nineteen in 1882. A few years earlier, in 1877, his son Michael (Meir) had
been arrested for political activity and, in 1879, exiled to Siberia. During
this period Michael lived with a non-Jewish woman and later converted
to Christianity. After his release from Siberia in 1885 he married her.
David Aberbach mentions that Michael's conversion, "created a scandal
among the Jews in the Pale, not only because of the taboo on conversion
and intermarriage but also because of Abramovitsh's position as a leading Jewish educator and writer. Much as he grieved for his son, he did
not sit *shive* or say *kaddish* for him, as one can imagine Mendele doing if
his son had converted. He kept in close touch with him, to the detriment
of his reputation: in fact, largely for this reason and amid much contro-
versy, he was denied election as an honorary member of the Odessa Hebrew Literary Society."[17] At around the same time, Abramovitsh was
made the victim of blackmail by a man from Berditchev who had been
caricatured in Abramovitsh's play *Di takse* (The Meat Tax). Finally, the
large scale pogroms of 1881–1882 no doubt aggravated Abramovitsh's
depressed mood and were, very likely, an important reason for his continued writer's block which lasted until the mid-1880s.[18]

Abramovitsh returned to writing in Hebrew in 1886 with short
stories about current events related to the upheaval in Jewish life.[19] As
part of this literary comeback in Hebrew, Abramovitsh published his
Sketches to My Biography in Nahum Sokolov's *Sefer zikaron le-sofrei yisra'el hakhaim itanu kayom* (1889, A Memoir Book of Contemporary Jewish Writers). The sketch was included as the opening text in the section
titled "Autobiographien" (written in Latin letters). In it, thirteen of the
two hundred seventy Hebrew and Yiddish writers included were represented by autobiographical texts.[20] Abramovitsh's sketch was at once
a brief autobiography, a literary manifesto, and a bibliographical entry
to his oeuvre. He perceived his autobiography as defined by his role as
a Jewish writer: the first encounter with his muse, his first published
article, how he became a Yiddish writer, and the final annotated bibliography of his works. Educational influences and major life cycle
events—even his father's sudden death—were only mentioned in pass-
ing and in terms of their impact on his literary life. Abramovitsh highlighted the inner struggle that led up to his decision to write in Yiddish.
He had disregarded the common attitude among Jewish writers with
regard to the dishonour of employing Yiddish as a literary medium.
The shift from Hebrew to Yiddish was such a crucial decision in Abramovitsh's literary career that twenty-five years after the fact he still felt a
need to vindicate himself.[21]

Shloyme reb khayims is the first and, most likely, the only Yiddish literary autobiography composed as a bilingual work. Mendele's "Ptikhta" was originally written in Hebrew and published in the journal *Pardes* in Odessa 1894, and later revised in Yiddish as "In yener tsayt" ("In That Time"). The second part *Shloyme reb khayims: A bild fun yidishn lebn in der lite* (Shloyme, the Son of Khayim: A Picture of Jewish Life in Lithuania) was originally serialized in the Yiddish weekly *Der yid* in 1899 and later revised in Hebrew as *Bayamin hahem*. This publication story is reflected in the distinctly different stylistic and narrative character of the work's two parts. Mendele's introduction was written for the intellectual readership of *Pardes,* the leading journal of Hebrew literature and Jewish thought, which published articles by Ahad Ha'am, the creator of spiritual Zionism, and the historian Shimon Dubnow. The first part of *Shloyme reb khayims* was published in *Der yid* (1899–1902), a Zionist weekly with a broad political and artistic agenda.[22] This weekly published some of the best Yiddish belle-lettres at the turn of the century, such as Peretz's Hasidic tales and part of Sholem Aleichem's Menakhem-Mendl stories. However, the main inspiration for the conception of *Shloyme reb khayims* originated with the Odessa circle of Jewish writers. Steve Zipperstein gives a compelling picture of the Odessa circle in which Ahad Ha'am and Abramovitsh played leading roles: "What served to animate the cultural lives of his [Ahad Ha'am] Odessa circle was the way in which—and only for the relatively brief period between the late 1880s and the turn of the century—a variety of intellectual, cultural and political factors coalesced there: Jewish and non-Jewish, political and literary, local and more generally Russian. . . . Odessa reinforced the belief that national identity was self-evident: permanent, secure, but also by no means immutable in its essential form. *Shtetl* culture was sufficiently distant to be rendered unoppressive yet close enough (just across town in the southern reaches of suburban Moldavanka) to serve as a nearly constant reminder of its wretched shortcomings, its vulnerability and needs."[23]

The group of Jewish writers in Odessa, consisting of "a small inner circle of no more than twenty young men,"[24] created a Jewish literary renaissance in Hebrew and Yiddish from the late 1880s to the turn of the century. However, these writers were marginalized and more or less unknown to the Jews of Odessa. Abramovitsh was the director of a reform Talmud Torah that reflected the progressive trends towards modernization of Jewish life and disintegration of traditional observance in Odessa. This was highlighted by the fact that, as early as the 1870s, ninety percent of the city's Jewish-owned shops were open on the Sabbath.[25] The transient character of the Odessa circle in the most liberal city in the Russian empire created the background for these writers' artistic output and utopian hopes for a radically different Jewish future.

Abramovitsh's turn to life-writing in the early 1890s in Odessa encapsulated the marginality and homelessness of the Odessa circle. Reb Shloyme's intellectual friends depicted in Mendele's "Ptikhta" were modelled on members of the Odessa circle. Severed from their origins in the traditional *shtetl* and with little cultural impact in their new urban environment, they increasingly turned their attention to traditional Jewish life. This created a cultural historical model for later Yiddish autobiographers in New York whose status as uprooted intellectuals— refugees and newly arrived immigrants—was similar to that of the Odessa circle. Looking back on their origins in the *shtetl* and formative years in the Eastern European metropolis, Yiddish writers in New York, like Abramovitsh in Odessa, would use life-writing as a vehicle to express their longings toward a life untouched by modernity. They created life-writing that became a counter-model and compensation for their insignificant existence in the metropolis: "these intellectuals evoke a longing of their own for the self-contained Jewish towns where they were once shunned, persecuted, and also important. The sadness in their writings is inspired by the view of what they left behind from the perspective of their new, painfully marginal urban perch."[26] This longing for "what they left behind" would provide a fertile inspiration for Yiddish life-writing in the twentieth century.

In a letter to Sholem Aleichem in 1902, Abramovitsh responded to Sholem Aleichem's request for biographical material: "regarding your request for my biography, I must laugh because of my troubles. You intend to honor me with a work which is now beyond my powers. . . . I have no time to breathe. That one writes, and another writes. Here for a school, there to give lectures, go be a *makher* [an important person] in a city! Oy, where does one find strength? Forget not that I am a grandfather, not a young man anymore, and furthermore, between us, a lazy bone, may it not happen to you."[27] Abramovitsh's inability to assemble material for his biography had less to do with a busy schedule, as he claims in the letter, than with his role as the founding "grandfather" of Yiddish literature in relationship to his "grandson," Sholem Aleichem, the creator of the myth. Abramovitsh considered it Sholem Aleichem's task to nourish this myth by writing his biography. Although the letter later makes references to Abramovitsh's "Hebrew autobiography"

(Sketches to My Biography), two novels *(Fishke der krumer* and *Di kliatshe)*, and one play *(Di takse)*, Abramovitsh does not mention his autobiographical novel, *Shloyme reb khayims,* or the "Ptikhta." Perhaps he felt that the incomplete character of this work, which he continued to work on until his death and never managed to finish, was inferior to his novels from the 1860s and 1870s. That Abramovitsh does not single out any part of *Shloyme reb khayims* indicates that he viewed it as part and parcel of his artistic work and not as a separate biographical source.

It is obvious, however, that the double character of *Shloyme reb khayims* as autobiographical novel distinguishes it from, say, the novels *Dos kleyne mentshele* and *Dos vintshfingerl,* in which autobiographical discourse is used in order to create a fiction of veracity and authenticity.[28] The more explicit ideological content of these works is well served by the use of autobiographical discourse, which lends credence to the life experiences presented by fictional autobiographers. In *Shloyme reb khayims,* on the other hand, Abramovitsh presented autobiographical material in the form of a novel in order to depict his origins as an artist in the traditional *shtetl* and his later acculturation as a Jewish writer. The proper name in the title signifies the work's link to an extra-literary reality. Shloyme is a slight variation of Abramovitsh's real name, Sholem, Sholemke. His father's name, Khayim, is similarly Abramovitsh's father's first name: Khayim-Moyshe Broyde. The proper name in the title is a traditional designation of the ancestry of a male Jew, Shloyme son of Khayim. Several of the characters in the story, such as the *melamed* Lippe Ruven (whose real name was Yosef Ruven), are modelled after historical characters. His father's occupation as *parnes* (one of the elected heads of the community), responsible for the meat tax, also corresponds to the historical data available about Abramovitsh's father. In his article "Mendele's Parents and Siblings" (1937), Max Weinreich demonstrates that Shloyme's siblings described in chapter one and sixteen of *Shloyme reb khayims* are modelled on Abramovitsh's siblings, although their names have been changed in the book. The episode with Shloyme's sister Lea, who divorced her husband (chapter 16), corresponds to the facts that Weinreich gathered from interviewing Abramovitsh's surviving family members in the 1930s. This reading of *Shloyme reb khayims* as a major source of biographical information about Abramovitsh's childhood and family characterizes the dominant critical approach to this work, for example Shmuel Niger (1936; 1970) and David Aberbach (1989).[29]

In reading both parts of *Shloyme reb khayims,* we can delineate four phases of Abramovitsh' life story: his childhood (ages seven to thirteen), which was brought to an abrupt end by his father's untimely death; his years as a wandering *yeshive* student (ages thirteen to seventeen); his first Hebrew writings at age seventeen; and his old age at sixty-odd years as writer, teacher, Talmud Torah principal surrounded by Jewish intellectuals in his Odessa apartment. Abramovitsh's life between late adolescence and old age is only hinted at in Mendele's "Ptikhta" in his depiction of Reb Shloyme's literary activities in Glupsk. The crucial turning point of Reb Shloyme's life—his father's death— occurs in early adolescence. A couple of years later, this traumatic event is followed by Shloyme's break with the religious tradition when he begins to write Hebrew poetry (chapter 1). The polarity between Reb Shloyme's childhood in the *shtetl* K. and his old age in Odessa is the narrative axis that defines his life story.[30] These distinct life phases highlight the way in which Reb Shloyme grew from a child of the *shtetl* into the key literary figure of the Odessa circle.[31]

In *Sketches to My Biography,* Abramovitsh described the origin of the Mendele figure as that part of his creative self that ridicules and unmasks people: "And a wonderful thing: when I started to write and finished the first thing—Satan came to me, that is the scoffer who now rules in me in the form of *Mendele Moykher Sforim,* and talked me into ridiculing people and tearing away their masks."[32] Given his own admittedly destructive impulses to caricature others, it becomes understandable why Abramovitsh had to protect his autobiographical stand-in, Reb Shloyme in *Shloyme reb khayims.* This character's resistance to the pressure of Mendele, and the other intellectuals who want him to write his autobiography, can be seen as a reflection of Abramovitsh/ Reb Shloyme's defence against Mendele's mocking gaze. Thus, Abramovitsh could establish an artistic equilibrium between the two sides of his artistic self: Mendele and Reb Shloyme. On the one hand, he unmasked his current and past life as Jewish intellectual in a satirical way in Mendele's "Ptikhta." On the other, he embellished Reb Shloyme's account of bygone days, interweaving his artistic origins in childhood with ethnographic images in *Shloyme reb khayims: A bild fun yidishn lebn in der lite.*

In Mendele's introduction, Abramovitsh creates a self-portrait through a complex web of altering points of view, represented by narrative voices belonging to fictive and semi-autobiographical characters. Abramovitsh imagines how he would appear if someone else were telling his story, or, in the words of Philippe Lejeune, he "attempts to retrieve the discourse that others might pronounce concerning him, so as to impose upon them in the end the image of himself he believes to be true."[33] Philippe Lejeune distinguishes between two kinds of autobiographical techniques or "fictive fictions": the witness narrative and the dialogue. The former establishes a point of view, or discourse, defined by a "fictive witness," from whose point of view the autobiographer is portrayed. The latter refers to the dialogues between a semi-autobiographical and a fictive character that describe the autobiographer from different perspectives.

The autobiographer's play with alternating perspectives is based on the fundamental fact that it is impossible to create a self-portrait or "write an autobiography without constructing and communicating a point of view towards oneself."[34] In autobiographies that employ a "fictive witness," the autobiographer is depicted in the third person as in a novel or a biography. The autobiographer simultaneously employs varying points of view by using one or more fictive characters, each of whom portrays his life story differently. This elaborate play with narrative perspective becomes a prop that in no way undermines the autobiographer's control and intention. By manipulating the fictive witness account, the autobiographer can evade and highlight painful memories. Lejeune's insights apply both to the ways Abramovitsh created his own "fictive witness," Mendele's "Ptikhta," and to the novelistic account of his semi-autobiographical character, Reb Shloyme. The best-known examples of the relatively few autobiographies written entirely in the third person are Victor Hugo's *Mes fils* (1874), Henry Adams' *The Education of Henry Adams* (1907), and Norman Mailer's *The Armies of the Night* (1968). Lejeune concludes: "The third person is almost always used in a contrastive and local manner in texts that also use the first person. This contrast ensures the effectiveness of the figure. It can involve either an exceptional use of the third person or a deliberate alternation between the third and first person."[35] A typical example of the autobiography in the third person with a "fictitious witness" as narrator is *The Autobiography of Alice B. Toklas* (1933), Gertrude Stein's fictional autobiography of her secretary Alice Toklas.

In the "Ptikhta," Mendele narrates how he arrived in N (in the Hebrew version *Shikhor* [black], referring to Odessa's location by The Black Sea) where he visits the well-known writer Reb Shloyme. Thus, Abramovitsh creates an autobiographical self-portrait in the discursive framework of his primary literary character. Mendele becomes a "fictive witness", chronicling Reb Shloyme's past literary activities in Glupsk and his current life as aging writer surrounded by fellow authors in Odessa. Secondly, the dramatic dialogue between Mendele and Reb Shloyme enables Abramovitsh to view his autobiographical project from varying points of view. Through Mendele's rhetorical style, we are presented with the discussion between Reb Shloyme and the other writers. In the end, Reb Shloyme succumbs to the intellectuals' arguments about the importance of writing his autobiography only because Mendele suggests that he will take care of the logistics of publishing the manuscript.[36] Abramovitsh depicts his alter ego Reb Shloyme as evading the writing and publication of his autobiography, and Mendele as the one who finally convinces Reb Shloyme to do so.

The "Ptikhta," which constitutes approximately one-sixth of *Shloyme reb khayims*, is Mendele's longest monologue in all of Abramovitsh's works. Although the introduction is conducted entirely in Mendele's words, it is only on the first evening of the encounter between Mendele and Reb Shloyme that the former appears as its narrator. On the second day, Mendele is reduced to a minor character who, like the rest of the intellectuals, comments on Reb Shloyme's agonizing monologue. Only in the final paragraphs of the introduction does Mendele reappear in his traditional role as salesman of holy books and publisher of "authentic accounts." There is a clear shift between the rhetorical character of Mendele's monologue on the first day (51–65), and Reb Shloyme's torturous self-examination on the second day (65–79).[37] On the first day, Mendele's voice is in the foreground satirizing the intellectuals as well as the traditional *shtetl* Jews. With loyalties to no one, Mendele is free to unmask and mock the various types of Jews by accentuating their absurdities. On the second day, Mendele retreats to the role of audience to Reb Shloyme's soul searching monologue. This rhetorical shift in the middle of the introduction is crucial for an understanding of the work's autobiographical character. It is crystallized when freezing air from the storm outside seeps into Reb Shloyme's smoke-filled room and interrupts the intellectual conversation. Reb Shloyme's wife and daughters have already left the room shortly after Mendele's arrival, as the men begin to talk about *divre-toyre*, matters relating to literature and philosophy. The disappearance of the women is not noticed by the men until their voices are heard in the hall.

Then Mendele compares the relationship between men and women among ordinary Jews and among traditional and secular *talmide-khakhomim* (Talmud scholars). He concludes that only among the former do women enjoy some kind of equality; among the latter, they are completely submissive. That is the case with Reb Shloyme's wife and daughters, who appear as silent props with no distinct qualities of their own until the *yeshive* student arrives. Suddenly, the male intellectuals' attention is focussed on their absence: "We, Talmud scholars, were so involved in discussing our affairs that we did not know whether they [Reb Shloyme's wife and daughters] were still there or had gone, until their voices, the furious draft, and the sound of slamming doors in the hall startled us as from a deep sleep. After a moment, one of the daughters came in and whispered to her father, 'Father, some boy is here . . . he wants to stay overnight in the school.'"[38] This sudden awakening is related to the female realm of Shloyme's childhood, which has been repressed in his life as Jewish writer. Significantly, the first chapter of *Shloyme reb khayims* depicts his mother and sisters' painful conversation after their social decline in the town of Mlinitse. It is through the female lenses of emotional loss, pain, and nurturing that we are first introduced to Shloyme. The intellectual, male realm in the "Ptikhta" is a state of refuge and being out of touch with reality because it excludes the "female realm" of emotional depth, sexuality, and childhood.[39]

Mendele observes that the climate has recently changed as radically as the unpredictably fluctuating stock market. He then compares the present generation of modern Jews to chameleons, constantly changing their identities and cultural fashions. Like the abstract exchange of money on the stock market, opinions and ideological statements have become commodities in an abstract discourse. On a more fundamental level, the present time, as Reb Shloyme characterizes it, is "a stormy time [*a tsayt fun geviter*], the world is turning. . . . It is not an auspicious time [*eys-rotsn*], brothers."[40] Even the weather behaves strangely and unpredictably. This refers to the time after the pogroms of 1881–1882 that shattered the Jewish intellectuals' belief in the possibility of Jewish integration and emancipation in Russian society.

The repressed reality, represented by the silent women around the table and the seventeen-year-old Talmud student from Lithuania, triggers Reb Shloyme's self-examination, his autobiographical quest. Looking back on his life, Reb Shloyme characterizes it in terms of a storm metaphor: "My life is a turbulent ocean, my days and years are raging waves, and my soul is the storm-battered boat."[41] This metaphor is related to his primary experience of oneness with nature as a child during a storm: "That was the time when my eyes were opened and I was revealed to myself completely as I am" ("Ikh antplek mikh tsu mir

aleyn in gantsn vi ikh bin").[42] The storm image is an example of a "meta-
phor of self,"[43] signifying dislocation, mobility and self-revelation in
nature as emblematic qualities of Reb Shloyme's self and life story. Reb
Shloyme's idealized account of his childhood, based on enlightened
Jewish values and proximity to nature, is meant as an antidote to the
Jewish intellectuals' alienation from traditional female sensibilities.

But before Reb Shloyme can write his autobiographical account originating with his first self-conscious moment as a child in a storm—an
image that "hot zikh mir ayngeshnitn in hartsn"[44] ("has carved itself
into my heart")—he must overcome three internal objections to this
project. As mentioned earlier, these objections can be viewed as Reb
Shloyme's evasive approach to his autobiography, rationalizing his
account's lack of introspection. But they are also included in the
"Ptikhta" to delineate the parameters of a Jewish autobiographical discourse. By looking carefully at Reb Shloyme's objections against writing
his autobiography, and at how his friends refute them, we can learn how
Abramovitsh conceived of a Jewish autobiographical discourse in
Shloyme reb khayims. Reb Shloyme's first objection outlines a universal
discourse in which the Jews play no part. Success and achievement, unlimited by any restrictions in economic, political, and sexual terms, ex-
clude Jews because of their circumscribed, confined ghetto life. Thus, a
Jewish autobiographer must be aware of his material's lack of universal-
ity, and of his self-portrait as a public act portraying a Jewish collective.
A Jewish autobiographer must be careful not to give in to self-hate by focussing on the deficiencies of Jewish life. He must acknowledge Jewish
oppression by focussing on the spiritual qualities behind the degrading
material conditions of Jewish poverty and persecution. As Marcus
Moseley points out, Abramovitsh highlights "the utter incompatibility
of the life-history of a East European Jew with . . . the West European
autobiographical genre." At the same time, he distances his work with
"relentless irony" from the kind of Gentile life style which originated
with the Russian gentry autobiography exemplified by Tolstoy's *Childhood* (1852–1857).[45]

Reb Shloyme's second objection deals with the difficulty of separating the individual from the collective in traditional Jewish society. Reb
Shloyme compares the social life of ants to that of the *shtetl* Jews. There
is no distinction between the group and the individual. Individual expression can only occur through the typical pattern mapped out by the
group: "We are an anthill, each one like the other, all the same. In books
on natural history, scientists devote a separate chapter to the genus of

ants as a whole, but not to the individual ant."[46] ("Mir zenen an eyde fun milbn, vos vi eyne, azoy di andere, ale glaykh. In der natur ge-shikhte, zoologye, vert geredt vegn dem min milbn beklal, ober nisht vegn etlekher milb bazunder.") Although such a positivistic approach to human life is refuted by one of the intellectuals emphasizing each individual as unique, Reb Shloyme's remark is typical of his resistance to going beyond the characteristic group behaviour by exploring his own individuality.[47] The last objection that Reb Shloyme raises against his autobiographical project concerns the tedious logistics of its publication. As a response, Mendele offers his services as publisher and editor, enabling Reb Shloyme to write his account without worrying about making it available as a published text.

Reb Shloyme's first two objections created a normative Yiddish auto-biographical discourse until Y. L. Peretz radically redefined it in *Mayne zikhroynes*. According to Reb Shloyme, the Jewish autobiographer is dis-inclined to contemplate his individuality because the notion of individuality is foreign to traditional Jewish society: "but my life alone, looked at separately, in what respect has it deserved, and what kind of news does it entail, that entitles it to being recorded? What has happened to me, has happened to thousands among us; it's a familiar story. Is there any other people in the world among whom the way of life of every individual [*der gantser shteyger lebn fun etlekhn bazunder*], from the moment he comes into the world until his last breath, goes on and on according to a single pattern [*nusekh*] as it does among us, Jewish children?"[48] Here Abramovitsh views the individual as an undifferentiated part of the Jewish collective. In Odessa, Reb Shloyme's individuality has been dismantled from the traditional way of life in the *shtetl*. The first precursor to this sense of being disconnected from the Jewish collective was Shloyme's self-revelation in the storm that set him apart as an individual in childhood. Reb Shloyme views his self-portrait as inseparable from a picture of the Jews as a national group. Forces within and without the Jewish community threaten the survival of Jewish life through assimilation and anti-Semitism. As a result, the auto-biographer must provide a balanced picture that strengthens Jewish dignity and points to paths of spiritual renewal. Abramovitsh wrote *Shloyme reb khayims* in 1890s Odessa, where anti-Semitic sentiments were the order of the day. The pogroms of 1881–1882, which led to a Jewish mass exodus from the Pale of Settlement, were still in recent memory. A few years later, the next wave of pogroms (Kishenev in 1903, and Odessa in 1905) would force Abramovitsh to leave Odessa in the most humiliating way. He was forced to hide from the pogromists and shortly after decided to leave Odessa for Switzerland.[49] This threat to Jewish existence is expressed by one of the intellectuals. He responds to Reb Shloyme's objection by arguing that the beauty of Jewish spiritual life ought to be the focus of a more idealized account emphasizing the spiritual "essence" behind the bleak Jewish reality. Thus, autobiography is turned into ethnography, and becomes a means of resurrecting a way of life threatened by extinction. The autobiographer's *raison d'être* becomes his ability to rescue the collective, ethnographic customs as authentically as possible.[50]

The ethnographic and confessional modes are closely interwoven in *Shloyme reb khayims*. The balance between these two intentions—the social-historical and the autobiographical—has, to a large extent, determined the narrative structure of Reb Shloyme's account. Abramovitsh's reworking of *Dos vintshfingerl* for Sholem Aleichem's *Di yidishe folksbibliotek* employed a third person narrative and emphasized the work as reflecting a social historical reality. In *Shloyme reb khayims*, Abramovitsh continued this novelistic approach through the use of a third person narrative and detailed descriptions of ethnographic customs and artifacts.[51] Yiddish writers I. Aksenfeld (1787–1866) and I. M. Dik (1814–1893) employed ethnographic depictions as a means of displaying the corruption and backwardness of Jewish life they believed would be replaced by enlightenment and capitalist progress.[52] But instead of completely discarding the old way of life, these *maskilim* took pleasure in depicting its ethnographic customs and artifacts. They depicted the preparation for Pesach; the *shterntikhl* (traditional lady's head covering [*Dos shterntikhl* was the title of the first modern Yiddish novel by I. Aksenfeld, published in 1861]), superstitious beliefs, and so on. They discovered the immense artistic and entertaining potential in this material. They even endorsed the historical significance of documenting the ethnography of a Jewish civilization that they considered on the verge of extinction. The contradiction between these *maskilim*'s ideology and the ethnographic material's artistic potential created a paradoxical artistic practice that defined nineteenth-century Yiddish literature.

The same paradox was also evident in the *maskilim*'s use of Yiddish as a literary vehicle in their ideological warfare against the orthodox religious establishment. The *maskilim*'s main reason for using what they considered the debased, primitive Yiddish language was entirely instrumental. Yiddish made it possible for them to reach a large Jewish audience, primarily women and men without sufficient knowledge of

Hebrew and the non-Jewish vernacular (Polish, Russian, or German). But the *maskilim*'s artistic mastery of the colloquial richness of Yiddish often transcended their original intention for using Yiddish as a literary medium. *Shloyme reb khayims* belongs to this main trend in nineteenth-century Yiddish literature coloured by the neo-romantic trends of the 1890s. The work is to a large extent a typical Enlightenment novel in its critical and satirical depiction of Jewish life. As in other such Yiddish novels, the same artistic delight in replicating customs and superstitious beliefs is evident in Abramovitsh' depiction of his mother's *tkhines* (penitential prayer), the "Napoleon's hat" designed by his father, Toybe-Sosye's *sabobones* (superstitions), and so on. But the satirical approach to Jewish *shtetl* life is toned down in comparison to Abramovitsh's works from the 1860s and 1870s. At times even apologetic and nostalgic tonalities can be detected in the work's depiction of Jewish superstition and powerlessness. *Shloyme reb khayims* was written at a time of great Jewish national and cultural resurgence. The neo-Romantic trends in Yiddish literature depicted the traditional *shtetl* more favourably and even, primarily in the case of Y. L. Peretz, adapted narrative forms and settings originating in a Hasidic universe. Abramovitsh's critical attitude to these new trends is expressed in Mendele's satirical depiction of the Jewish intellectuals in the "Ptikhta." Abramovitsh maintained his adherence to Enlightenment ideology and artistic practise. This is evident in the portrait of Shloyme's development, which demonstrates how a religious education inhibits his artistic growth by turning him into a *dortiker* (otherworldly person), an individual disconnected from his historical and physical reality.

The actual chronological beginning of Reb Shloyme's account in chapter two consists of elaborate descriptions of Reb Khayim's home, its furniture and social life. Several paragraphs are introduced with the words *"lozn kinds-kinder visn"* (let your grand-children know) emphasizing Abramovitsh' historical intent. A more subtle ethnographical style in *Shloyme reb khayims* is the satirical depiction of the powerless Jewish response to the tsar's decrees. One example of this is Reb Khayim's invention of the *napoleonke* (the Napoleon's hat) in response to the tsar's decree forbidding the Jews to wear their traditional hats. Reb Khayim saves the Jews from being forced to dress like "Germans" (i.e., Europeanized Jews), which would mean relinquishing their Jewish identity: "in the history should be recorded the name, Reb Khayim the First, who invented it."[53] Abramovitsh ironically transforms history from a record of the deeds of great kings and warriors to that of a *shtetl balebos'* (small town householder) creativity in maintaining distinct Jewish clothing in the face of the Gentile power's attempt to eradicate it.

The decline of the *shtetl* K. is the result of yet another of the tsar's decrees, the "Clothing Decree" forbidding women to shave their heads and making the kerchief used as female head covering superfluous. The economic and social life of K. is based on the manufacturing of cloth for women's kerchiefs. By forcing the Jews to abolish the kerchief, the tsar deals the *shtetl* an economic deathblow from which it never recovers. Reb Khayim's high status, derived from his administration of the meat tax, becomes the target of Jewish criticism that ultimately leads to his sickness and death. Again Abramovitsh exposes the fragile economic and social basis of Jewish *shtetl* life in the Pale of Settlement. The traditional Jewish prayers, fasts and other religious paraphernalia in times of crisis once again reveal Jews' inability to change their existential misery. Abramovitsh demonstrates how the forces that lead to Reb Khayim's death and his family's social decline originate in a general state of Jewish powerlessness and superstition.

A final example of Abramovitsh's use of folklore in *Shloyme reb khayims* is the image of the *yeytser-hore* (the evil inclination) employed in its traditional meaning: the "evil inclination" tempting the young Jewish male to leave "the righteous path." This betrayal of Shloyme's traditional upbringing is presented as a positive phenomenon that gives him the courage to go beyond his predestined path. Later, after his father's death, in the second part of the book, the *yeytser-hore* literally keeps him alive by weathering off his suicidal moods. The *yeytser-hore* ignites Shloyme's imagination, his desire to write: "If the evil inclination had not approached him unexpectedly, like a redeeming angel, reviving him with its sharp means of arousal—spurring him on, blowing on the nearly extinguished spark of his fiery, sensitive soul, igniting in him the feeling of solidly attached friendship, and giving him desire to live—if not the *yeytser-hore* with its means, Shloyme would long ago not have been in this world, and, as a matter of course, his current life story would not have seen the light of day."[54] Abramovitsh depicts the *yeytser-hore* tenderly, as yet another folkloristic artefact from "a bygone age." The *yeytser-hore* literally keeps Shloymele alive through his difficult years as a *yeshive* student and later propels his writing. This concept clearly belongs to a traditional mind set which excludes the radical subversion of Mendele's discourse.

Childhood accounts have comprised a fundamental feature of the modern autobiography since Rousseau first depicted this stage as a phase of life which must be understood on its own terms.[55] Typically, the Romantic idea of childhood views the child as the bearer of qualities such as imagination and sensuality. This motif emphasizes the similarity between the child and the artist and becomes an indispensable hallmark of the autobiography after Rousseau. Richard N. Coe defines the childhood account as a sub-genre of the autobiography in which the self is depicted "from first consciousness to full maturity over an allotted span (normally) of some fifteen to eighteen years."[56] Coe mentions that this time span can be abbreviated: "because one section of the experience, typically in wartime or revolutionary situations, was so intense that the whole process of maturation was speeded up to a quite abnormal extent; because, for socio-historical, mythological, agricultural, or other reasons, the cyclical pattern of the year takes precedence over the linear chronology of development; or finally because the writer wishes to analyse the formation of one isolated element in his identity."[57]

The childhood account as, to paraphrase the title of James Joyce's autobiographical novel from 1914–1915, "the portrait of the artist as child and young man," separates it from the bildungsroman. The latter relates the development of the protagonist's self from his first awareness of himself to the point when he is harmoniously integrated into society (the archetypical bildungsroman is Goethe's *Wilhelm Meister's Lehrjahre* (1777–1829). The childhood account, on the other hand, portrays the narrator's self from his first awareness of himself through his transformation into an artist. The narrative ends when the autobiographer becomes an artist situated outside "respectable" society, which then is criticized and condemned "in terms of the self."[58] The childhood account's emphasis on the child as writer-to-be has, since Rousseau, made it into the preferred autobiographical sub-genre of poets and fiction writers. In his analysis of *Shloyme reb khayims*, the Soviet Yiddish critic Aaron Gurshteyn points out that "as a work about the growth of a child . . . it is one of the most important works in Yiddish literature."[59] Gurshteyn demonstrates how the depiction of the child is patterned on an educational program for Emancipation through the child's encounter with nature, sexuality and the lowest rung on the social ladder, the childlike, artistic artisans in the *shtetl*. Gurshteyn's reading focuses on the child's inner emancipation from the spiritual oppression of *shtetl* obscurantism and feudalism, modelled on Rousseau's idea of the "natural" child. Abramovitsh depicts his childhood by employing the Romanticist notion of the innocent child who intuitively understands animals and plants and communicates directly with nature.[60] The experience of the child's proximity to nature is fundamentally different than the restrictive, rational, adult world and is repeated in slightly different variations throughout Reb Shloyme's account. The Rousseauian "natural child" provides the perspective from which the intellectual *khevre* (group) in the "Ptikhta" and traditional male Jewish society are criticized. Shloyme's identification with the marginalized artisan-artists establishes an alternative to traditional Jewish male socialization.

The work's childhood theme first appears in the beginning of the "Ptikhta." Although Mendele has not seen Reb Shloyme in years and realizes that they have both aged, he nevertheless characterizes Reb Shloyme as youthful, with burning eyes and fervor of speech, in short, *eyn alt-yingl* (an old-lad). Later the same evening after the incident with the poor *yeshive* student, Reb Shloyme's physical appearance changes to such an extent that Mendele hardly recognizes his friend: "In front of me sits an old, weak man, a broken vessel [*tsebrokhener sharbn*], and the face is heavily wrinkled."[61] Having been confronted with his painful years as a wandering *yeshive* student and the traumatic loss of his father, Reb Shloyme now looks old. This quality of being simultaneously a youngster and an old man characterizes a number of the positive characters in Reb Shloyme's account, such as Lippe Ruven, Itsik the Smith and Hershl Keyles the Carpenter. They are referred to as *alt-yinglekh* (old-lads) because of their love of animals, children, nature and artistic inclinations. Belonging to the bottom of the *shtetl* hierarchy of *melamdim* (religious school teachers) and *bal-melokhes* (artisans), they are even marginalized from these groups because of their carefree childish behaviour. As such they become alternative father figures for Shloyme.

Reb Khayim's background, marriage and present life, as an influential *balebos* (patriarch) responsible for the meat tax, is depicted in chapter two and three as typically representative of the Jewish establishment in K. In contrast, Shloyme is introduced in chapter four through his talent for mimicking other people. This is the first indication of Shloyme's artistic affinity for parody and satire, which the mature Abramovitsh developed to perfection through the medium of Mendele. Shloyme's relationship to his *melamed* (religious school teacher), Lippe Ruven with "the passion of an artist" *(der bren fun a kinstler)* who draws, carves and works on artistic assignments while teaching him, is depicted in idealized terms. This kind of education is unique in the *shtetl*, where the norm is a master-slave relationship between teacher and pupil, with corporal punishment as the most prevalent pedagogical method.

Reb Khayim has assigned Lippe Ruven to teach Shloyme the Bible, emphasizing the development of the child's fantasy and imagination. The Bible is here contrasted with the Talmud's arid intellectual logic belonging to the sterile, adult world. This idealized picture of the birth of the artist as child exemplifies Abramovitsh's view on what constitutes a proper education. It is fundamentally different from the degenerated, mind crippling *kheyder* depicted in all its corrupting consequences in *Dos kleyne mentshele*. Itsik the Smith and Hershl Keyles the Carpenter deviate from the Jewish male adult norm because of their wild bohemian behavior, exemplified in the scene where Hershl Kayles plays the violin for the children. The traditional *shtetl* childhood is only a brief dream; youth disappears quickly and adult life starts at the threshold of puberty when the adolescent is married off.

The end of childhood is marked by the death of Shloyme's father, which forces him to look for ways to sustain himself as a wandering *yeshive* student. Suddenly Shloyme is faced with the worries of an adult; his childhood's intuitive affinity with nature is relegated to the past: "Paralysed he suddenly stands in the middle of the field, where he used to walk, his forehead is wrinkled, his face hazy from new thoughts. His soul is somewhere else, far from woods, charm, beauty, God's wonder, which not long ago was so close to his heart! Now he broods about practical purpose [*takhles*]."[62] The liberation from being forced to search out a *takhles* as wandering *yeshive* student is presented in the first chapter. At this moment the narrative of alienation, loss and suffering culminating at the end of part one and continuing through part two, is brought to an end. This first chapter indicates the beginning of a new narrative about his artistic origins that radically changes Shloyme's life. Shloyme writes his first Hebrew poems, roaming in the woods near the town Mlinitse, a few miles from K, after having returned to his mother who has married the miller of the little town. Abramovitsh shows that the liberation from adulthood, after the termination of childhood, has already been predetermined at the child's first moment of self-revelation in nature in the "Ptikhta." In order for Shloyme to reconnect with this primordial experience of himself in nature, he must break away from the restrictive realm of traditional Jewish male society by emulating the creativity of the child artisans.

Reb Shloyme's account begins and ends at Passover, pointing to his childhood account as governed by cyclical temporality. The death of Shloyme's father is supplanted by the birth of his artist self at the liberating time of Passover, the spring holiday celebrating the Jewish Exodus from Egypt. Only by transcending the linear chronology of the adult world—goal oriented *takhles* inexorably leading towards death—is Shloyme able to enter his childhood's cyclical time. This can only be accomplished through his use of literary tropes as a means of imagining what has been irretrievably lost.

For many Yiddish autobiographers the loss of one or both parents became a central theme of their quest.[63] They depicted the death of one or both parents as a metaphor for the loss of being rooted in a traditional family they had left behind in the pursuit of a literary career.[64] The devastating experience of being orphaned at a young age is a central theme in the first part of *Shloyme reb khayims* and colors the second part's description of Shloyme's *yeshive* years. Although a more direct expression of grief and pain is conveyed in the second part, this theme is, much like part one, crafted into a bildungsroman about a protagonist from bygone days: "May one be protected, God of the universe, from such loneliness which Shloymele felt upon his return to the *shtetl*. Loneliness is bitter in every form, but there are differences of degree and of kind. There exists a lonely condition that in itself, without any comparison with earlier, is bitter enough. Pity on the unlucky fellow who has never experienced a good hour in his life; who is lonely all the time like a stone, a stranger in the world. But there is a big difference between being a stranger and being estranged. Apart from the bitter taste of being a stranger, being estranged has an even more sharp taste—a terrible bitterness which is increasingly aggravated in comparison with the good, happy bygone years, and Shloymele's loneliness belonged exactly to this latter kind."[65] This voice is intent upon conveying Shloymele's experience of alienation and loneliness as compared to "the happy bygone days." It is an epic voice concerned with the flow and rhythm of the narrative and as such artistically self-conscious in its depiction of a complex internal reality. At the same time the quote summarizes the main theme of exile and estrangement that figures so prominently in the "Ptikhta." Abramovitsh's choice of this artistic voice and the third person novel for his autobiography in *Shloyme reb khayims* reflects his lack of aspiration towards exploring his life and self in a more intimate way. Two main features of *Shloyme reb khayims* established its canonical status as the first Yiddish literary autobiography. First, Abramovitsh inscribed his life story in a novel featuring Mendele Moykher Sforim. Abramovitsh defined life-writing as yet another expression of the fiction-making process governed by suspense, multiple perspectives, chronology, and contrast. Framing *Shloyme reb khayims* as a novel created a paradigm for Yiddish life writing that became highly influential in the development of the genre. Even more important was the second main feature introduced in *Shloyme reb khayims:* the self was conceived as both uniquely individual and representative of a collective way of life threatened by extinction.

2

A Whistle of Defiance

Peretz is the leader of the period, more correctly would it be to say: the centre of the period, a center of influences. Everything is mirrored in him, and reflected back from him like in a magnifying glass. He is not a founder of a literary school, because he was, to the end of his life, an explorer [*zukher*]. . . . He continuously switched from style to style.

> H. D. Nomberg, "A Literary Generation" (1919)[1]

Peretz was silent for a moment; then he said almost to himself: I am only envious of two writers, Shakespeare and Sholem Aleichem.

> Y. Y. Trunk, *Poyln: zikhroynes un bilder*, vol. 5 (1949)[2]

Sholem Aleichem mentioned in a 1895 letter to the Yiddish writer Mordechai Spektor that, "the best novel is a person's life, and my life is very rich in various episodes, characters and types,—I have decided to begin describing my life (autobiography) at length from my birth until age twenty. I intend to publish my autobiography in your *Hoyz-fraynd* [a Yiddish literary journal edited by Spektor]. You probably understand that simply describing how I ate, learned, ran around, jumped—I won't do that. I will select the richest episodes which will appear regularly, step by step, and those that will have a particular interest not only for myself but also for others."[3] The most likely impetus for Sholem Aleichem's autobiographical plan, which took nearly twenty years to implement with the publication of *Funem yarid*, was Abramovitsh's "Ptikhta," published in Hebrew the previous year (1894).[4] However, this epistolary reference to life-writing did not have any immediate consequences, except for a short autobiographical sketch written in 1903 in response to the Hebrew writer Ravnitsky.[5] It is, however, interesting as

Sholem Aleichem's first conception of the link between fiction and life-writing ("the best novel is a person's life"). Although Sholem Aleichem later declared that he wanted to depict the first fifty years of his life in ten volumes, the 1895 letter's intention to cover only the first twenty years of his life turned out to be more accurate.[6]

Sholem Aleichem's autobiographical sketch from 1903, "To My Biography" was modelled on Abramovitsh's "Sketches to My Biography." Unlike Abramovitsh, who also focused on the Jewish writers' resistance against writing in Yiddish, Sholem Aleichem simply mentions that he began writing in the language of Mendele Moykher-Sforim and sent his first story "Di ibergekhapte briv" (Overheard Letters) to the first Yiddish newspaper in Russia, *Folksblat*, in 1883. The fourteen years separating the two sketches had revolutionized the status of Yiddish literature from one of marginality to that of an established vibrant literature with three classical writers. Sholem Aleichem's sketch outlines the main events of his personal and artistic life as later depicted in *Funem yarid*. Clearly, Sholem Aleichem's autobiographical project was already crystallized in 1903, although it was not begun until five years later.

Sholem Aleichem's work on his memoirs consisted of two aborted attempts in 1908 and 1913, resulting in only a partial realization of the project. Both times it was the onset of a serious illness that triggered Sholem Aleichem's return to his autobiographical project. At the age of fifty, Sholem Aleichem suffered his first acute episode of open pulmonary tuberculosis at the end of the summer of 1908.[7] In the introduction to *Funem yarid*, he links this life-threatening event with his decision to write his autobiography. Sholem Aleichem referred to his autobiography as a testament (*tsvoe*). In a dedication to his children written in February 1916, he called the work: "my book of books, the Song of Songs of my soul."[8] Only after he settled in New York in 1915, seriously ill with tuberculosis, did he begin this project by writing the first three parts of the projected multi-volume work.

Several critics have mentioned the vast cultural and ideological gulf that separated the Kiev stock broker Sholem Rabinovitsh from the Yiddish writer Sholem Aleichem.[9] However, the true distinction between these two actually transcended the difference between Sholem Rabinovitsh and his artistic pseudonym. As a writer, Rabinovitsh was subsumed and, to a large extent, effaced by his creation Sholem Aleichem. Therefore, it was fitting that in the introduction to *Funem yarid*, the writer distinguished between Sholem Aleichem *der shrayber* and Sholem Aleichem *dem mentshn*: "I'll talk about myself in the third person. [That means] I, Sholem Aleichem the writer [*der shrayber*], will tell the true story of Sholem Aleichem the man [*dem mentshn*], informally and without adornments and embellishments as if an absolute stranger [*a zaytiker parshoyn, a vild-fremder*] were talking, yet one who accompanied him everywhere, even to the seven circles of hell. . . . And may He who gives man strength to remember one's entire life grant that I omit nothing and nobody during my fifty years at the great fair."[10] Similar remarks referring to Dante's seven circles of hell appear in the introductions to *Menakhem mendl* and *Motl peyse dem khazns* (1907–1916, Motl the Son of Cantor Peyse).[11] As such, Sholem Aleichem *dem mentshn* can be equated to fictional characters such as Menakhem Mendl and Motl because of their identical relationship to Sholem Aleichem *der shrayber*. The choice of a third person novelistic account is obviously influenced by *Shloyme reb khayims*. But whereas Abramovitsh elaborates on the distinction between Mendele and Reb Shloyme as separate characters inhabiting fundamentally different cultural and social realms, Sholem Aleichem *der shrayber* effaces his alter ego in *Funem yarid*. The distinction between Sholem Aleichem *der shrayber* and Sholem Aleichem *dem mentshn* becomes instead a question of different aspects of the same persona.[12]

A passage in "The Crisis," the final chapter of the third volume of *Funem yarid* marking the end of Sholem Aleichem's childhood years, is unusually self-revealing. Sholem Aleichem attempts to explore the personal reasons for his many disappointments and losses which "left a scar on the soul forever" *(a krel in der neshome oyf eybik)*:

Whenever the author of this autobiography descends to the deep catacombs of his distant childhood, brings forth memories of bygone periods, delves into his later experiences, from the big world market place which is called "life" and considers all this soberly [*klorer kop*] and judiciously [*kaltn moyekh*], he marvels at his ability to survive so many merciless beatings, cruel deceptions and bitter disappointments—and still remain hale and hearty for fresh beatings, further deceptions and even greater disappointments. The blows themselves weren't as terrible as the disappointments and deceptions. You can recover from a beating, but a disappointment leaves a scar on the soul forever. Sholem had experienced spiritual disappointments and financial deceptions. As will be shown in future chapters, he knew how it felt to lose a fortune quickly per the advice of all kinds of Menachem Mendls. He can say with a clear conscience that he was less shaken by the monetary loss than by other people's deceit and by his loss of trust in others. The disappointment is what always embittered him and drove him to the grave.[13]

These observations are triggered by having been betrayed and rejected by the cantor's daughter with whom the young Sholem is in love. She later runs away with a clerk and converts to Catholicism. This episode crystallizes a number of devastating experiences resulting from Sholem Aleichem's trusting character. Behind these experiences looms the major loss of his childhood: his mother's death from cholera right after Sholem's *bar-mitsve*. None of these formative events are discussed in a reflective manner, except in the quotation above, where Sholem Aleichem acknowledges the pain and suffering inflicted upon him. Sholem Aleichem's ability to bounce back after having been deceived by con men and the unexpected death of his mother is due to his talent for transforming deception and loss into hilarious stories about the absurdity of human existence.[14] One of Sholem's earliest lessons, taught him by his childhood friend Shmulik the Orphan, was to search for the hidden treasure. Like Shmulik, Sholem learns how to recreate reality so that it yields consolation, hope and narrative magic. This talent enables him to cope with the loss of being orphaned and provides him with an outlet for his artistic talent for mimicking and parodying other people.

The distrust of others is the most excruciating experience of his life. However, the character Sholem Aleichem is obviously insufficient to the task of confronting this distrust with a "clear head" and "cold mind," instead of employing it as means for humorous storytelling. Sholem Aleichem's effectiveness as a literary character is based on the reader's trust in his ability to make people open up to him as a listener and a confidant. To show distrust and betrayal to be central to the formation of his artistic identity would undermine the identity of Sholem Aleichem. Thus the drive towards autobiographical self-reflection that Sholem Aleichem expresses in the above quote is in fact antithetical to his essential qualities. In order to maintain his artistic integrity he must avoid understanding the "deeper catacombs of childhood," in "the seven circles of hell." Thus, *Funem yarid* only allows us to unravel the formative events in Sholem Aleichem's life and artistic career in a very indirect way.

The Yiddish writer Linetski's short autobiographical sketch *Funem yarid* (1909) provided Sholem Aleichem with the title and central metaphor of his autobiographical novel.[15] The fair signalled the bustling center of the *shtetl*, the communal public space that, rather than the private space of the self, was the focus of the book. Linetski even provided the proof-text for Sholem Aleichem's declaration in his introduction to *Funem yarid* by stating the sexual impropriety of "revealing the naked I for the audience" *(heroysfirn dem naketn ikh farn publikum)*.[16] In the introduction, Sholem Aleichem points out that to "[w]rite your autobiography"—the real story, not an invented tale—"is easier said than done. It means taking stock [*opgebn din-vekhezbn*] of your entire life for your readers and confessing [*zogn vide*] to the whole world."[17] Sholem Aleichem distances himself from the traditional Jewish confession, or *vide*, that is, the two times an orthodox Jew is commanded to confess his or her sins aloud: the deathbed confession and Jewish communal repentance on Yom Kippur (The Day of Atonement). This confessional aspect of life-writing is also related to a non-Jewish literary tradition originating with Rousseau. Sholem Aleichem rejects both of these approaches as inadequate for *Funem yarid*. Instead, he models his autobiography on *Shloyme reb khayims* in the form of a third person novel that focuses on the writer's life as a prism of Jewish cultural history in the Pale of Settlement. Mapping the "deep catacombs" of childhood, and tracing its meanings for the writer's work and life belongs to a fundamentally different discourse that originates with Peretz. In *Mayne zikhroynes* (My Memoirs), published in 1913–1914, at the same time as *Funem yarid*, Peretz would employ confessional modes as a way of expressing the unconscious part of his self beyond the public realm of Jewish society.

Sholem Aleichem's correspondence reveals interesting details about the evolving character of *Funem yarid* between 1908 and 1916. Six or seven chapters were completed in 1908 and, according to his son-in-law, the Hebrew and Yiddish writer Y. D. Berkovitsh, mailed to Yiddish writer Dovid Pinski in New York. However, Pinski could not find a newspaper willing to accept the work.[18] Sholem Aleichem's income during the last decade of his life was dependent on the salary he received from serialized novels and other feuilletons published in the Hebrew and Yiddish press. After 1908, in addition to supporting a big family, Sholem Aleichem required constant medical supervision and extended convalescence in the resort town of Nervi in Italy. In other words, the impetus to write his autobiography competed with his bread-and-butter work for the Yiddish press. Yiddish readers expected Sholem Aleichem to turn out humorous stories addressing contemporary issues instead of indulging in multi-volume childhood reminiscences.

The second time Sholem Aleichem turned to his autobiography was in January 1913. Inspired by the recent publication of Yekhezkel Kotik's *Mayne zikhroynes*, he wrote the first version of the initial fifty-one chapters.[19] Some of these were translated into Hebrew by Berkovitsh and published in *Hatsefirah* in 1913–1914 with the title "Sefer hayaldut" (The Book of Childhood).[20] Two other attempts at finding a publisher for his autobiography in the spring and summer of 1913 proved fruitless. The first possibility was the newly established monthly *Di yidishe velt*, edited by Shmuel Niger and Dovid Bergelson. In a letter to Niger dated March 31, 1913, Sholem Aleichem mentions that Bergelson's attitude towards publishing his memoirs is positive and that he might be willing to pay him a respectable salary for them. However, another member of the editorial board, Zelig Kalmanovitsh rejected the work.[21] The second option was the businessman Shmuel Shrira, who offered to pay a monthly salary and sponsor the publication of the entire work in book form. After lengthy written negotiations in the spring and summer 1913, Shrira abandoned the project. Particularly interesting is a letter to Shrira on April 30, 1913, in which Sholem Aleichem outlined the work's cultural historical significance:

[I]n the meantime, it is only a beginning, the Creation, from my childhood, how the chicken was hatched out of the egg, a kind of "embryo" as it is called in books. Moving forward, it will become broader and deeper, the horizons will spread out, types and images will increase like the sand on the seashore. By the way, my own personality will also become clear, as human being, and after that, as writer—and in this fashion we will come to the real thing, to Yiddish literature with its prophets, true and false, with its works, worthy and shallow etc. But much more than the literary world will be depicted. Before the reader's eyes will pass complete cinematographic images from the secular world of commerce. The whole stock exchange with its actual and fantastic Menakhem Mendls, based on my twenty-three-year-old debut on the Kiev (Yehupetser) stock exchange until today. A whole chain of movements in our communal life with our communal leaders will be unravelled: *hasidim, misnagdim,* assimilationists, nationalists, Lovers of Zion, Zionists, Territorialists, Socialists—everything that I have lived through . . . to sum up, it is not my biography, but the biography of our little Jewish world.[22]

At the same time, shortly after Sholem Aleichem's autobiography had been rejected for publication by *Di yidishe velt*, the monthly's editorial board invited Peretz to submit his autobiography. The first seven chapters of Peretz's *Mayne zikhroynes* were published in instalments from May to December of 1913 in *Di yidishe velt*. Although Sholem Aleichem later published the last chapter of Tevye, "Lekh Lekha" in *Di yidishe velt*, his reputation as not "only" a humorist but also as a serious writer had not yet taken hold among the Jewish intelligentsia. A critical re-evaluation of Sholem Aleichem among the young Yiddish literati first occurred in the decade following his death in 1916. This is evident from Shmuel Niger's introduction to his monograph about Sholem Aleichem (1928).[23] As a result, Sholem Aleichem's *Funem yarid* was caught between a rock and a hard place. It was not considered artful enough to be included in the highbrow journal *Di yidishe velt*, yet not *shund* (trashy) enough to be accepted as a serialized novel by the Yiddish press.

Particularly revealing in this regard is a letter from Sholem Aleichem to the Yiddish writer Yankev Dinezon on June 9, 1913. In it, the writer indignantly rejects Dinezon's allegations, purported by the literary critic Bal-Makhshoves, that Shmuel Y. Yatzkan, the editor of the Yiddish daily *Haynt* in Warsaw, had turned Sholem Aleichem into a *shund* writer: "Sholem Aleichem has never sold his pen for money. He always writes for 'its own sake' [*lishma*]. Good or bad—that is a question of taste and a feeling. But he loves his work with his whole heart and with his whole soul [*bekol levevo vebekol nafsho*], and regardless of how much he is paid, it cannot pay for his health and his soul and the blood which he pours into every line, into every word! Sickness and ill health and a shorter life are the result of his writing, regardless of his productivity and his light style. Several chapters of his novel, which the wise Bal-Makhshoves calls 'second hand goods,' have been revised at least ten times."[24] Ironically, Sholem Aleichem began his literary career with a crusade against *shund* in *Shomer's mishpet* (1888). Now as a seasoned writer, he is forced to defend his artistic integrity against criticism of being a hired hack. As he is fully aware, the origin of this view originated with Dinezon's friend and literary hero, Peretz. Sholem Aleichem's resentment of the Jewish cultural hero of the day is expressed indirectly in the same letter: "I think that the atmosphere in Warsaw is, pardon me for saying so, rotten" ("Ikh meyn az di atmosfere in varshe iz, mekhile, azoy fareypesht"). The young Yiddish literati affiliated with Peretz, and the popular Yiddish press, although diametrically opposed in their literary politics, agreed on one thing: Sholem Aleichem was a humorist, and not in any way to be considered a high-brow writer like Peretz and Abramovitsh. The latter published one of his autobiographical sketches in *Di yidishe velt* in 1914 and, in the same year, serialized the unfinished second part of *Shloyme reb khayims* in Yatzkan's *Haynt*.[25]

Sholem Aleichem's final turn to autobiography occurred after his dramatic escape from a Northern German resort town to neutral Denmark at the outbreak of World War I. During his 1914 summer lecture tour through Russia he was received as a celebrity writer and a leading representative of Russian Jewry, whose fate he now narrowly escaped. Although he was worshipped by crowds of Russian Jews in Copenhagen and on board the ship to New York, his situation was not fundamentally different from that of other Jewish refugees.[26] The insular, luxurious life he had been leading since 1908 in the resort towns of Switzerland, Italy and Germany had been abruptly terminated by the outbreak of World War I. In addition to disrupting his creative life and his steady income as a contributor to the Yiddish press in Russia, he was forced to relocate his family to New York. That was the only place where he could continue the affiliation with the Yiddish press that was crucial in supporting his family. He was suddenly plunged into the cauldron of Jewish immigrant life in New York as a refugee from Russia in the winter of 1915.

This dislocation played an important role in his decision to devote his best creative energies during the last one and a half years of his life to the completion of *Funem yarid*. The contract he signed with the New York Yiddish daily *Der tog* required him to publish one segment of the autobiography every week in addition to his humorous stories. *Der tog* was willing to take on the commercially risky endeavour of publishing *Funem yarid* for the privilege of having Sholem Aleichem as staff writer. However, the newspaper's lack of enthusiasm about *Funem yarid* was evident during the serialization of the work. Sholem Aleichem was expected to make money for the newspaper by giving his readers humorous *feuilletons*. A childhood memoir about the old country did not fit *Der tog*'s commercial calculations.[27]

The freedom to explore his earliest memories in *Funem yarid* helped Sholem Aleichem to distance himself from both his immediate surroundings in New York and the fate of his friends and readers in Europe. As a result, *Funem yarid* became suffused with nostalgia in the original meaning of the word: it became an artistic outlet for Sholem Aleichem's homesickness. Suzanne Vromen points out that the term *nostalgia* was originally coined by Johannes Hofer as a medical term in a Swiss thesis from 1688: "Hofer's thesis was intended to translate the emotional phenomenon into a medical one and the new term was, appropriately based on Greek words: "return home" and "sorrow." The pathological model is also evident in the German term *Heimweh* and the English word *homesickness*."[28] Both the commonly held views of nostalgia as a regressive, pathological return to the past and as a creative, liberating outlet are on display in *Funem yarid*.

Sholem Aleichem created an autobiographical counter-life embedded in an idealized version of his childhood. This image excluded any troubling memories about anti-Semitism and conflict with the non-Jewish world. Dan Miron points out that any reference to the Catholic Church in Voronke has been erased from *Funem yarid*. Unlike Wolf Rabinovitsh's memoir of his brother Sholem Aleichem, which paints a much more accurate historical picture of Voronke replete with priests and monastery, *Funem yarid* refashions the mythological image of the *shtetl* in Yiddish literature in the nineteenth century.[29] Sholem Aleichem's portrayed a lost childhood paradise disconnected from his present life. This tendency nostalgically to recreate the past was exacerbated by Sholem Aleichem's status, working on *Funem yarid* in New York, as an exile.

However, *Funem yarid* must not be reduced to an escapist response to the outbreak of the war, or to the author's refugee status in New York, as some Soviet Yiddish critics have done.[30] Berkovitsh's melodramatic depiction of his adored master's last year and a half in New York in the *Sholem aleykhem bukh* (1926) was part of his effort to perpetuate Sholem Aleichem's own myth about himself.[31] This myth can be summed up by the poem that Sholem Aleichem crafted in 1905 and that later was inscribed on his tombstone:

> Do ligt a yid, a posheter,
> Geshribn yidish-taytsh far vayber,
> Un farn prostn folk hot er—
> Geven a humorist a shrayber.
>
> Dos gantse lebn oysgelakht,
> Geshlogn mit der velt kapores.
> Di gantse velt hot gut gemakht
> Un er—oy vey—geven af tsores!
>
> Un dafke demolt, ven der oylem hot
> Gelakht, geklatsht un fleg zikh freyen,
> Hot er gekrenkt—dos veyst nor got—
> Besod, az keyner zol nit zen.
>
> Here lies a simple Jew,
> who wrote *yidish-taytsh* for women,
> and for the common people—
> he was a humorist-writer.
>
> He ridiculed all of life;
> reviled the world.

The whole world made out very well,
and he—alas—had troubles!

And precisely when his audience
was laughing, applauding, and having a good time,
he was ailing—only God knows this—
in secret, so no one would see.

This poem is vintage Sholem Aleichem in its theatrical and operatic style, or in Cynthia Ozick's words, its "sweep of aria."[32] The clown's crying face behind the joyful mask is a conventional trope used to create a myth about Sholem Aleichem as a folk writer and a humorist. This image is turned into an anachronism through the use of the term *yidish-taytsh*, a pre-modern name for Yiddish employed in old Yiddish literature and usually combined with a formulaic address to "women and unlearned men." The poem uses this outmoded literary convention to link Sholem Aleichem's artistic self to a concept of Yiddish literature as folksy, anachronistic and entertaining. Unlike Abramovitsh's Mendele figure, Sholem Aleichem was crafted as a persona that excluded any separate identity beyond the delightful expression on the clown's mask. The Sholem Aleichem persona distorted the autobiographical truth of *Funem yarid* while, as with his other major novels such as *Motl peyse dem khazns* and *Tevye der milkhiker*, magnifying the work's mythological quality.[33]

In *Funem yarid*, Sholem Aleichem confronted the formative events of his life: the search for the treasure; how he became a writer; how he found the love of his life; the social decline of his family; becoming an orphan at age thirteen. These important events form the narrative building blocks of a picaresque novel. What Dan Miron calls "the Kasrilevkezation of most of his *shtetl* depictions"[34] is evident in *Funem yarid*. (Kasrilevke was the name of Sholem Aleichem's quintessential fictive *shtetl*.) Instead of attempting to depict autobiographical and social-historical events truthfully, the book addresses the central myths of Sholem Aleichem's work in the form and style of a novel.

Like the rest of Sholem Aleichem's work, the central myth is the treasure (*oytser*). The importance of this myth is crystallized at Sholem's exit from the *shtetl* Voronke after his father's failure in business forced the family to relocate. Upon leaving Voronke, Sholem recalls how his childhood friend Shmulik the Orphan first told him about the hidden treasure. He imagines how he would use the treasure to help his family and the poor people in the *shtetl*. When Gergeleh the Thief, one of the poorest kids in the *shtetl*, appears, Sholem decides to tell him about the treasure. Gergeleh cuts him short: he wants something concrete, not fairy tales about hidden treasures. As a result, Sholem gives him a pair of old boots, which Gergeleh angrily rejects. He was looking forward to at least brand new boots or a hint at where the treasure is hidden. The autobiographer reflects on the incident: "It was a silly incident—but how much aggravation it caused. Gergeleh's flight embittered Sholem's farewells to this village and poisoned all the joy of his first big, beautiful long trip. Try as he might to blot out the image of his humiliated friend, Sholem remained haunted by it. The scene repeated itself in his mind's eye and crimped his heart. "You've humiliated and shamed a poor friend."[35] Sholem Aleichem's Kasrilevke idyll, his childhood paradise, suddenly collapses. The curtain falls and the estrangement of the autobiographer from his origin as a prodigal son of the *shtetl* is revealed in all its stark reality. Neither the myth of the treasure nor the old boots will change anything in the life of Gergeleh the Thief. In fact, Sholem Aleichem views the *shtetl* itself as an abandoned orphan who only deserves pity and compassion. Even as a child Sholem did not belong to the same realm as Gergeleh the Thief, but he inhabited an imaginary *shtetl* that he transformed into the locus of mythological images such as treasures and larger-than-life characters.

The specific character of the origin of Sholem's artistic identity is related in two episodes in chapters fifty-two and fifty-three. In the first episode, he is caught writing on the wall of a house on Sabbath afternoon by his orthodox uncle Pinye. His debut as writer consists of copying a famous Russian song and illustrating it with the picture of a round-faced little man on the wall of a house. This transgression is severely punished, and Sholem is given the pejorative name *pisatel* ("author" in Russian) by his teachers. In the next chapter, a contradictory version of the Jewish writer is presented. Sholem watches his father and other leaders of the community laugh heartily on a *shabes* afternoon as they read an old Yiddish storybook. Unlike his first Russian writing, these Yiddish stories do not subversively undermine religious and cultural norms; rather, they are enjoyed as entertainment by Jewish middle-class men on the holiest day of the week. Watching this scene, Sholem Aleichem makes it clear that his "profoundest wish was that, God willing, when he grew up and became an adult, he too would write a book that would make Jews laugh and good-naturedly curse the author."[36]

The next stop on Sholem Aleichem's journey to becoming a Yiddish writer is his three years as secretary for the rich Jewish landowner

Loyev. As in a fairy-tale, the hero is, after many trials, finally given the ultimate prize: a secure position at the top of the social pyramid with time and leisure to devote most of his time to literary work, while dating his future wife, Loyev's daughter Olga. However, after three years the love affair is called off by Olga's father, when Sholem's love letters fall, against the lovers' wishes, into Loyev's hands. At this point, Sholem Aleichem stops the narrative with two dotted lines and makes an aside about his hero: "What do these dots mean? They stand for a long, dark night. Everything was wrapped in a thick mist. The lonely wanderer was groping for his way. He kept stumbling over stones or falling into a pit. He fell, scrambled up, continued on his path, tripped over another stone and fell into another pit, taking no notice of the bright world around him. He did foolish things, made mistakes, one greater than the other. A blindfolded man cannot possibly find the right road. A blindfolded man must go astray—and Sholem went astray. Until he found himself."[37] What is glossed over in this aside is precisely the very stuff of modern autobiography: the failures, the doubts on the road to self-knowledge, the person behind his artistic representation. As Hana Wirth Nesher points out, "[T]he autobiography is often an attempt at setting the record straight, of telling the 'facts.'" She mentions that the particular ways in which this attempt is accomplished "will depend on the extent to which the autobiographer presents his or her life as representative of a collective identity or as a unique subject who has been heretofore either unknown or known but misrepresented."[38] Clearly, Sholem Aleichem lacked the desire to reveal or confess anything about his "true" life except insofar as it served as a symbol for the life of the collective.

Sholem Aleichem's fictionalized his life history in *Funem yarid* by making it an intrinsic part of his mythological Kasrilevke. His death prevented him from implementing his grandiose plan for a multivolume memoir of cultural historical scope. A much more complex, indepth portrait of the man behind the Sholem Aleichem persona can be pieced together from Sholem Aleichem's rich correspondence and Y. D. Berkovitsh's intimate portrait of his father-in-law in his memoirs. However, even in Sholem Aleichem's personal letters the tendency to hide behind literary devices and the unmistakable tenor of his voice is evident. As the Yiddish critic Shmuel Niger pointed out, *Funem yarid* became a model for Yiddish autobiography, a lesson not in self-revelation and self-exploration, but in how to disguise oneself: "an autobiography is either a disguised apology or a confession (*vide*). The intention in both cases is not so much the palm of the hand which is exposed as the two palms which are disguised (complete confessional autobiographies [*vide-oytobiografyes*] such as the holy Augustine, Rousseau or Tolstoy are exceptions)."[39] Superseding Abramovitsh's self-critical, brooding "Ptikhta" and elaborate bildungsroman *Shloyme reb khayims* in popularity, the adventures of *Funem yarid*'s picaresque hero, depicted in small, upbeat instalments, became the point of departure for Yiddish life-writing, particularly after the Holocaust.[40]

Paul E. Eakin points out that the "modern autobiography seems to have emerged concurrently with—and is perhaps a symbolic manifestation of—people's acquisition of a distinctly personal space in which to live, rooms of their own, in which . . . the bourgeois values of privacy, intimacy, and 'home' could flower."[41] It would take a self-conscious modernist such as I. L. Peretz to introduce the intimacy of "personal space" by rejecting Abramovitsh's master trope of Yiddish literature as a theatrical performance, even in the case of internal monologue.[42] Peretz's autobiographical innovation was a result of his modernization of Yiddish literature, which transformed Yiddish literature from a medium for entertainment and enlightenment into a vehicle of artistic self-expression. This shift between Abramovitsh and Sholem Aleichem's novelistic lives and Peretz's loosely structured set of reminiscences contributed to the formation of Yiddish literary modernism.[43]

Two characteristics set Peretz's autobiographical method apart from that of *Shloyme reb khayims* and *Funem yarid*. Peretz intends *Mayne zikhroynes* to be a *shlisl* (key) to his work. Personal reminiscences are included only to the extent that they highlight his literary works and their aesthetics. Secondly, Peretz's autobiographical account is structured by memories that he uncovers through the process of writing. The magnet that pulls these memory-fragments, or, in Peretz's words, *ayzn shtoyb* (iron dust), from their hidden existence in the self are the facts, ideas, and moods associated with them. These reminiscences and their association with specific facts, ideas, and moods are used to exemplify the autobiographer's artistic credo.[44]

Mayne zikhroynes outlines the process of transforming autobiographical memories into building blocks for literary works. It narrates a particular version of his life, the origin of the artist in childhood, "which I once more go over in my mind on the way from child to writer."[45] In the beginning of every chapter, critical passages present a particular existential or artistic complex that is then exemplified in a series of reminiscences. Peretz narrates his life story in the first person and never changes narrative perspective or views himself as representative of collective historical and cultural phenomenon the way Abramovitsh does in *Shloyme reb khayims*. Writing at the age of sixty, Peretz still envisions himself creating new works in the future, "if there is time, I will build and fill a new barn."[46] Unlike Reb Shloyme who similarly looked back at his life from the vantage point of his sixty-odd years, Peretz does not present a *khezhbn hanefesh* (spiritual stocktaking). Rather, his autobiography is a critical description of his artistic achievements and their origin in his life story. In the prologue, the modern quest for exhibitionist self-revelation is rejected as *opfal* (trash). Although Peretz's autobiography also rejects a traditional religious world view, he still adheres to a moral ethos that excludes the public display of *zindikayt* (sinfulness), acts that transgress certain ethical standards.[47] The image of the religious Jew who goes to the *mikve* (the ritual bath) to purify himself before prayer is compared to the artist who must purify himself of "sinful" thoughts before he can express himself creatively. In Peretz's universe, the artist's search for meaning takes place introspectively in the artist's dialogue with the hidden part of his self.

The novel as proof-text for the autobiographies of Abramovitsh and Sholem Aleichem is absent in *Mayne zikhroynes*. Peretz never wrote a novel, and excelled primarily as a short story writer and playwright. His only other long prose work, *Bilder fun a provints rayze* (1891, Pictures from a Journey in the Provinces), consists of a series of impressionistic pieces rather than a coherent narrative. In a letter to Shmuel Niger, the editor of *Di yidishe velt*, in which the work was serialized in 1913, Peretz insisted that the discrete chapters of his autobiography comprised the basic unit of the work: "First of all, you must understand that I present the work in chapters, because that is the form in which they pour out of me, and dividing them, you make me completely confused and I think the reader even more so."[48] Peretz's immediate audience for his autobiography was his literary disciples, young Yiddish writers and critics such as Shmuel Niger and Dovid Bergelson. They were both on the editorial staff of the monthly *Di yidishe velt* (Vilna), which serialized the first seven chapters of *Mayne zikhroynes* in 1913 (nr. 5–12).[49] At the end of chapter seven, Peretz mentions that his arranged marriage completes the first part of his autobiography. The eighth chapter, published in the Warsaw journal *Dos lebn* in 1914 (nr. 51, 63, 69), was intended as the first chapter of a projected second part of the autobiography left unfinished at the time of Peretz's sudden death in 1915.

Peretz sought to depict his life's major themes in distinct chapters through the juxtaposition of different sections that present reminiscences, their connection to his artistic work, and meta-poetic reflections. In this regard, Peretz is indebted to a Romantic biographical approach in which "synecdochic episodes represent the whole of the character and life of the subject."[50] The narrative in *Mayne zikhroynes* is propelled by life-cycle events, beginning with Peretz as child prodigy and ending with his arranged marriage. The reminiscences appear as a narrative sequence of obstacles on the autobiographer's spiritual journey. Folk mythology such as "the dog as guardian," "the three sisters," "the *pardes*" (orchard), "the key to the library," and "the whistle" are utilized in order to reflect the archetypical character of the autobiographer's existential quest. The final chapter of the unfinished autobiography gives a detailed description of Peretz's wedding and ends with the epiphany in the Swiss mountains. Chronologically, this epiphany belongs to a much later life phase and appears as the revelatory climax in the autobiographer's search for artistic truth.

The titles of the introduction and eight chapters illustrate the major themes of the work (childhood, education, enlightenment, sexuality, death, and marriage) and indicate that the Haskalah autobiography is the narrative proof-text.[51] However, Peretz also points out that the Haskalah ideas never struck root in Zamosc because of its rabbi, Moshe Wahl, and the lack of an intellectual Gentile population with which the *maskilim* could exchange ideas. The autobiographer's development was not triggered by Haskalah ideas or other ideological trends but by his unconscious, sexual desires and the existential angst to which he sought answers in kabbalistic and other religious texts.[52] His "conversion" from religious Jew to freethinker is described in terms of a folk tale hero's encounter with archetypical situations, such as his romantic involvement with the three sisters, his entry into the orchard *(pardes)*, his confrontation with death, and the visit to their *besmedresh* (prayer and study house), the Gentile library. Instead of running away from home to seek his fortune in the big city, Peretz is moved by his mother's tears to stay home and he eventually accepts an arranged marriage. The typical Haskalah narrative has been reconstructed in two ways. The protagonist's inner crisis develops as a series of confrontations with outer and inner obstacles and not as a result of ideological "conversion." Secondly, instead of leaving town in order to join the Enlightenment in the city, he succumbs to his mother's emotional pressure and remains at home. The main conflict between father and son in modern autobiography is in

Peretz's autobiography replaced by the son's filial attachment to his mother. According to Ruth Wisse, the episode with Peretz's mother weeping at his bedside "conveys something of the legendary mother Rachel, weeping for her children as they pass by her tomb into exile."[53] This observation points to the importance of the mother-son relationship for Peretz's self-conception as artist. Peretz viewed his loyalty to his mother as his life's most important formative influence. The centrality of the mother-son relationship is also evident in Glatshteyn's Yash books and Chaim Grade's *Der mames shabosim* (see chapters 4 and 5).

Peretz emphasizes his particular artistic awakening and existential crisis rather than the typical story of the abandonment of faith for Haskalah. His father in-law Lichtenfeld's conventional Haskalah ideas are not able to provide answers to his existential angst.[54] In the last chapter, Peretz's artistic quest is momentarily answered through his epiphany in the Swiss mountains, outside the Jewish realm. The shepherd's *hefker fayf* (whistle of defiance) is, for a short while, able to pull him out of his lethargic mood after a nearly fatal heart attack. Peretz stresses his autobiography's function as a meta-poetic tool for critical exploration. It utilizes a complex style and sophisticated vocabulary to discuss topics such as *tsayt gayst* (the spirit of the time, or zeitgeist), memory, symbol, transcendence, and the split between rationality and emotion. Like his Romantic predecessors at the beginning of the nineteenth-century such as Goethe and Wordsworth, Peretz makes his autobiography a critical discourse about the relationship between his life and work: "Romantic literary biography came to see itself not as a historicist tool, or an instrument of moral and didactic utility, or a vehicle devoted to the exploration of character and personality, but as an agent for theories of criticism, history, genre, genius, and culture."[55] This meta-poetic aspect of the autobiography originates with Peretz's later critical essays,[56] which introduce Peretz's neo-Romantic and Nietzschean theory of the artist as prophet and called for a return to classical Jewish sources (*tsurik tsu der bibl* [back to the Bible]). Several of the critical categories discussed in *Mayne zikhroynes* were first theorized in these earlier essays. The condensed style of *Mayne zikhroynes* or, in Yankev Glatshteyn's words, its "kaleidoscope of thinking,"[57] originated in a fundamentally different approach to literature than that of Abramovitsh and Sholem Aleichem.

In a series of letters to Sholem Aleichem (1888–1889), the editor of *Di yidishe folks-bibliotek*, where Peretz's literary debut, the poem *Monish*, was first published, Peretz outlined his literary credo in contrast to that of Sholem Aleichem. In one of these letters written in Hebrew, Peretz confused Sholem Aleichem with Abramovitsh: "while claiming to know the former's 'work' and 'aim,' he was reacting to the latter's *Travels of Benjamin the Third* and *The Nag*, which he had read in Polish translation. This is another illustration of the indifference of Yiddish writers to their colleagues and to Yiddish literature in general until the 1890s."[58] Peretz points out that he writes for his own pleasure and if he thinks of a reader, that reader belongs to "a higher level of society, it is the person who has read and learned in a living language."[59] Peretz distinguishes between his own individualism and modernism, addressing Jewish intellectuals familiar with European literature and the work of Sholem Aleichem. He characterizes Sholem Aleichem as a writer for a more uneducated Jewish audience who seeks to entertain and enlighten "the audience who speak jargon in jargon-land."[60] Peretz emphasizes the potential of literature as a means of exploring uncharted human experiences. It was crucial for Peretz that Yiddish be developed into a sophisticated medium for literary and critical discourse.[61] Peretz envisioned his reader to be a person like himself. He hoped that would enable him to attract the estranged Jewish intellectual to modern Yiddish culture. The odds were squarely against such an endeavour, as there was no such intellectual readership in Peretz's time. An interesting observation by the Yiddish writer Yente Zerdatsky about the contemporary readership of Peretz' work in a 1920 article highlights this fact: "Yes, the whole people feel that he [Peretz] is important, but who are his readers? The workers are engaged in their struggle and do not have time to become absorbed in his work. The students are assimilationists, they do not know any Hebrew and do not want to know about Yiddish. . . . [H]e is read and appreciated by a *yeshive* student who ponders holy books and a pale dreamy girl who kills time at her rich parents' house and gets pleasure from the Yiddish word."[62] Peretz believed optimistically that his example as a leading Jewish intellectual would create an educated Yiddish readership. This hope was partially fulfilled in interwar Warsaw, Vilna, Kiev and New York. In his 1945 essay "Peretz's Heritage," Yankev Glatshteyn glorified the memory of Peretz as "the Rambam of the nineteenth century"[63]: "If his audience for the autobiography was invented, it reflected the optimism of a great artist and the deep belief in the renaissance of Yiddish literature."[64]

The first three chapters of his autobiography open as Peretz begins attending *kheyder*, supervised by a series of *melamdim* (religious elementary teachers). They continue with his "exile" to the little town Shebreshin near Zamosc, and conclude with the end of his *kheyder* education.

The title of the introduction and chapter two, *nepldike kinder-yorn* (foggy childhood years) encapsulates Peretz's portrait of himself as child. In contrast to Abramovitsh and Sholem Aleichem's depiction of their childhood, in which they communed with nature and artist-artisans, Peretz's childhood is depicted as a passive, half-conscious phase of life. The child is defenseless, depicted as a being shaped by adults, and with a consciousness without defined structure. The *kheyder* is run by sadistic *melamdim* who rarely teach anything that makes an impact on the child. As a result, he rebelliously wages war against his *melamdim*. From the beginning, the child is presented as an *ile* (a child prodigy) who passes with distinction the initiation ritual for studying the *khumesh* (the Pentateuch).[65] This is one of the few times Peretz describes his scholarly potential. Another is the crucial moment when Mikhl Fidler asks him the *pshat* (the literal meaning) of a sentence in a kabbalistic book. His scholarly training as an *ile* stands him in good stead: he answers correctly and is handed the key to the Gentile library. Peretz depicts himself as having been destined to become a leader and an intellectual tower of strength in the Jewish community. At the same time, the portrait emphasizes his *enfant terrible* character and stresses his emotional rather than his rational capacity.

Peretz mentions that his poem *Monish* (1888) may be considered the literary proof-text of his life story. But unlike *Monish*, the emphasis in the autobiography is on the child's rebellion against his teachers rather than on sexual temptation. The origin of the artist in childhood is related to this sense of going against the grain and not fitting in. In most autobiographies the parents loom large, but in Peretz's *Mayne zikhroynes* his mother and father are only a significant presence at the very beginning. They then retreat into the background, only to reappear at crucial moments in his life. Two important examples are his mother's weeping at his bedside the night before his planned departure and the trip to the woods with his father, while "the bride from the ruin" is getting married. Their formative effect on him is reduced to symbolic generalities:"My father's 'They can't put the whole world in jail' and my mother's 'pious at Ayzikl's expense' were the two seeds that once implanted in my youthful soul, took deep root there and later bore fruit in everything I wrote."[66] As a prodigal son Peretz emphasizes the importance of his parents' heritage for his literary work. The death of his father, usually a traumatic event wrought with cosmic significance in childhood autobiographies, is skipped over in a parenthesis: "My father (he is not alive anymore)."[67] The boy's relationship to his mother, on the other hand, is the most significant parental influence. It determines the ambivalence of loyalty and defiance that characterizes Peretz's separation from his parents and his later artistic identity.

The autobiography presents several idealized father figures who are depicted in a mythological fashion. These include F. G., and the rabbi of Zamosc, Moyshe Wahl. In the middle of describing the figure F. G., Peretz interrupts himself in order to present meta-poetical ideas, thereby establishing a contrast between the fable, or folk tale, and a mimetic depiction of reality. He mentions that he could check his memories about F. G. by asking his friend, Yitskhok, the current doctor in Zamosc. However, Peretz does not want this reality check because he is searching for a mythological, "higher" truth. Here Peretz outlines his neo-romantic credo by defining autobiography as creative reconstruction of memories disconnected from any mimetic reality. Similar to the folk tale and the fable, the autobiography must focus on the transcendent reality beyond the observable reality. It must create a truer, fuller picture out of the chaotic events of life: "Man bends his will and hides his true face and does what he wants. People have a nose, sense the essence and the fundamental quality of a human being [*dem etsem-inyen fun mentsh*], and characterize him by what he would have done had he been true to himself; what he would have radiated into the world if random obstacles had not interfered. . . . The stories about holy men after their death [*okhrey mos keydoshim*] are also shaped in this way. Once the accidents and trivial acts, "acts because of economical necessity," because of anger, a victorious moment—disappear, sink into forgetfulness, a soul appears, an almost naked one . . . and people dress it in appropriate cloths, and whole human beings appear; whole, strong, not like the precarious shadows they were in their life time [*gantse, shtarke, nisht vakldike shotns, vi baym lebn*]."[68] The last sentence echoes Shloyme's monologue in the drama *Di goldene keyt* (The Golden Chain)—"we great, great Jews / Sabbath-holiday Jews"[69]—as a vision of the great personality who transcends the confines of everyday reality. This utopian myth of the superhuman, which is an important theme in Peretz's *Khsidish* (Hasidic) tales and *Di goldene keyt*, becomes problematic in his autobiography. His life story must, to a certain extent, be embedded in a particular time and place in order to convincingly convey the authenticity of its origin and development. Peretz includes the historical and the mythological approach and demonstrates how the former provides raw material for the artistic recreation of the latter.

Another example of this is Peretz's portrait of his friend from Shebreshin. This reminiscence depicts the child's love for an older peer as a protector and as surrogate family in a hostile environment. It is contrasted with Peretz's later encounter with this friend who, in the meantime, has become worn down by worries over *parnose* (making a living). These two images are incompatible in Peretz's universe because the latter undermines the mythological authority of the former: "Worries about earning a living, terrible worries [*dayges-parnose*]. . . . I feel compassion for him, but I nevertheless avoid him. In my heart I see a beautiful picture of a dear friend; every time I see him this image is darkened, overshadowed, and I want to protect it as a treasure . . . so I avoid him [*mayd ikh im oys*]."[70] This meta-poetic credo is outlined at the beginning of chapter three, in which the autobiographer addresses one of his readers. Characteristically, this is a well-educated reader who is familiar only with Peretz's work in Russian and German translation. This imagined reader also knows current critical concepts that he is capable of applying to Peretz's work. This is Peretz's ideal reader, educated in a "living language" and with whom he can discuss his neo-romantic credo. Unlike Abramovitsh, Peretz is not concerned with how the image of himself as a Jewish artist might be misused for anti-Jewish purposes. Peretz's universalism is reflected in his self-consciousness as a modern artist intent upon protecting his autonomy and artistic vision. The self is seen as a fully formed universe whose creative potential must be developed separate from its surroundings by protecting it from the randomness of daily life. The autonomous self, which Peretz calls *mayn inerlekhkayt* (my inwardness), is that inner realm from which the artist retrieves hidden memories. As a result, the self's interaction with its social environment becomes a battle between the will to remain self-sufficient and the attempts from the outside to breach "the walls" of the self: "My private self [*mayn inerlekhkeyt*] I protect from the slightest incursion. All hell may break loose, but I keep myself intact [*es regnt mit al dos beyz; inerlekh ver ikh nisht nas*]."[71]

Through this protective measure, Peretz is able to refine and re-create the idealized images, "the treasures", stored in his memory. The walled city of Zamosc, a feudal relic replete with fortress, is the physical and spiritual environment that provided a model for Peretz's self-conception. Like Abramovitsh, he must remind the contemporary reader of the historical distance that makes his childhood appear unintelligible. The anachronistic surroundings prevent him from developing into an artist. Doors to exciting new worlds are guarded by dogs; his father and *melamdim* control his behaviour and the town walls inhibit his access to nature: "A Jewish child, born in a fortress! Walled in from forest and field by gates and ramparts. . . ."[72] At the same time, Zamosc provides material from a glorified past with imposing heroic deeds. The cantonist (a Jewish soldier forced to serve twenty-five years in the tsar's army) in the town, for example, becomes the model for a section of the short story "Dray matones" (Three Gifts). The importance of story-telling far transcends learning Torah and introduces the child to the flight of the imagination. The first section's central theme, the child's re-bellion against authority, can be summarized in an episode at the end of chapter three. The young Peretz hangs a picture of Napoleon and his wife on the wall in order to tease the *melamed*, whose traditional reli-giosity forbids him to look at a picture of a woman. This act crystallizes the child's identification with the mythical charisma of the majestic per-sonality. It becomes his way of defying and transcending Jewish life's restrictive mediocrity.

Chapters four to seven focus on the young Peretz's encounter with the Haskalah movement. Two sections in chapter five about Rabbi Moyshe Wahl and Peretz as an old writer in his Warsaw apartment highlight the main theme of this section: the impact of the Haskalah movement on Peretz's artistic development. Rabbi Wahl is depicted as a great personality who is above any ideological struggle.[73] The rabbi has full authority over his congregation, who respect his learning and fol-low his directives as sanctioned by God. His unimposing physical stat-ure and affinity for children increase his charisma and authority. He leads his flock wisely and with an open-mindedness that even includes poring over secular books such as the Hebrew translation of Eugene Sue's *Mysteries of Paris* (1858). Due to the greatness of his personality, the religious and ideological battles dividing so many Jewish communities are avoided in Zamosc. Neither the *maskilim* nor the *hasidim* can chal-lenge Rabbi Wahl, and he becomes an ideal figure in Peretz's identifica-tion with the great personality. In the next section, Peretz interrupts the narrative about his childhood to insert an account of himself as an aging writer. It is prefaced with reminiscences about the six-fingered *melamed*. This character is described as a *groyser pashtn* (a literal minded person), who is an expert in expounding the literal meaning of the Talmud.[74] Peretz is horrified by the *melamed*'s six fingers and, as a result, he is un-usually compliant the whole semester. This reminiscence, repeated later on, seems to reflect Peretz's fascination with grotesque images. The *melamed*'s deformed hands embody the individual's uniqueness that also characterizes Rabbi Wahl and Peretz's image of himself as artist.

The section that follows includes a discussion of Peretz's literary career and his role as literary and spiritual guide for young writers in his home in Warsaw, the *peretsistn-nest* (nest of the Peretzists). Peretz points out that through his example many young writers succeeded in becoming literary "names," especially the ones "who did not let themselves be led." He then tells the story of a young writer who came to visit him in Warsaw in order to seek his advice about his short story entitled "Der tsaytgayst" (the spirit of the time, or zeitgeist). This title does not refer to the Haskalah but to radical political movements such as the Bund. In a play on words, the young writer is called *der tsaytgast* (time guest), a visitor from the heated ideological battles on the political front. The story describes a big watch, *der veltzeyger* (world watch), that hangs between heaven and earth. This watch symbolizing the *tsaytgayst* is trying to take over Heaven but only succeeds in reaching the *kise hakoved* (God's throne). Then the *tsaytgayst* sees a flower and picks it. This allegory can be viewed as the story of the Romantic artist who, en route to conquering the world with his mission to redefine all values, becomes distracted by a *blo-bliml* (blue flower). This is also the hallowed Romanticist symbol of poetry coined by the German poet Novalis (1772–1801). In a critical article the Yiddish writer Nomberg mentioned that Peretz viewed romantic longing as the main theme of his work. Actually accomplishing any object of desire would immediately strip it of its enticing qualities and turn it into "dirt." Longing from a distance was the only thing that could maintain the ideal image of a flower, love, or radical ideology.[75]

By placing this reminiscence after the one about Moyshe Wahl, Peretz emphasizes his own role in "the golden chain" of Jewish leadership. At the same time, he exposes the superficiality of ideologies as artistic motivation.[76] As a result of such an ideological concept, autobiography becomes a reflection of the collective Jewish destiny as in the *maskil* Yankev Reyfman's unfinished autobiography.[77] In it, the autobiographer is born twice, once on Yom Kippur and again on *ti'shebov*. On the other hand, it can also become Rousseauian self-exposure, the "sins of our youth" (the title of M. L. Lilyenblum's Hebrew autobiography from 1876), as Peretz calls his early confessional poems to one of the three sisters.[78] Neither of these autobiographical approaches is expansive enough to reflect the image of the six-fingered *melamed*, the horrifying, crippled irrationality at the heart of the self. Peretz utilizes a modernist style of contrast and symbolism in order to expose the Haskalah's limitation as an ideological movement. The individual's unconscious part is viewed as his primary artistic subject matter. "The spirit of the time," as reflected in the Haskalah or radical political movements, is presented as a secondary influence. It lacks the power to fundamentally affect the inner life of the "great personality."

The formative experiences in Peretz's adolescence, the encounters with the three sisters and his entrance into the orchard (*pardes*) activate memories of death (chapters 5 and 6). Peretz depicts an inner road to enlightenment on which he is confronted with sexuality and death as "trials" before he can be entrusted with the "treasure": the key to the Gentile library. Freudian terminology, which was part of the intellectual zeitgeist in the early 1910s, has informed Peretz's concept of the unconscious part of the self, explicated in the frequent use of the term "from under the conscious threshold." This unconscious aspect consists of chaotic sexual instincts which can be "mined," or made conscious through an associative method: "The problems that absorbed me grew like wild mushrooms in that restless, full of premonition trembling chaos [*tohuvevohu*] from under 'the conscious threshold' where the sexual instincts wake. Without my knowledge, and irrespective of my will, the male animal [*di khaye mansparshoyn*] emerged and colored all that had once been black and white in a rainbow of shades, mostly blood red and purple."[79] A close reading of the episodes with the three sisters reveals a universe of Freudian dream elements, projections and symbols. The encounters take place on the "narrow and dark" stairs on which the young Peretz descends with burning eyes. We are led down into a narrow dark space of sexual desires as in a dream. The first encounter ends with a kiss, and Peretz mentions that he did not go as far in sexual sin as did his character Monish, who was condemned to hell. As a child he had hit the second sister, "the bride from the ruin," on the cheek with a stone leaving a scar. Now, trembling, he touches the scar and promises that even if he had knocked out one of her eyes he would continue to love her.[80] The third encounter with the tuberculosis-ridden youngest sister reaches a climax when Peretz kisses her lips and thus defies the risk of being contaminated. Here he transcends all normative boundaries by kissing an unmarried girl who is dying. Yet Peretz emphasizes ironically that this account is not meant as a confession of the "sins of youth."[81] Rather, it must be seen as an important part of his inner journey toward artistic maturity.

The final two events in chapter five re-establish ego-control after his dream-like fulfilment of sexual desires. Peretz's father takes him into the woods where peasants are chopping trees that are later floated down river to the Vistula and sold as timber. This fatherly task has to do with *takhles* (practical purpose) and economical benefit. When a peasant chops a tree "something tears in my heart." Peretz leaves in a state of shock, shivering until he falls asleep in a house in the woods. This reaction to chopping trees is determined by something that relates to his previous sexual desires and to the fact that his "bride from the ruin" is getting married at the same time. It can be seen as symbolic castration, a punishment for lack of ego-control over his unconscious sexual desires. The super-ego is reinstated in the final episode of the chapter when the young Peretz unconsciously rebels against the highest authority in Zamosc, Rabbi Wahl. In an act of displacement, he intends to hit the town fool but hits the rabbi instead. Confronted by the rabbi, he promises never to hit anybody and to keep his rebellious acts (particularly the sexual) within the realm of acceptable social and religious behaviour.

Peretz utilizes Jewish proof-texts to describe his inner journey: the Garden of Eden narrative in Bereshit (Genesis) and the Talmudic story about the *pardes* (99–100).[82] He emphasizes psychological transformation as a necessary preparation for his shift of world view, enlightenment/knowledge, which takes place in the library. *Pardes* can, according to medieval kabbalistic sources, be viewed as an acronym— *p-r-d-s*—signifying four different ways of reading Scriptural texts: *pshat* (the literal), *remez* (the allegorical), *drash* (the homiletical), and *sod* (the mystical).[83] All readings must intersect in order for a full understanding of the scriptural text, or, in this case, the self and life story as textual figuration in an autobiography. The different stylistic and thematic parts of *Mayne zikhroynes* can be seen as a meditative reflection on these four ways of reading. The reminiscences belong to the literal reading *(pshat)*, which is interpreted in meta-poetic reflection *(drash)*. The mythical elements (idealized images and folk tale devices) belong to an allegorical reading *(remez)* hinting at a "mystical" reality *(sod)*, which is addressed in the epiphany at the end.

Peretz characterizes his autobiography as "a bundle of keys to my works" emphasizing the centrality of the key image.[84] Only sexual maturation can open the letter code that blocks access to the unconscious part of the self, the origin of artistic creativity:"On my pure, childish heart hangs a lock with scattered letters . . . who knows, when and whose hand will find the right combination, open and make fire, holy or foreign, on the little altar. . . . I am still a girl, my bride from the ruin—a boy."[85] This condition of being locked out, or not being in touch with parts of the self, is repeated in an image of the garden as "a locked Gentile paradise" *(goyish farshlosenem gan-eydn)*. Similarly, the entrance to the library can only occur once Peretz is provided with a key to its door.[86] The chaos of the library in which books in different languages, genres, and fields stand next to each other without any apparent order corresponds to the young Peretz's inner confusion. The chaos in his heart and the chaos of the Gentile library will provide the future artist with the raw material for his artistic creations. In order to gain access to it, however, he must confront those inner psychological barriers that prevent him from being fully in touch with his unconscious creative potential.

Entering the *pardes*, Peretz conducts an inner philosophical debate about the cosmological character of death as expounded by the great Jewish thinkers in the Talmud (Bruria), the Middle-Ages (Rambam), and the founder of Hasidism, the Besht. He reminisces about his childhood experiences confronting dying people. They are described with an intimate, unsentimental, comical directness. This contradicts Nomberg's observation that Peretz sought to repress thoughts about death, and his assertion that it is doubtful that "he [Peretz], in his life, saw a corpse."[87] Rather, as mentioned earlier, Peretz was drawn towards the decadent fascination with death inherited from the Romantics. In order to spell out the letters in his unconsciousness, Peretz must finally confront death. The Romantic artist is born in his exposure to the horrifying, uncanny, irrational modes of existence. By letting oneself be plunged into *tohovevohu* (chaos), the Romantic artist negates the mediocre world of ordinary human beings.[88]

The *fayf* (the whistle of defiance) appears for the first time at the end of the *pardes* section in chapter seven. Peretz tells the story of his charitable Uncle Lipa who drowned in the river. At the funeral procession his wife Yente appeared in a state of madness, but showing no sign of grief, when "suddenly she tore off her wig, and from the mouth—a whistle."[89] Losing her devout husband unleashes this outburst of antinomian behaviour. It is as if traditional religious values have lost their meaning for her after his sudden death. In the final chapter Peretz uses a similar strategy of defiance when he is dragged through his arranged marriage. At the end of chapter seven, Mikhl Fidler appears as a corpse with a lantern in his hand. This gothic image completes the section on death, creating the surreal atmosphere in which Peretz enters the Gentile library. Peretz ascends a lighted stairway leading up to the attic library, reversing the dark, descending stairs in the section with the three sisters.

Biblical imagery (the pillar of cloud and pillar of fire) is the first thing that comes to mind when he looks into the library. Although he is entering "their *besmedresh*" and has lost his faith, he is still steeped in traditional Jewish images and associations. In the library, Peretz symbolically experiences the transmigration of souls described in the kabbalistic passage that Mikhl Fidler asked him to interpret earlier: reading grants Peretz the ability to enter other people's minds. The library is like a bustling market, filled with groups of people talking and arguing. Dialogues of characters in novels become "a crack through which to look into a human soul." For the first time, the young Peretz is able to overcome his isolation by gaining access to an imaginary community of characters and ideas in secular non-Jewish books.

In the final chapter, Peretz consents to the arranged wedding in the hope that his future father-in-law, the *maskil* Gabriel Yehuda Lichtenfeld will appease his existential hunger: "he would explain all my evil dreams; answer all my questions about God and the world."[90] Lichtenfeld turns out be a rather conventional *maskil* who later helps the young Peretz to publish his first Hebrew poems. Although Peretz dismisses his literary debut as embarrassing and shameful, it is obvious that his consent to get married is motivated by his desire that Lichtenfeld serve as a literary midwife. On one hand, Peretz wants to please his parents, fulfilling his obligation as a loyal son who has been offered a beneficial wedding contract. On the other, the wedding as business transaction is depicted as an absurd theatre, in which he participates out of loyalty to his parents. His rebellious character finds other outlets: he behaves weirdly in the synagogue, posing as Napoleon.[91] On the Sabbath he wants to break the religious law against picking flowers yet is unable to do so. He transgresses the religious obligation to fast on his wedding day but the food he eats is salty and inedible. This conflict between rebellious self-assertion and loyalty to his parents is never resolved. He maintains a middle position between religious observance and enlightened rejection.

Compared to *Shloyme reb khayims*, Peretz's autobiography demonstrates an important shift in focus. In the former, childhood serves as the locus of the mature autobiographer's longing for a period of life unspoiled by modernity, a natural realm of inner freedom. In Peretz's autobiography, the child is not significantly different from the adult, nor is he more deserving of "authentic" insights and closeness to nature. Childhood is a dim, unstructured phase of life that only becomes interesting when the child takes charge of himself and learns to defy the adult world. For Peretz, adolescence becomes the archetypical phase of life in which parental values are challenged by the adolescent who strives to fulfil his inner potential. Patricia Meyer Spacks argues that this shift in focus from childhood to adolescence characterizes one of the main differences between nineteenth and twentieth-century autobiography: "If childhood could be associated, in the last century, with irresponsible and innocent happiness, the ideal state of being cared for and indulged, in our time adolescence means permitted defiance and difference. It means other things too, of course, but its potency as a central image for human development depends heavily on its definition as the period in which one discovers or creates an identity separate from and significantly opposed to that of one's elder: for many, particularly in retrospect, an exciting activity."[92] Adolescence is regarded here as a phase of life onto which the autobiographer retrospectively projects his sense of unlimited possibilities and freedom. Peretz's adolescent rebellion is never translated into a social act that transforms his life. Rather it is depicted as an untouchable inner state of defiance that typifies his artistic self-image. He learns to compartmentalize his life between adolescent megalomania and a conventional life as loyal son and exponent of his family and people. This dual loyalty to revolutionary change, as inspired by the latest cultural trends in the Gentile world (Freud, Nietzsche, symbolism, neo-Romanticism) and to his Jewish upbringing and education is reflected in the autobiography's mixture of stylistic and thematic elements belonging to both the *heymishe oytser* (the homey treasure) and their *besmedresh* (House of Study). Peretz presents himself as being equally at home in the Jewish and the Gentile worlds and makes this double loyalty the foundation of his artistic identity.

After the *khupe* (wedding), Peretz first hears the *sheygets* (the Gentile lad) whistle a cry of defiance. This whistle becomes the representation of artistic freedom, and the autobiographer contrasts it to the alienating wedding ceremony, his first sexual experience on the wedding night, and the humiliating moment when the newlyweds wake up in the morning "like two small fish which . . . wriggled into one net."[93] He carries the sound of this whistle with him during the coming years.[94] It becomes the emotional keynote of his work as a mature writer: "a spirit of defiance [*a shtikl hefker*] took hold inside me for many, many years. . . . [T]hrough Zamosc, Apt, Tsoyzmer, Warsaw, Great Poland, and back to Warsaw . . . in many of my writings is it possible to hear this whistle."[95] Unlike Abramovitsh and Sholem Aleichem, Peretz did not attempt to recreate a wholeness of the mythical and mimetic elements in his *shtetl* image. Instead Peretz, as Dan Miron points out, "strove entirely to place the elements in their contradiction, in their inability to be compatible."[96] The rupture between myth and mimesis that was reflected in the fragmented narrative style of Peretz's first major prose work, *Bilder fun a provints rayze*, inaugurated Yiddish modernism and made him the central Yiddish writer of his generation. In 1913 and 1914, at the end of his literary career, Peretz conveyed the same artistic vision in *Mayne zikhroynes*.

Peretz broke most of the rules for autobiographical self-portrayal established by Abramovitsh and Sholem Aleichem. He abandoned their omniscient epic, narrative voice in favour of his own subjective, idiosyncratic, and colloquial. Although he still adhered to a basic chronological sequence in the depiction of his childhood and adolescence, Peretz's artistic method was determined by associations and digressions, presented without apparent order. Instead of only subsuming his self as part of an epic, master narrative about how a child of the *shtetl* became a writer, Peretz also depicted his chaotic inner world and its idealized images of people and places. He abandoned mimetic accuracy and used instead his neo-Romanticist credo as a frame of reference for his reminiscences.

Peretz's autobiography became the first Yiddish successor to the hallowed tradition of Romantic autobiographies to present the writer's literary credo as central to his life story (Goethe, Wordsworth, Bialik.) The different novelistic models for autobiographical self-representation in *Shloyme reb khayims* and *Funem yarid*—the bildungsroman and artist's novel—were in Peretz's autobiography replaced with Romantic and Symbolist models. Peretz located the origin of the writer in a state of rebellious defiance, which he developed in childhood and later made into his trademark in adolescence. Interestingly, though, this defiance against what Peretz considered a mediocre middle class upbringing in the feudal environment of Zamosc did not lead to a break with his parents' traditional way of life. Peretz insisted on the balance between loyalty towards his parents and his own inner world. These dual loyalties led to self-inflicted misery, which is most vividly depicted in Peretz's first miserable marriage. Peretz's influence as autobiographer on future generations of Yiddish writers is visible in all the areas outlined above. His personal style and disregard for any fixed narrative patterns presented a subjective and non-mimetic approach. This opened a vast area of self-analysis for future Yiddish autobiographers. Peretz's compromise between rebellious defiance and loyalty to his Jewish background also became paradigmatic for future Yiddish autobiographers such as Jonah Rosenfeld, Yankev Glatshteyn, I. B. Singer and Chaim Grade. They were not limited by Peretz's *yidishkeyt* ethos, and were therefore able to express a much more penetrating and candid picture of the Jewish family and their own sexuality.

Part II

In America

3

The Trials of a Yiddish Writer

Jonah Rosenfeld was not appreciated by Yiddish criticism. I believe
that Rosenfeld will first be discovered by a younger generation that
has no knowledge of the earlier accounts and falsehoods. Then it will
be revealed that this allegedly primitive person was a sophisticated
writer, and one of our best.[1]

      Yitskhok Varshavski (Isaac Bashevis Singer)

Most people travel over a frozen river steadily and certainly, as if there
was not a frightening depth underneath . . . but I . . . I was constantly
uncertain even in my uncertainty.[2]

      Jonah Rosenfeld

In his article "America in the Memoir Literature" (1945), the Yiddish
critic Y. A. Rontsh mentioned that the 1930s and early 1940s were particularly rich in autobiographies by Yiddish writers in America: "Recently
there is a plethora of memoirs in Yiddish America. This is a sign that our
literature is getting older; a result of the anniversaries. Yankev Milkh's
Memoirs in the *Morgn-Frayhayt*; Peretz Hirshbeyn's in *Tog*; Osip Dimov's
in the *Forverts*; Mordechai Dantsis' in *Tog*; and more and more are prepared. A. Raboy has published his memoirs in the *Morgn-Frayhayt*. Yankev Glatshteyn's *Yash* is an original memoir of artistic scope."[3] These
Yiddish writers who immigrated to the United States between 1899 and
1914 wrote autobiographical works that expressed the artistic centrality
of their earliest, formative years in the *shtetls* of Eastern Europe. Ruth R.
Wisse's observation that the Yiddish poets Di yunge (the young ones)
"in their estrangement from America . . . sought an alternate fictional
homeland, and re-created themselves in the atmosphere they had left

behind."[4] applies to the Yiddish autobiographer in America as well. The American Yiddish writer's loyalty to the Old World as his primary artistic source of inspiration was expressed sarcastically by the American Yiddish poet Moyshe Leyb Halpern in the poem "Di letste" (1924, The Last):

> May her right leg wither
> If she plucks a harp
> By strange waters
> Or forget the dear dung heap
> That had once been her homeland.[5]

Jonah Rosenfeld's *Eyner aleyn* (1940, All Alone) and Yankev Glatshteyn's *Ven yash iz geforn* (1938, *Homeward Bound*), and *Ven yash iz gekumen* (1940, *Homecoming by Twilight*) were arguably the most artistically innovative autobiographies of Yiddish writers in America during this period. These works accentuated modernist fragmentation by fusing genres such as the travelogue, the novel and the *shund roman* (trashy novel) with autobiographical modes. Glatshteyn and Rosenfeld modernized the Yiddish autobiography's image of the Old World by avoiding nostalgic and sentimental approaches to Eastern European Jewry. The Yash books and *Eyner aleyn* were exceptional among autobiographies by Yiddish writers in America because of the personal urgency with which they recreated the Old World, transforming it into an artistic arena for autobiographical self-confrontation. The exigency with which Rosenfeld wrote *Eyner aleyn* originated in his conflict with Abraham Cahan, the editor-in-chief of the *Forverts,* who refused to print Rosenfeld's stories during the last ten years of his life (1934–1944). Rosenfeld's portrait in *Eyner aleyn* of his troubled relationship with his *balebos* (boss) more than forty years earlier in Odessa were fuelled by his conflict with Cahan. This drama is revealed in a series of unpublished letters between Rosenfeld and Cahan that I discuss below. As I will demonstrate, the book's narrative voice and themes must, to a large extent, be viewed as Rosenfeld's artistic response to his exclusion from the *Forverts* while he was at the height of his creative powers in the second half of the 1930s. As noticed by the Yiddish critic Nachman Mayzel, *Eyner aleyn* belongs to the Yiddish autobiographical genre in its portrait of the artist as child and young man.[6] Inspired by Peretz's autobiography, Glatshteyn and Rosenfeld did not only recreate images of times and places from bygone days; they also took on a self-analytic and meta-poetic perspective.

Eyner aleyn combined a complex, introspective style with suspenseful drama situated in an authentic Old World setting. Rosenfeld took his experience as an apprentice to a Jewish turner in mid-1890s Odessa and transformed it into a powerful metaphor of a self severed from family and community, *eyner aleyn* (all alone). He presented a self-portrait in the form of a *roman*, a love story, through which his adolescent protagonist discovered his first intimations of sexuality, social protest, and artistic inclination. Through his autobiographical character Jonah's struggle to protect his moral values and his very self from his foster family's destructive influence, Rosenfeld revealed the Jewish family's greediness, brutality, and perversity.

Rosenfeld had personal scores to settle, accusing the cold-hearted, insensitive *balebos* and his family of making his apprenticeship miserable. He demonstrated how his host family dehumanized him by treating him worse than a dog, and took revenge by calling them pejorative names such as *mamzerkhl* (bastard), *ye'makh-shmoynik* (scoundrel), *kelevnik* (dog), *a groysgufiker* (big ass), *malekh hamoves* (angel of death), *a gazln* (thief), *rotseakh* (murderer), and *a kolboynik* (rascal).[7] But Rosenfeld also openly revealed his own brutality and sexual passion. These feelings, and their impact on other people, were not only depicted as survival strategies in an inhumane environment, but also as the result of his coming of age. Like the Rousseauian confession, Rosenfeld's dictum was autobiographical honesty, which he turned against himself and his opponents.

In Rousseau's *Confessions*, the intended audience for the book is the multitude, the faceless masses—"the numberless legion of my fellow men gather round me, and hear my confessions"—who are plotting against the autobiographer and spreading the worst lies about his person. His *Confessions* is a long defense speech by a persecuted and misunderstood literary and philosophical celebrity. This apologetic stance defines Rousseau's self-presentation, or in the words of Elizabeth Bruss "the autobiographer's identity is bound up with the notion of 'being misunderstood,' both by former friends and by his immediate audience."[8] Similarly, *Eyner aleyn* is a personal crusade against the people who mistreated and abused Rosenfeld in adolescence. The combination of social accusation, personal apologetics, and Rosenfeld's self-depiction as the sole bearer of positive moral values pitted against a vulgar, primitive and amoral family links *Eyner aleyn* to the Rousseauian autobiographical quest.

Rosenfeld was left with traumatic psychological scars, along with the loss of family and status, as a result of being orphaned at a young age. Like Abramovitsh's autobiographical alter ego, Reb Shloyme, who was also orphaned at *bar mitsve* age, Rosenfeld sought to come to terms with painful memories through a confessional and accusatory narrative. Except for allusions to his orphanhood, *Eyner aleyn* is characterized by the absence of childhood memories. The protagonist's "blind spot" regarding his childhood serves to portray him as a marginal loner with a troubled past. He, like a character in a novel, enters the narrative with a set of predestined characteristics. Rosenfeld depicts his autobiographical past by condensing it into an adolescent love story. However, unlike Abramovitsh's use of the bildungsroman and artist's novel to depict the origin and development of Shloyme from child to adolescent/artist, Rosenfeld candidly focuses on the particular developments of his self in early adolescence in the form of an autobiographical *roman*.

The double meaning of the word *roman* in Yiddish, referring both to a novel and to a romance, appears several times in the book: "this is the first chapter of my beautiful novel/romance" (120) and "in the second part of my sweet novel/romance" (130). This play with the novelistic character of the supposedly autobiographical events is part of the book's fascination. On the surface, the book consists of autobiographical episodes without any cohesion or development. But a closer reading shows that the sexual attraction between Jonah and *dos meydele* (the girl), the daughter of his boss, constitutes the book's master narrative. As a result of this infatuation, Jonah allows himself to be apprenticed to the *balebos* despite his brother's warnings that "you will not lick any honey at their place" (11). This *roman* is brought to a sudden, dramatic end when *dos meydele*'s clothes accidentally catch on fire, nearly killing her, while she and Jonah are playing a game of sexual hide-and-seek. This love story provides Rosenfeld with the narrative framework needed to depict many key events in his adolescence: his dehumanisation and rebellion against his boss; his relationship to the socialist worker Eliyohu; visits to his crippled brother and cousin; and excursions in Odessa.

Like Peretz in *Mayne zikhroynes,* Rosenfeld deals with adolescence as the central period of life, taking Peretz's *hefker-yung* (defiant adolescent) a step further into the borderland between normality and insanity. Rosenfeld explores the fine nuances of sexual intrigue in his relationship to *dos meydele,* and the slave-master relationship between himself and his boss as it evolves in small daily episodes. Like Peretz, Rosenfeld freely explores the irrational and pathological realm of human behaviour without having to emphasize the collective aspects of his autobiographical past. In his review, A. Mukdoni points out that the apprentice is representative of his class, and the book can be seen as a parable of social and political oppression: "It is not autobiographical in the sense that it only deals with Jonah Rosenfeld as a apprentice with a turner; instead you have tens of thousand apprentices who were sold into slavery; you have a political system which legitimizes this kind of slavery in modern times."[9] This piece reflects the dominant attitude among Yiddish critics to the autobiography as representative of collective features. Rosenfeld compares the treatment of the Jews in the tsarist army—one of the most feared experiences among Eastern European Jews because of forced Gentile indoctrination and brutality—with his own *inkvisitsyes* (inquisitions) in the *balebos*'s family. One of the first of these *inkvisitsyes* is his exposure to the family members while they are emptying their bowels in the toilet: "But that was nothing compared to the familiarity [*heymishkeyt*] they showed me on the first night when I arrived. A wife would even be ashamed to show her husband such 'familiarity' shortly after their wedding, and a mother is ashamed to do it in front of her son and a daughter in front of her father. . . . They did not realize that they ought to be ashamed. Besides, an apprentice, is that a human being? He is similar to an animal [*kebeheyme nedmo*]. . . . [D]oes one need to be ashamed in front of an animal, or a horse to do 'the human thing' in the stable in front of the horse's eyes?"[10]

Rosenfeld depicts the Jewish family as a microcosm through which psychological repression is revealed in all its pathology and deformity. The anti-Semitic victimization of the Jews exemplified in the tsarist army's brutality has been replaced by a shift of focus to the crippling, interpersonal dynamics in the Jewish family. As a result, anti-Semitism in Odessa at the turn of the century, which frequently erupted in violent attacks, is not mentioned at all in *Eyner aleyn*.[11] In his review of the book, Kalman Marmor compared *Eyner aleyn* to Abramovitsh's *Dos kleyne mentshele*, which also deals with an artisan's humiliating treatment of apprentices. He pointed out that "Mendele's apprentice lived in a paradise" compared with Rosenfeld's physical and spiritual oppression. Although Abramovitsh's portrait of the apprentice in *Shloyme reb khayims* depicts a much earlier period (the 1840s), it nevertheless presents a traditional view of the apprentice in Jewish Eastern Europe. This can be considered part of Rosenfeld's frame of reference in *Eyner aleyn*: "An apprentice with any artisan had to carry slops for years, help out the boss' wife at home and got slaps and beatings like a piece of wood. He learned a craft like the plague; as a result he could practise it like a plague. In addition he was a bungler, a bitter, unhappy person. He liked to drink because of his misery. His hands were ready to beat, some times honouring even his own wife with a beating. Pity on the apprentices, poor ones, who fell into his hands! And who, alas, were the kids who came to such a person in order to learn a craft? Orphans, poor, abandoned, who never went to *kheyder*, without knowledge of Hebrew— ignorant people."[12]

Rosenfeld's artistic career was inaugurated by Peretz, who, on a visit to Odessa in 1902, heard Rosenfeld read his story "Dos lern-yingl: a bild fun toker lebn" (The apprentice—a picture of turner life).[13] As a result, the story became Rosenfeld's debut and was published in *Der fraynd* in 1904. That same year, Y. M. Weissenberg also made his debut under the auspices of Peretz. Weissenberg based his work on a harsh naturalist depiction of Jewish working-class life, emphasizing social protest and class conflict. Unlike that of Weissenberg, Rosenfeld's depiction of social problems emphasized the warped psychological character of the Jewish working-class family and individual.[14] According to Nachman Mayzel, Peretz advised the young Rosenfeld "[C]onstantly tell what you know . . . and depict what is familiar to you."[15] Peretz's idea was to empower Jewish workers through literature that would reflect the social injustice perpetrated against them. He wanted to develop a Yiddish literature that would be a part of the Jewish workers' liberation, one that would encourage their aspiration toward universal humanistic values. Unlike most of their contemporaries, Jonah Rosenfeld and Y. M. Weissenberg were not initially exposed to Haskalah literature in Hebrew. Nor, for that matter, were they originally inspired by German and Russian literature. Instead, they drew literary inspiration primarily from their own experiences as workers.[16]

The centrality of autobiographical texts in Rosenfeld's oeuvre is apparent in the fact that his longest works prior to *Eyner aleyn* were fictive and autobiographical diaries. In the documentary diary *Fun mayn togbukh* (1924, From My Diary), Rosenfeld depicted his return to Kovel from Kiev in 1919 during the Russian civil war. Rosenfeld regarded this text and *Er un zey, a tog-bukh fun a gevezenem shrayber* (1927, He and She, a Diary of a Former Writer) as his best works. Together with the autobiographical texts in volume 5 of Rosenfeld's *Gezamlte verk* (1924) titled *Ikh* (I), they indicate the importance of autobiographical writings in Rosenfeld's work.[17] The title story, "Ikh," written in the early 1920s, depicts Rosenfeld's artistic origin. Similarly to *Eyner aleyn*, the autobiographical hero arrives as a stranger in a household that has no interest in him. During the four weeks before his being drafted into the tsar's army, the reason for his brief sojourn with his family, Jonah develops a close relationship with his cousin Etl, the daughter of the household. By taking care of him and supporting him through this anxious time, she becomes like a sister to him. The approaching draft forces Jonah to re-evaluate his previous life: "at that time something unexpected took place: a sudden, violent transformation of my spiritual 'I.'" He falls in love "but I did not know in whom, whether in the girl, or in myself." Etl's role as mirror and extension of Jonah's self underlines his narcissism. She enables him to embrace his own self lovingly by listening to his elevated talks and enthusiastically supporting his first writing. Jonah does not belong to either the Jewish conscripts in the House of Study or the Gentile conscripts getting drunk in the local inn.[18] He feels lonelier than ever and realizes that he cannot continue his usual life. In the story's climactic scene, Jonah tells Etl that he wants to write a letter to her fiancée. When Etl arrives with pen and paper, Jonah breaks a small mirror and chews pieces of it. Through this act, he hurts himself so he can appear unfit for the draft. He has decided to take charge of his life by trying to avoid conscription. At that moment, he grabs the pen and starts writing to a stranger: "The hand which had never written to anybody; the hand which since age twelve (since *kheyder*) had never held a pen, moved quickly . . . forgot to whom, for what and when; it moved quickly [*s'iz avek a gang*]; in quick rhythm, at the same time my heart was in uproar."[19] The text, which Etl reads afterwards, is an cry of loneliness and isolation, a release of inner pressure. This is the first time Jonah has written anything; indeed, at this point he does not even know that such a thing as *shraybekhts* (artistic scribbling) exists. On the day he is drafted, Etl escorts him, fasting like a bride on her wedding day. He is not conscripted, and leaves the family immediately thereafter without any desire to continue the love affair with Etl. Her role as his literary midwife has been fulfilled, and Jonah can return to Odessa with the new sense of himself as potential writer.

Rosenfeld immigrated to America in 1921 and became a regular contributor to the American Yiddish journals *Di tsukunft* and *Der veker* and, in particular, the daily *Forverts*. During the final seven years of his life, Rosenfeld suffered from stomach cancer, from which he died in 1944. In this last period, Rosenfeld was excluded from publishing stories in *Forverts* because of a conflict with its editor, Abraham Cahan, who believed that Rosenfeld's stories about life in America were not on the same level as his writings about the old country. Rosenfeld had a different opinion

about his last stories, and would not heed Abraham Cahan's requirements. The result was that the *Forverts* continued to receive Rosenfeld's
stories, paid the full salary for them, but never printed them.

Quite a different picture of this conflict is revealed in a series of unpublished letters that Rosenfeld and Cahan exchanged between 1931
and 1942, and in a published letter sent by Rosenfeld to the Yiddish
writer B. Vladek in 1937.[20] The letter to Vladek, written right after an
operation for stomach cancer, conveys how worried Rosenfeld was
about his financial situation. He expresses concern that the *Forverts* did
not pay Rosenfeld his full salary and that he has not received payment
for the chapters from his *roman (Eyner aleyn)* that were to be printed
in *Tsukunft*.[21] But the question of American vs. European stories as the
source of the conflict between Cahan and Rosenfeld is not mentioned
in the correspondence. From the beginning of the conflict with Cahan
in 1935 until Rosenfeld's death in 1944, he only published a few stories
and two preliminary chapters from *Eyner aleyn* in the *Tsukunft*.[22] A five-
page, typewritten letter from Rosenfeld addressed to "Abraham Cahan
(editor of the greatest Yiddish newspaper in the world)" sets the tone
for Rosenfeld's biting attack on Cahan. According to the writer, Cahan
had refused to print his submissions to the *Forverts* for several years,
which culminated in a falling-out between them. At the end of the
letter, Rosenfeld explicitly compares Cahan to his former *balebos* in
Odessa, who even had a similar name: "In the letter that I wrote to you
four years ago (if I am not mistaken, it is already five), I did, inciden-
tally, come across a very mysterious coincidence that the name of my
boss, whose apprentice I was, was also Avrom, and wonder of wonders: Kohen! And he beat me for four whole years with sticks and poles,
but despite that I came out alive, unharmed [*dokh bin ikh aroys mit gantse
beyner*]. That is precisely the way you will succeed in spiritually killing
me [*gaystik tsuderhargenen*], which is to say, you will not succeed."[23] Despite his exclusion from the *Forverts*, Rosenfeld assures Cahan that he is
still writing extensively. He points out that the editor might succeed at
excluding him from the *Forverts*'s pages by providing Rosenfeld with a
lifelong annual retirement bonus, but he will never silence him. Rosenfeld ends the letter with a mysterious warning: "Cahan, even if you win
you will lose. . . . Remember, you are playing with fire." Just as forty
years earlier Rosenfeld as a young apprentice in Odessa defended his
moral integrity, so will he now fight Cahan's unjust demands and inhumane treatment. In a letter dated September 25, 1941, Rosenfeld uses
the word *inkvisitsyes* to describe his feeling of being persecuted by

Cahan. This word is also frequently used in *Eyner aleyn* regarding Jonah's sufferings in the *balebos'* family. Although the phrase *ir shpilt zikh mit fayer* (you are playing with fire) is an ordinary figure of speech, a warning signal, it is also reminiscent of Rosenfeld's personal story. This can be seen in the episode at the end of *Eyner aleyn* in which *dos meydele* catches on fire during a sexually charged game orchestrated by Jonah. The letter indicates that the internalized anger and moral self-righteousness originating in his apprenticeship in Odessa was triggered again more than forty years later by Cahan's insensitive treatment of Rosenfeld's work. Again, Rosenfeld is pitted against personal brutality, hatred, coarseness. In this state of mind, he began to write *Eyner aleyn* in 1937.

Eyner aleyn, which is divided into two parts, begins with the encounter between Jonah and the *balebos,* an episode that is equated to "the outbreak of a storm, that is how my master's smile was deeply engraved in my memory" (6). Rosenfeld establishes the present moment of recall as a narrative perspective that involves the *zikorn* (memory) on which past events are *ayngeshnitn* (carved). This is repeated in the second part of the book: "I will remember forever; forever will my joy remain engraved" (133). Unlike a more conventional autobiography, which typically recalls the first conscious moment in childhood, Rosenfeld begins his book with a metaphor that equates the *balebos's* smile with the initial flash of lightning before the outbreak of a storm.[24] This metaphor crystallizes the basic tenets of the autobiographical narrative: Jonah's struggle to erase the smile by showing that he is worthy of being an apprentice; that he is a man and not a child. To achieve this developmental goal by trying to win the respect of his father figure, the *balebos,* he is forced to live through a "stormy" period of personal humiliation, depicted as a sexual and psychological trial. Rosenfeld subtly shifts the reader's expectations of an autobiography to that of a novel by placing himself at the centre of a romantic drama. It is *dos meydele's* sexual attractiveness that enables him to muster enough strength to convince the *balebos* that he is fit for the job.

At the end of part 1, the narrator makes an aside to the reader by comparing his own narrative with sensationalised newspaper articles: "It is not without reason that the newspaper reporters, poor things, scream that life is the biggest *shund* writer when they present a particular sensation, and thus, evidently, they intend to anticipate the 'reader's' objection in case people won't believe their sensation. Yes, the biggest '*shund*-things' happened in my 'apprenticeship,' which the reader will discover in the second part."[25] What happens in the "real world" as it is reflected in the daily press belongs to the same *shund* universe that characterizes serialized potboilers and trashy novels. The narrator points out that features such as the romantic intrigue, narrative suspense, and personal vendettas depicted in the Yiddish press also characterize the narrative of his apprenticeship. The narrator concludes by asserting that even if he had indeed made up the entire story, he could not have conjured a more artistically true ending. In the final pages of the book, he uses an aside typical of the *shund roman* in which the narrator promises to fulfil the reader's interest in the destiny of one of the main characters: "But because many of the readers would want to know what happened to the girl, if she was maimed forever, or if she recovered after this incident, I will tell about it for their sake."[26] Thus, Rosenfeld addresses serious literary themes and aesthetic concerns in a talkative, intimate style, replete with informal asides to the reader, through the fusion of an introspective Rousseauian autobiography and stylistic features of a *shund roman*.[27]

One of the ways in which the narrator exposes the *balebos*'s level of ignorance is by revealing his employer's lack of Jewish learning. In the synagogue and at the *shive-minyen* (the seven day mourning period after the death of a relative) following the death of the boss's mother, Jonah challenges the *balebos* with questions about ritual observance.[28] He openly ridicules the *balebos* by repeating his mispronunciation of Hebrew during prayer (263). In a more indirect way, the narrator employs Hebrew to indicate his Jewish learning, and to provide a scriptural sub-text for his sufferings. The *balebos*'s workshop is called *beys-avodim* (85, house of bondage) and Jonah an *aved knaani* (19, Canaanite slave). When his brother and friend come to visit him at the workshop, Jonah cries out in despair: "to whom have you sold me?" (192), echoing the story of Joseph in Genesis. The *balebos* as a latter-day Pharaoh who has enslaved the young Jonah/Yosef is one scriptural sub-text of the book. In addition, Jonah uses the imagery of the *akeyde* (the binding of Isaac) to convey his sense of being sacrificed by the *balebos*. He equates the workshop to a *mizbeakh* (altar) on which he is "condemned to death" (30). Later, upon returning to the *balebos* after having disappeared for several days, he describes it to his brother in this way: "Just as if you lead me to the *akeyde*" (358).

Jonah meets the worker Eliyohu, who introduces him to clandestine socialist gatherings, encouraging Jonah to espouse socialist values. At the same time, the Jewish world connects Jonah to his childhood and to his deceased parents. It is only within a Jewish context that Jonah is able to maintain a modicum of status and power over his *balebos*. Because he is a *cohen* (descendant of the High Priest who receives special honors in the synagogue), he is allowed to leave the workshop when someone in the courtyard dies. (According to Jewish law, a *cohen* may not be under the same roof as a corpse.) His Jewish background gives him the moral upper hand, in many situations, and the inner confidence that saves him from self-destruction. At the same time, Jonah's knowledge of Jewish religious practice is also used to further humiliate him, such as when he is asked to recite the blessing over wine on a Friday night but is then sent back to the anteroom without being allowed to eat with the family.

The narrator presents the characters' Russian speech in order to give a faithful depiction of trilingual Jewish Odessa (Yiddish, Hebrew, and Russian). The Russian language signifies the world of the Gentiles as well as the cultural *Bildung* to which the young Jonah aspires in the end of the book. The narrator's translation of phrases and songs from Russian into Yiddish reveals the vast cultural distance between Jonah's Jewish universe and the Gentile world. Thus, the narrator graphically outlines Jonah's development from an adolescent with a scant knowledge of Russian into a mature writer with a competent mastery of this language. In his review of *Eyner aleyn*, Kalmor Marmor points out that learning Russian meant more than learning a language; it meant a cultural road to enlightenment for many Jews. In an interview, Rosenfeld admitted his ignorance of world literature except for Russian literature; his favourite writers were Chekhov and Gorky.[29]

The boss's son Itsik uses truncated, incomprehensible speech, signifying the spiritual deformity of the Jewish proletarian family. This is paralleled by Jonah's hunchbacked elder brother whose disability symbolizes his failure as breadwinner (he is unable to take care of Jonah) and as a father (his twins die in childbirth). The hunchbacked brother's impotence is also apparent in his inability to implement his threats against the *balebos*'s maltreatment of Jonah. In the workshop, *dos meydele* freely exposes her breasts in front of Jonah without any repercussions from her father. Later, she is attracted to a landowner because he embodies the Gentile world of romantic intrigues and riches. Instead of preventing this contact, her father uses her sexual attractiveness as an incentive for his business. Jonah responds with contempt to this lack of dignity and adherence to Jewish moral principles.

Jonah's orphanhood becomes a metaphor for the rupture and dislocation resulting from the break-up of traditional Jewish values. Like

Abramovitsh's Shloyme in *Shloyme reb khayims,* who struggles to maintain his social status based on *zkhus oves* (the merits of ancestors) following his father's death, Jonah fights against social injustice by defending the traditional religious and moral values with which he was brought up. By the end of the book, socialism and culture have become moral replacements for the traditional Jewish values. The book's central metaphor of the self is crystallized in an episode in which Jonah works through the night in order to repay borrowed money: "Despite how lonely you feel during the day, it is nothing compared to the loneliness when you are awake and all alone, and the rest of the world is deeply asleep. You get the impression that you are severed; isolated from the entire world and all its inhabitants. You are an orphan, an orphan of the world [*velt-yosem*], but only you know it. The rest of the world does not know it, because the world is sunken into nightly rest and sleep."[30] This nocturnal experience represents perfectly Jonah's situation on both the individual and the universal level. The chapter begins with the sentence "Ikh fil zikh vi a nekhtiker" (I feel confused/out of place). The narrator equates this feeling of confusion and displacement with that of insomniacs and survivors of catastrophes, stuck in the realm of waking dreams and past memories. He experiences a feeling of estrangement from his body and his work, initiating an introspective moment, an epiphany in which pictures and memories from his early childhood appear without censorship. He sees two burning lights connected to memories, "which rose like the resurrection of the dead" (324); even his dead parents appear as in a dream. The two burning lights signify both the *yortsayt* (memorial) candles lit after their death and the Sabbath candles, which illuminate the inner sanctum of the Jewish family. This access to past memories expands his consciousness and points to his greatest personal tragedy, the loss of his parents.

In the next episode, the daughter of the house appears near the workshop to take a glass of water from the faucet there. Silently, Jonah and the girl embrace: "We stand, already fused together as one person with a single desire, and we breathe on each other with fire, and both of us begin to lose our bearings" (326). This erotic moment is interrupted by the sound of cloister bells. The girl "woke up as if from a bad dream" and quickly leaves the room. Jonah regrets that he did not take sexual advantage of the moment. He is filled with envy toward the families who are turning on lamps in the courtyard in order to get ready for a new day: "Only I, all alone, am condemned by the world and by people" (327). By focussing on his first confusing experiences as an apprentice, prior to establishing his social identity as an adult, Rosenfeld made this feeling of loneliness and isolation his "metaphor of self." As an adolescent rebelling against parental authority and groping for new values, his situation is further exacerbated. Jonah becomes a figure without an identity in a family that refuses to name him. Either they talk about him in the third person or call him *dos lern yingl* (the apprentice), reducing him to a nonentity who is worse off than *dinstn un meshorsim* (57, maids and servants). He is haunted by feelings of guilt, an inferiority complex, and the need for emotional attention. Rosenfeld's autobiographical method depicts the relative boundaries between normality and pathology. During a conversation with Yokhanan Tverski in 1937, in a rare instance of artistic self-reflection, Rosenfeld formulated what could be called his literary credo:

Without having a big selection of "types," I must be content with the situations in which I place my characters. And as a result, each "type" ceases to be a "type." For in reality, the typical kind does not exist! . . . It means that the type exists only as long as he lives in normal circumstances. If you place him in new, totally different circumstances, he begins to act abnormally: that is, in such a way you would not expect a person who belongs to this or that group of people would behave. And in complicated, entangled situations it becomes possible to watch how the biggest heroes become confused, and the smartest do not know what to do.[31]

The transformation of social norms creates situations in which otherwise normal people behave strangely or even pathologically. This is particularly evident in periods of radical social change as a result of urbanization, secularization, and emigration, and in the aftermath of personal tragedies such as the death of parents. Rosenfeld's autobiographical method seeks to explore the potential for deviant behaviour by individuals removed from their normal social environment and placed in unprecedented, extreme situations.

This theme is exemplified by the mask motif that first appears when the *balebos* punishes Jonah by smearing red paint on his face. Instead of ridiculing him, *dos meydele* takes pleasure in his looks, allowing him to joke with her "because that was not me" (174). In the following episode, Jonah knocks over a bottle of polish. When the *balebos* stretches out his hand to punish him, Jonah spontaneously smears red polish on his own face: "Feeling the mask on my face, which simultaneously both cooled and pained me, I felt a strange defiance [*hefker-gefil*], and began to show such tricks [*kuntsn un shtukes*] that, in any other circumstances, I would not have been allowed to show in the presence of the *balebos*."[32]

He begins to clap his hands, to imitate different animal sounds, and to behave like a dog. *Dos meydele* is clearly aroused by this behavior, and Jonah starts to bite her leg "like a person going wild with passion" (180). In this episode, Jonah discovers that the act of disguise both serves as a means of liberation from his slave role in the family and allows him to express sexual feelings towards *dos meydele*. This *hefker gefil* (defiant, lawless feeling) enables him to break out of his role as outcast by becoming a prankster, the object of laughter.

The next episode takes place on Christmas, when *dos meydele* dresses up like a *maloroseyske* (a Ukrainian woman) looking like an *emese shikse* (182, a genuine non-Jewish woman). On this particular day, it is the custom for children to wear masks, walk around in the courtyard and ask for money. Although *dos meydele* does not participate in this custom, she nevertheless dons a mask and looks out the window. Later she gives the mask to Jonah as a gift for his services as letter carrier to her secret boyfriend. At this point in the story, Jonah and *dos meydele* have developed a relationship based on mutual aid: he delivers letters to her boyfriend and she protects him from the *balebos*'s anger. This game of secret undertakings behind the adults' backs is symbolized by the mask. Jonah learns about disguise as a means of deceit and manipulation, providing him with the first key to breaking out of his slavery. Sitting with Eliyohu in the inn, Jonah sees his reflection multiplied in the mirrors, the endless potentiality of social identities. He compares this to his lack of identity in the *balebos*'s workshop: "I was not only one 'I,' but a lot of 'I's,' which I saw in the mirror on both sides. Suddenly such a restoration [*oyfrikhtung*]! . . . 'There' I am not even once an 'I,' and I do not occupy a place anywhere, and here I occupy so many places" (219).

After the visit at the inn, Eliyohu takes Jonah on a trip to a factory outside the city. There he disguises himself as a priest and leads a burial procession of mourning workers that, at the end, turns out to be a clandestine socialist demonstration. Once more, the act of disguise is employed as a strategy for subversive activity, one that has a liberating effect. The mask as a means of personal and political liberation can also be used with fatal consequences. Jonah dons the mask in front of the old grandmother, resulting in an aggravation of her health. Even the doctor's assurance that she is old "and is about to die of old age" (250) does not prevent Jonah from feeling guilty of killing her. On top of having poisoned the family's dog in the courtyard as revenge against the family, Jonah feels that "that would already have been my second murder" (257). The mask instructs Jonah about the adult world of social roles. It also teaches him to use disguise as a means of transcending an oppressive social reality.

An important theme in most autobiographies of Yiddish writers is the way in which the authors discover their talent for writing. This theme is indirectly conveyed in the section in which Jonah decides to visit the woman who buys *di shpendelekh*, the small pieces of wood that Jonah has been assigned to make for the *balebos*, in order to find a place to spend the night. He remembers that this woman knows several writers in Odessa and, as an excuse to approach her, he asks to borrow a book:

The Jewish woman told me that she knew a writer whose name was "Mendele Moykher-Sforim." How does this woman know the writer who has such a strange name? Because her son . . . studied in the Talmud Torah where this Mendele was the supervisor, so this Mendele Moykher-Sforim gave her one of his books with the name "The Mare," so she could read it. . . . Recently she got to know another writer who wrote in Hebrew, and this writer's name was Moyshe Leyb Lilyenblum. How did she learn about Moyshe Leyb Lilyenblum? Again the same story: her husband was a member of the Burial Society. As is well known, Moshe Leyb Lilyenblum was a warden in the Odessa Burial Society, so he also gave her one of his books, although this one she was not able to read. Therefore she relished another book, *The Polish Lad* by Y. Y. Linetski, who was also an inhabitant of Odessa.[33]

Rosenfeld points out that until this moment he did not know about writing as a profession. It is no coincidence that a woman opens his eyes to the world of Yiddish and Hebrew letters in Odessa. She belongs to the same uneducated stratum of workers as Jonah and is further culturally handicapped by her gender (she is unable to read Lilyenblum's Hebrew book). Jonah and his *balebos* belong on the other side of the social divide that separates the Jewish intellectuals from the Jewish working class. The works mentioned in the passage above—Abramovitsh's *Di kliatshe* (1873, The Mare) and Linetski's *Dos poylishe yingl*—represent the satirical and realist trends in Yiddish literature. Rosenfeld uncompromising expose of the Odessa Jewish community's violent and backward character as a mirror of a similarly prosperous and assimilated Jewish community in the 1930s U.S. was indebted to Abramovitsh and Linetski's works.[34]

As a worker in the *balebos*'s traditional household, Jonah is excluded from secular Jewish culture. As a result, his outlook on the world of learning is still a product of his traditional religious upbringing. At the Seder table at Passover to which this "literary" woman invites him, Jonah proudly announces that his father was a writer *(a shrayber)*.

When the daughter thinks he means a *pisatel* (the Russian word for writer), her mother points out that for Jonah, a writer teaches small children to write (a *melamed*). Without understanding this distinction, Jonah points out that his father knew German and actually read the Haggadah in German. He gives an example of what he regards as cultured speech, German, but it sounds ridiculous to this family. For them, it is Russian—not German—that is the language of high culture. The family bursts out laughing, and Jonah cries until he is gently carried out of the room, humiliated because of his cultural ignorance. This scene points to the similarity between the proletarian and woman autobiographer (of any class background), who are alike excluded from the male-dominated cultural domain through upbringing and education. As a result, the male worker and the woman writer must rely on their own inner world and experiences as their primary creative source of inspiration.[35] In the 1937 interview with Y. Tverski, Rosenfeld expressed this feeling of social protest that originated in childhood and the primacy of autobiographical experiences as artistic inspiration:

[T]he manner of writing I "pump" from myself, but the theme is something completely different. That originates mostly in encounters with people. . . . Truly, I remember myself at three years or even earlier . . . but if you spend your best years, that is, the earliest, in the "workshop" (and until age thirteen in the little, desolate *shtetl* that numbers perhaps a hundred and fifty houses) . . . if you see such a limited number of people in a narrow grey life—have you ever noticed the stew-like emptiness that originates in poor kitchens where little is cooked and little is aired? . . . When each day of your best years is like crawling out of a mirror as an imitation of yesterday. . . . Yes, if you see only such a life, you cannot, as I realized myself, go too far with your themes.[36]

Rosenfeld's picture of Odessa in the 1890s is filtered through his emotionally deprived adolescent hero in the throes of socialist awakening, exposed to the brutality of his *balebos*. Forty years later, Rosenfeld relived a similar personal drama in his relationship with *Forverts'* editor Abraham Cahan. Once again, he was confronted by a tyrannical individual who had the power to control his work and his personal life. This time, he replied with the only weapon he knew as a writer: he transformed both the anger against the rich and powerful that he inherited from childhood and the personal injury sustained in his apprenticeship into a brilliant piece of autobiographical fiction. In a letter to Cahan written in 1935, Rosenfeld listed some of Cahan's criticisms of his literary style: "a story that can be retold without ingenuity, without speculations [*nit gekintslt, on griblerayen*]."[37] Although he angrily refused to abide by Cahan's aesthetic requirements, he nevertheless made *Eyner aleyn* more accessible to the Yiddish reader by structuring it as a series of smaller episodes with narrative suspense. Most importantly, he used the technique of asides to the reader, typical of the Yiddish *shund roman*, and the style of the colloquial literary monologue originating with Abramovitsh and Sholem Aleichem. Like them, he turned the act of speech in the first-person singular into a storytelling performance, directly addressing the reader as a part of the literary discourse. As he stated in the 1935 letter, a Yiddish writer dependent on his monthly salary from the Yiddish press could not afford to write for "the few intellectual readers." However, it was impossible for a writer of Jonah Rosenfeld's stature and character to abandon his themes and introspective style. In a letter from September 25, 1941, a year after the publication of *Eyner aleyn*, Rosenfeld—after a conciliatory gesture from Cahan—requests that Cahan read his new autobiographical work in progress about his early childhood.[38] Aware of Cahan's bad mood "in the very unfavourable situation on the Russian front," he ends the letter "hoping that the craziness [*meshugas*] is all over ('all over' also means in regard to my writing). I remain with the best feelings toward you." However, according to Cahan, autobiographical introspection, even wrapped in *shund* elements and presented in the colloquial style of the Yiddish literary monologue, was not fit to be printed in the *Forverts* in the middle of the war. Rosenfeld continued to be excluded from "the greatest Yiddish newspaper in the world" until his death in 1944. Despite the good reviews received by *Eyner aleyn*,[39] the terminally ill Rosenfeld never saw his most important work serialized in the *Forverts*.[40]

What was at stake in the conflict between Rosenfeld and Cahan was more than personal animosity. It was not merely that Rosenfeld was confronted with the most powerful, autocratic dictator in American Yiddish letters, known for his unpredictable and ruthless whims. More importantly, Cahan represented the conventional literary taste that made *Forverts*' literary instalments one of its most important features in attracting a Yiddish mass readership. Rosenfeld's introspective, subtle psychological stories did not possess the narrative drive and subject matter that made the work of I. J. Singer, Sholem Ash (until he was banned by Cahan in the early 1940s) and, later, Isaac Bashevis Singer the centerpieces of *Forverts*' literary supplements.[41]

Peretz had envisioned a modern Yiddish literature that would fuse the newest literary trends in Europe with uniquely Jewish cultural and social concerns. Rosenfeld remained loyal to Peretz's literary credo to the end of his life. For him literary art was self-expression and auto-biographical introspection rooted in a working class Jewish context. Cahan, on the other hand, represented the American *allrightnik,* which primarily viewed prose literature as entertainment and nostalgia about the "old world." It allowed very limited room for artistic experimentation beyond social realist content and style. Unlike Isaac Bashevis Singer and Yankev Glatshteyn (the former initially under the auspices of Cahan), Rosenfeld did not manage to remake himself as a Yiddish artist in America. *Eyner aleyn* was his last testimony to a Peretzian literary credo that had been made obsolete by the radically new conditions for American Yiddish literature in the 1930s.

As David G. Roskies points out, from the anger that runs like a red thread through modern Yiddish literature "came a negotiated return to the discarded past, a passionate desire to rebuild the culture out of its shards."[42] *Eyner aleyn* should be read in this light: as an artistic re-creation of Odessa in the 1890s, depicted through the angry eyes and ears of an adolescent protagonist caught in the throes of a socially determined inferiority complex and beginning to experience a rudimentary awareness of proletarian class consciousness.

What is more, writing in New York in the late 1930s about what must have seemed a very distant time and place, Rosenfeld was also articulating his role as chronicler. Walking in the Moldavanka neighborhood, with its prostitutes and thieves, the *lumpenproletariat* corresponding to his own poverty-stricken childhood in a Ukrainian *shtetl,* the narrator makes an aside: he characterizes the poor workers as *Gorkis heldn* (Gorky's heros) and continues: "Yes, I had the luck to meet some of them personally before I had heard Gorky's name, and, in general, before I knew that such a 'profession' [*melokhe*] as writing existed" (114). Here the autobiographer presents his memories as untouched by any later literary crafting process. They bear unmediated and authentic testimony to a way of life that has been obliterated as a result of World War I, pogroms, and the Bolshevik revolution of 1917. As one of its few surviving witnesses, Rosenfeld presents himself as a Yiddish Gorky whose work will remain as a chronicle of Jewish working-class life in 1890s Odessa. Watching workers in the Odessa harbour carrying heavy sacks up and down the stairs to a ship, Jonah compares them with the biblical Jacob's dream about the ladder to heaven: "Although I knew that they were not angels, I nevertheless looked at them . . . well, like some other kinds of people, although I knew (and saw) that it was the same kind of people that swarmed the whole area" (118).

Although the angelic side of human nature is much less pronounced in the book than its darker side, Jonah nevertheless experiences moments of human compassion. After having been beaten ruthlessly by his boss, suffering from pain and self-hatred, dreaming of revenge and suicide, the appearance of a tray with tea and bread makes him feel appreciated again. Once outside the workshop, Jonah and his boss's unequal relationship is momentarily replaced by their equal roles as workers in a work team. Covered by dust from polishing the stones, they suddenly look alike and their funny appearance unites them in laughter: "That created an intimate feeling towards him. Yes, that was the first time I had such a feeling. And this feeling became more tangible, when we both began to look grey from the grey dust, so that within approximately an hour we both looked as we were carved out of stone. He, a father-statue—I, his child" (373). The proletarian solidarity only lasts a few moments; then the usual alienating distance returns. Rosenfeld succeeded in voicing his anger about poverty and social injustice by creating an imaginary Eastern European homeland that brought a formerly vibrant civilization to life in fascinating detail.

4

An American Yiddish Poet
Visits Poland, 1934

It has rightly been said that all great works of literature found a genre
or dissolve one—that they are, in other words, special cases. . . . From
its structure, which is fiction, autobiography, and commentary in one,
to the syntax of endless sentences (the Nile of language, which here
overflows and fructifies the regions of truth), everything transcends
the norm.

      Walter Benjamin, "The Image of Proust" (1929)[1]

Writers generally postpone their memoirs to old age, and that is a big
shame, because one must write about youth with youthful passion
and with youthful beliefs. And the older writer is often a very tired
editor of his own memories.

      Yankev Glatshteyn, *In tokh genumen: Eseyen 1945–1947*[2]

Yankev Glatshteyn's two Yash books (1938, 1940) provided an analysis
and exposition of the universal condition of exile, dislocation, and
growing fear of war in the inter-war period. They reflected Glatshteyn's
crisis as a Yiddish writer midway through his career, during a period
when increasing anti-Semitism threatened the very survival of the Jewish people.[3] His trip to Poland in the summer of 1934 forced him to confront Polish-Jewish poverty and the fear of anti-Semitism from which he
had been free during his twenty years in America. Provided with a first-
hand impression of the old world from his nine-week trip, he set out to
write the projected Yash trilogy.[4] In writing the Yash books, Glatshteyn
reclaimed his origin as a Polish Jew from Lublin. (He would later name
a collection of poems *A yid fun lublin* [1966, A Jew from Lublin].) He

restored an important part of his self and life story and also developed a more explicitly Jewish literary credo. The latter would later enable him to respond to the Holocaust as a self-consciously Jewish artist. Dov Sadan mentions that Glatshteyn radically changed after his encounter with his native city, which was like coming face to face with Jewish collective fate.[5] The enthusiastic reception of the Yash books—the second volume received the prestigious Louis Lamed prize for Yiddish literature in 1940—marked a turning point in the poet's popularity.

With the exception of Dov Sadan, and more recently Dan Miron, Ruth R. Wisse and Leah Garrett, literary scholars have either ignored the Yash books or diminished their significance as sketchy travel impressions or as a poet's not-always-successful attempt at writing prose.[6] Glatshteyn's contemporaries considered him to be a poet primarily, one who wrote journalism and literary criticism on the side. However, in order to understand the Yash books' important role in Glatshteyn's oeuvre and Yiddish literature, it is pertinent to view them as a poet's autobiographical quest to come to terms with himself and his craft. Glatshteyn turned to autobiographical narrative in the Yash books out of a creative longing that his poetry did not satisfy.[7]

Jewish autobiographies in America such as Mary Antin's *The Promised Land* (1912) and Abraham Cahan's *Bleter fun mayn lebn* (1926–1931, Pages of My Life) depict the individual's development from childhood to adulthood as part of a master narrative of Jewish migration from the *shtetl* toward individual freedom in the Promised Land. Glatshteyn reinvented himself in the Yash books in a fundamentally different way, questioning the basic assumption of integration and abandonment of ethnic difference in the American melting pot. Glatshteyn's books insist "that assimilation and modernization take place in ethnic and even ethnocentric forms."[8] The Yiddish writer's exchange with the American cultural world was a one-way street in the 1930s and 1940s, summarized in Glatstheyn's famous comment: "What does it mean to be a poet of an abandoned culture? It means that I have to be aware of Auden but Auden need never have heard of me."[9] This situation did not change until the 1950s, a decade that saw a significant increase in English translations of Yiddish literature.[10] The Yash books, however, were not translated into English until the 1960s and then only in abridged versions.[11] Writing in Yiddish meant being part of an international community of Yiddish letters which, in the inter-war period, spanned three centers: New York, Warsaw and Moscow.[12] It also meant addressing a Jewish audience particularly receptive to Jewish cultural expression and content.

Being a Jewish writer in English, on the other hand, signified that Jewish concerns and literary models were less than central. This distinction between the American Jewish writer in English and Yiddish was dramatically accentuated during and after the Holocaust.[13]

As pointed out by Ewa Morawska in her comparative study of Jewish and Slavic representations of the Old Country in America between 1880 and 1930, "Jews . . . were from the beginning far more America-oriented (than Polish, Ukrainian, Slovak, Hungarian immigrants) [and] . . . ventured much more outside the immigrant world and the dominant society."[14] Slavic immigrants developed an ethnic identity centered round the concept of the *Vaterland* (fatherland), whereas the Jewish immigrants build their ethnic distinctiveness on a "gradual idealization of *Heimat*—the local Old Country homeland, generalized as 'the *shtetl*" and counterpoised with the larger (Gentile) society."[15] The distinction between belonging to a European nation state and to the Jewish minority was highlighted in an exemplary way in the contrast between the Yash books and Louis Adamic's *The Native's Return* (1934).[16] Adamic's travelogue was published shortly before Glatshteyn began to serialize his Yash book in the journal *Inzikh*.[17] Sponsored by the Guggenheim Foundation, Adamic depicted the return to his homeland after nineteen years in America. The successful writer was received by Yugoslav politicians and artists who celebrated the return of their native son. In order to portray his trip to visit his dying mother in Lublin in the summer of 1934, Glatshteyn's artistic method had to be radically different. Glatshteyn introduced the work in the journal *Inzikh*, which serialized the first part of the planned Yash trilogy (this introduction was not included in the 1938 book): "Without laurel wreaths, without preparing an audience in advance, without a ready-made form and without the newly awakened attachment to one's own land, it will be a lot harder to relate the nine and a half weeks of my poor, bachelor Odyssey. But—with your patience and permission."[18] Glatshteyn' s trip was highly insignificant at a time "when any female teacher can grant herself the luxury of traveling every summer."[19] The Yiddish reader was saturated with poetic and fictional accounts of the old world: "The *shtetl* has already been praised, set into rhyme and spiced up."[20] Most importantly, Poland as part of tsarist Russia, which Glatshteyn left in 1914, and *Polonya restituta*, the newly independent Poland to which he returned in 1934, did not qualify as a homeland for the expatriated Jewish writer. Glatshteyn's artistic solution in the Yash books was to employ modernist techniques, narrative fragmentation and fusion of different genres such as the travelogue, the novel and the autobiography. B. Alkvit, one of Glatstheyn's *inzikhist* (introspectivist) compatriots, mentions in his review of *Ven yash iz geforn* that their artistic sensibilities were shaped by James Joyce, Marcel Proust, and Sigmund Freud.[21] The Yash books were similarly informed by modernism and psychoanalysis.

By choosing for his autobiographical alter ego the name Yash with its *heymish* (intimate), old world associations, Glatshteyn distanced himself from his earlier, more serious artistic pose as a modernist poet. Ruth R. Wisse points out the connection between a Polish tale by Marya Konopnicka and the Yash books: "The name Yash, which appears nowhere else but in the title, is a version of Janek, which, along with Jas or Jasio, is a variant of Jan."[22] This also relates to the Polish epigraph from Marya Konopnicka's poem "And When the King Went to War," which I discuss below. These references highlight the importance of Polish literature for Glatshteyn's artistic self-portrait in the Yash books. In addition, Glatshteyn's self-portrait transcended purely individual concerns in its similarity with a whole gallery of uprooted characters. Yash became representative as the central figure in the books' multifaceted collective tapestry: the voices and life stories of people he met on the ship to Europe, in the train from Paris to Lublin, and in the Jewish resort hotel outside Lublin.

In a 1955 interview with the Yiddish critic Abraham Tabatshnik, Glatshteyn characterized his poetry as a screen against exposure, not unlike Chinese poetry: "Precisely these frozen emotions, this very lack of a fuss about one's own feelings, is what always interested me in Chinese poetry."[23] In the same interview, Glatshteyn commented on the relationship between poetry and self-portrayal in connection with his deep admiration for the Yiddish poet Y. Y. Segal's work: "And as for personal lyrics, you can practically read his [Segal's] autobiography in his poems: his attitude to his children, his wife, his mistress, his friends, his mother, his father, and the most intimate occurrences. I envy him greatly, I cannot do the same. Why not, I don't know. I have a reticence, a feeling, let us say, of modesty. To write a poem openly about myself, or about my loves, or about my non-loves, feelings about my wife or to a beloved and things of that sort—I cannot write such self-revealing poems. Perhaps I would like to write them, but I have, as the psychologists say, a block."[24] This "psychological block" is highly significant for an understanding of the indirect, fragmented autobiographical account in the Yash books. Glatshteyn pointed to the connection between sexuality, modesty and autobiography as a psychological complex related to the process of alienation from his emotional life following his emigration to America. It was one expression of what he, in the above interview, called "re-emotionalization." This process is indicated in the depiction of the first tough lesson Yash learned upon arriving in New York at age seventeen. Yash's uncle did not meet the boat because he did not want to lose even one day of work.[25] Yash spends his first day in the new country looking for his uncle; his dream of the Promised Land becomes a nightmare: "A cry stuck in my throat. My hard welcome made me hibernate like a bear, and kept me on ice for several years" (193). Traumatized by this experience of abandonment, Yash hid his true emotions and identity behind a surface of hardness, irony, and distance during his first twenty years in America. Based on her conversations with Glatshteyn in the late 1960s, Ruth Whitman gives a slightly different version of these events that nevertheless supports the "autobiographical truth" of the account in the first Yash book: "Traveling third class on the S.S. Aquitania, Jacob arrived in New York in June 1914. He was met by his hunchbacked tubercular uncle, and brought home to the flat on the lower East Side where the entire family worked from dawn until midnight making cigars. Three days after he landed, Jacob got a job pasting felts on hammers in the Knabe piano factory near the docks. During the following six months he worked in fifty or sixty different factories. He shared a single bed with two cousins. To the young scholar and writer who had been the pet of his family and the pride of the Jewish community in Lublin, life in America was a sharp disillusionment."[26]

The autobiographical quest in the Yash books reflects the compromise between Glatshteyn's need for protection against self-exposure and his drive to restore his self and life story in order to recover parts of his emotional life stifled in America and, in a figurative sense, left behind in Lublin. The ambivalence between Glatshteyn's fascination with Y. Y. Segal's poetry and his inability to write such poetry himself was expressed in the Yash books. Glatshteyn candidly depicted parts of his life story in these novels, but he still "modestly" avoided exposing some of its most intimate and emotionally charged aspects. For example, he chose not to depict his encounter with his dying mother, whom he actually saw before her death.[27] There is a four week gap between the first and the second Yash book, enabling Glatshteyn to structure the excruciating experience of watching his mother die from a retrospective distance in *Ven yash iz gekumen*. Glatshteyn also decided to delete stories of his sexual development and family life, save for a few details.[28] Glatshteyn's negative view of I. B. Singer's work, particularly in regard to the latter's exposure of sexual adventures, must be viewed as a consequence of his life-long adherence to Peretz' ethos of *edlkeyt* (ethical refinement) as the defining norm of artistic expression.[29] Similar to Peretz, Glatshteyn went to a figurative *mikve* and purified himself of personal *opfal* (trash) prior to writing the Yash books.

Yash's return to Lublin to visit his dying mother was anticipated in the first book, which he dedicated to his mother, and her death and burial were retrospectively recalled in the second.[30] The symbolic function of the mother figure was reflected in the contrast between his dying mother's ears described as *gel vi voks* (166, yellow as wax) and his own *goldene oyrn* (193, golden ears). These ears, the organs of listening to other people's stories, represent the only quality that sets Yash apart from his fellow passengers on board the ship to Europe. His musical sensitivity to voices, their poetry and emotional character, is Yash's true inheritance from his mother. The synecdochic importance of ears evokes a central theme of decay and death versus creativity and life. This dichotomy is linked respectively to Polish and American Jewry and thematically unfolded in the second Yash book.

In the first four chapters of *Ven yash iz geforn* we follow Yash on board the transatlantic ocean liner from New York to France, and in the fifth and final chapter on the train ride from Paris, stopping in Berlin and Warsaw, until he reaches his destination, Lublin. The narrator Yash's role is as listener to the life stories of the people he encounters on the trip. One of the passengers, a Jew from Bogota, tells Yash that he, unlike the other passengers, has "golden ears": an ability to listen without interrupting. Nothing happens on the five-day trip over the Atlantic except for the passengers' flow of words, their self-indulgent monologues or agitated arguments with each other. Words have replaced real action and are used to show off, to justify an ideological stance or a lifestyle, to confide and entertain. Triggered by the passengers' talk, Yash's inner monologue delineates his own autobiographical account, which is interspersed among his depictions of the trip itself. He describes his hardship after coming to the United States as a young man; his *yikhes* (lineage) in the old country; childhood reminiscences about the Jewish Worker's movement in Lublin; the 1905 revolution and the Tsarist crack down; his immigration to the U.S.; memoirs of his adolescent experiences in the anti-Semitic Polish school system; and the final piece about his brother's death. The book contrasts two modes of literary discourse: the passengers' voices and life stories, and Yash's inner autobiographical monologue. The autobiographical mode is indicated by the name

Yash in the title,[31] and by the use of Glatshteyn's own name in the book: a passenger calls him *"gledi"* (29); the narrator's father calls him "Yankele" (106); and he is also referred to by his Russian name, "Yakov Isakovitsh Gliatshtein" (252). The two modes of literary discourse exist side by side without any interference. Glatshteyn separates these two literary styles to indicate Yash's need to hide his autobiographical monologue from the other passengers. Yash is part of the passengers' conversation, but only to the extent that he may listen and relate what he hears. He is never allowed to step forward as an individual in his own right and tell his own story on board the ship.

One of the passengers, an American editor, argues that a writer cannot write about the passengers on board the ship because they are not real human beings with ground under their feet: "A writer must have people and we are—passengers" (144). The coincidental character of the passengers on the ship—severed from their background, behaving cautiously and politely—excludes the development of real action. The only material left for the writer is the exchange of words, and Glatshteyn takes pleasure in relating the quirks and twists of the passengers' talk: "Not the action, but the dialogue creates the drama. The wrinkle of the words [*Der kneytsh fun di verter*], the voice, the expression" (264). Glatshteyn's depiction of the passengers' estrangement from one another is an allegory for Yash's Americanization. The intellectual sophistication he has achieved during his twenty years in America has changed him only superficially by endowing him with an intellectual vocabulary. Yash contrasts this Americanized part of himself with his life before coming to America: "Now the ship travels back to my youth, as if it would swim back again. The two decades in America are suddenly crushed [*tseribn gevorn*] between two hands. The essence is now the first years, which seek to tie on to everything which was destined [*bashert*] for me at home, like two hollowed halves of a toy that wants to be whole" (45). Yash is setting out on a quest to reconnect with his origins and recapture his status as a child of his city, Lublin. During the trip he peels off the shell of Americanization, depicted as a superficial lie and a digression from the existential core of his identity. Although he attempts to refuse to be overwhelmed by what he calls *oytobiografishe breklekh* (45, autobiographical pieces) that fall on him from all sides, he nevertheless sets out to restore himself as a whole human being: "But I began to restore myself, like I have never done in the twenty years in which I have been away from home" (45).

A central theme of the book is the conflict between the individual and the authoritarian mass movements of the 1930s, Nazism and Soviet Communism. The novel also comments on the Roosevelt's New Deal, which transformed society in the name of an ideology. The Soviet passengers are the most outspoken proponents of ideologies. Yash confronts them internally by recounting problems within the Jewish workers' movement in Lublin, which only served to split the Jewish community. Socialism did not fundamentally alter the Jewish oppression in Lublin, where Jews were scapegoats and victims of anti-Semitism. Yash compares the international melting pot aboard the ship with the superficiality and historical determinism of the mass ideologies of the day. Just as life in New York forces him to separate his individuality from the facade of Americanism, life as a Jew compels him to reject the optimism of the radical social movements. There is no lesson from his Jewish upbringing in Lublin other than that the Jews will be the first victims in a new world order. The core of Yash's identity is his Jewishness, which consists of an all-encompassing fear of the *goyim* rooted in him since early childhood. It was this very fear, in fact, that spurred him to leave home and immigrate to the United States. Yash thought that he could leave behind this fear and transform himself into a new human being, just as the mass movements intend to achieve major social transformation. He paid the price of having to repress his emotional life; he became a half-person, a synthetic human being. The trip represents a reversal of this process. Yash again assumes the communal sense of fear experienced by Polish Jews. He is back to being that same frightened Lublin Jew that he was before emigrating to America: "But I ran away from my home town the way one flees from terror, because my home town has always been the essence of fear to me. A Jewish child is raised on fear. To us, our Gentiles are fear" (219).

Yash also confronts authoritarian tendencies and beliefs in historical determinism among Jews. When he arrives in Paris he learns that the Hebrew writer Bialik has just died in Palestine. Yash recalls a meeting for Yiddish writers a few years earlier at which Bialik denounced the future of Yiddish in the name of the Zionist revival of Hebrew. Bialik was ready to sacrifice an entire segment of the Jewish people for his Zionist vision, or as Yash expresses it: "You don't want to go to the slaughter?! You wretched, pitiful thing! But you will be slaughtered anyway" (214). The political climate in the Jewish community mirrors the polarized political situation in the world: "the Jewish people are led intensely by leaders—led with energy, pomp and circumstance, and fervor [*klaptararam un bren*]" (36). Yash's trip, on the other hand, is not ideologically motivated, but initiated by the news about his dying mother. Upon disembarking, the narrator suddenly discovers Jewish faces he had not noticed on board the ship. They openly appear ready to set out to their various destinations in Europe. Now, it turns out, the American identity easily disappears and the true European nationality emerges: "Twenty, thirty, forty years worth of Americanization has been washed off their faces. Where does a Jew go? . . . Everybody goes home. Suddenly everybody has become "Rumainisized," "Polisized," and "Lithuanisized" (205, *farrumenisht, farpoylisht, farlitvisht*).

Glatshteyn uses a poem by the Polish writer Marya Konopnicka (1842–1910) as the epigraph for the book:

> And when Stach went to battle
> clear wells rippled,
> a field of corn ears rustled
> for longing, for misery . . .
>
> Stach received a mortal wound,
> While the king returned to his castle, healthy . . .

The epigraph functions thematically on two levels. First, it comments on Yash's trip: Smakh, the soldier in the poem, goes to war with longing and high hopes, but he is mortally wounded while the healthy emperor returns to his castle. Only Smakh, the individual, has been transformed in his struggle with death. Similarly, Yash has been through an emotional transformation brought about by facing his own mortality in the face of his dying mother. The power structure in the world represented by the emperor is unchallenged and the political war continues. Only Yash, the Yiddish writer, has been relieved of some of his illusionary ideological baggage. Secondly, the choice of a Marya Konopnicka poem is also thematically significant in a more indirect fashion. She was one of the leading representatives of the positivist trend in Polish society of the 1860s and 1870s, and was considered a philo-Semite as well as a populist who fought against the plight of the oppressed. One of her stories, "Mendl Dantsiker," was actually translated into Yiddish and used to introduce the third issue of Peretz's *Di yidishe bibliotek* (1895).[32] Glatshteyn's choice of the poem indicates that he wanted to present a more hopeful image of Polish-Jewish co-existence than the strained relationship of economical boycott and organized anti-Semitism in the 1930s. This interpretation is supported by the end of the book, in which Yash encounters a young

Pole on the train from Warsaw to Lublin. Yash's alienation from his Polish heritage is apparent when he apologizes for his broken Polish. The best indication that something has changed in the reborn republic of Poland is the way the young Pole pronounces the Polish word *zshid* (Jew): "he does say 'Jew,' but it comes out softly, without a bite."[33] At this point, Yash actually reveals an emotional memory to one of the people he encounters. In response to the young Pole who tells him that he is the only survivor of six siblings, Yash says that three of his own brothers died in infancy. For the first time on the trip there is true emotional understanding between Yash and one of the people he meets. The book ends with tears in the young Pole's eyes; his hand is on Yash's shoulder as they enter the Lublin train station.

But Yash is not only coming home to a Poland reborn, in which progressive young Poles reach out to Jews. (This image is thoroughly shattered as yet another illusion in *Ven yash iz gekumen*.) He is also returning to Jewish Poland, with its poverty, fear and starvation. The encounter with his three Warsaw cousins brutally reveals the Jewish-Polish legacy from which he has been estranged during his twenty years in America: "I have never thought about the last twenty years in terms of war, starvation, pogroms, fear, poverty, want—as I do now, looking at the three yellow faces" (255). Dreaming about a folkloristic, legendary *shtetl* replete with collective images of religious anti-Semitism and a *shabesdik* (Sabbath-like) atmosphere—a dream he has cherished and feared in his exile in America—he wakes up to the harsh reality of Jewish Poland while driving through Warsaw. The dream about a Jewish *shtetl* consists of religious symbols—the church bells, the priest, the Sabbath atmosphere—and folkloristic elements: the market place, the Jewish and Christian songs, and the water carrier. The Jewish fear of a pogrom is emphasized in the beginning and at the end in the image of the priest's hands that are looking bloody from the raspberries—a symbol of the crucified Jesus. Yash characterizes the dream as expressing his most intimate *(heymish)* feelings of fear, sadness and Jewish vulnerability in a Catholic anti-Semitic environment: "the sad tonality of my home" (249, *der troyeriker tonalitet fun der heym*).[34] This Jewish Poland is his true legacy and destiny and takes on biblical proportions: "Now my tongue actually cleaves to the roof of my mouth [*tsugeklept tsum gumen*], but I have never forgotten you, my Jewish-Poland. . . . Forget not my right hand, just like I have never forgotten you" (249).[35]

The autobiographical fragments in *Ven yash iz geforn* appear throughout the book as shorter or longer insertions in the travelogue.

There is a certain chronological order to them despite their seemingly improvised character. The first autobiographical section (46–49) depicts Yash's career as an employee for various companies. This section sets the tone for the book's anti-success story of Jewish acculturation in America. Yash's insignificance is revealed in his fearful passivity when he meets with the newspaper editor for whom he has worked for eight years: "My compromising, my talent, my three poor books of poetry, my convincing presence—everything pegged out because at the door of the room I clearly heard my wife wail and my three children beg that I, God forbid, wouldn't make any wrong move and not utter any insulting word" (41). Instead of standing his ground with self-respect, Yash is depicted as a *pater familias* who worries about his wife and children and is driven by the instinct for survival. The second autobiographical fragment about Yash's *yikhes* in Poland is triggered by the news of Hitler's murder of the SA leaders in 1934. Because Yash realizes that the news has no impact on the Gentile passengers, he wants to share it with a fellow Jew: "In this international paradise aboard the ship, the news of Hitler was the first which hit my Jewishness [*derlangt dem patsh iber mayn yidishkeyt*]" (43). Yash finds an old *balebatish* (genteel) Jew whose spiritual wisdom, reflected in his stately appearance, is contrasted to the typical hard-working American Jew without time for metaphysical reflection. This image of old world *yidishkeyt* initiates Yash's autobiographical quest: he is suddenly able to view his first seventeen-to-eighteen years in Lublin as connected to his visit home to see his dying mother. The collective threat to Jews exemplified by the news of Hitler confronts Yash with his Jewish origins and forces him, however reluctantly, to take stock of his life: "A flood of autobiographical fragments [*mabl fun oytobiografishe breklekh*] started to fall on me from all sides. I strongly resisted the temptation that already now, and not over twenty years later, I should place my first years under tweezers. What will I do at sixty, when literature under the pressure of the economic 'thirty-year war' probably will have completely lost its significance, and there will only remain the curiosity of old slanderers [*rekhilenitses*] to peek into each other's 'book of life' [*sefer hakhayim*]? But I began to restore myself, like I had not done it in the twenty years I had been away from home" (45). Here Glatshteyn presents a view of the autobiography as a medium of gossip and self-justification by old writers who analytically dissect their own lives. The autobiography as a problematic literary genre corresponds with an intellectual climate in which economical and political opinions have replaced artistic literature. Yash's sense of a collective threat to Jews makes him redefine the autobiography so that it becomes an instrument of true introspection and self-restoration.[36]

The third autobiographical section (86–109) is triggered by Yash's encounter with a group of Russians returning to the Soviet Union in high spirits, inspired by their vision of a Communist utopia. In the beginning of this section Glatshteyn reclaims his hometown's role in the Communist revolution and quotes one of the Yiddish revolutionary songs from his childhood. Then he reminisces about the naive belief he once had in revolutionary heroism, inspired by his grandfather's stories about the Polish uprising against the tsar in 1864. A reminiscence about a *ti'shebov* (a day of fasting and mourning in commemoration of the destruction of the first and second Temples in Jerusalem) during which the community was locked up in the synagogue while Cossacks pillaged in the street is followed by memories of newspaper pictures of Jewish pogrom victims. Clearly, the revolutionary movement is morally justified in fighting tsarist anti-Semitism. But instead of telling an optimistic story of Jewish revolutionary glory and heroism, Glatshteyn relates how the *nayer koykh* (new force), the socialist revolutionaries, terrorized the Jewish community.

The discrepancy between socialist ideals and reality is most poignantly revealed in the episode with Atlasovitsh. This young man from a good family with a talent for Talmud study, became instead a member of a socialist party. He was later assassinated for leaking secret party information to another socialist party. Yash was reading Dovid Edelshtat's socialist poems when he heard the shot that killed Atlasovitsh, and saw him bleeding to death in the street. At the funeral, Atlasovitsh's own father spit on his son's grave and screamed "may his name be blotted out." Yash holds the Jewish socialist movement responsible for the rifts between fathers and sons, workers and employers, religious and nonreligious. When the 1905 revolution finally breaks out, it is quickly and brutally suppressed by the tsarist military. The post-revolutionary period of disillusionment is characterized by increased poverty and intellectual escapism from a dreadful, hopeless reality. The socialist adventure turns out to be a tragic mistake. At the end of this section, Yash pathetically threatens his father with suicide if he does not buy him a ticket to America.

The fourth autobiographical section (166–93) completes the chronological sequence from the previous two autobiographical sections (Yash's childhood and adolescence) with a depiction of Yash's immigration to the U.S. in which is inserted a childhood train trip from Lublin to

Warsaw and back again. This section depicts the excitement and the anxiety of migrating from place to place. Similar to the previous auto-biographical sections, its narrative trope signifies longing after a goal, a belief in an ideal (the socialist revolution, the Promised Land), which turns out to be a devastating disappointment. The immigrants' physical and emotional hardship is presented at the beginning of this section. Although the ocean liner's third class deck is institutionally clean and far removed from the hellish poverty on the *imgrantishe tvishndek* (165, immigrant deck), it nevertheless makes Yash feel the immigrants' fear of being rejected and sent back. Then he watches the worn-out crippled toes of two Polish women reminding him of the letter from his aunt about his mother's *gele oyrn* (yellow ears). The past twenty years, from the moment he left her at the Lublin train station, are symbolized by the transformation of her ears from being attractive with enticing and decorative ear rings to becoming "yellow ears," representing the same decaying quality as the Polish women's toes. Then Yash reminisces about an increasingly anti-Semitic Lublin which threatens the middle class solidity of his father's business. The upward social mobility of his family is manifest in the money that paid for his ticket to America, saved up like *blutik gelt* (168, blood-stained money). It is also expressed by his idle life which he spent hanging out with a group of aspiring young artists and writers. Although Yash has already written "whole packages of poems and stories" (170), he considers himself nobody compared to the poet in the group who belongs to a rich, assimilated Polish-Jewish family. This poet openly plagiarizes other poets, but "God blessed him with sadness" (171).[37] This sadness is associated with poetry as European high art in contrast to America as the land of the *gele prese* (yellow press). Ruth Whitman provides biographical information about this early "Russian" moment in Glatshteyn's adolescence: "By the time he was thirteen or fourteen Jacob was part of a local group of young intellectuals who spent many evenings strolling together along the side of the street reserved only for the educated and upper classes. The proletariat, both Jewish and Gentile, by common consensus walked on the other side of the street. Glatstein spoke Russian with his friends rather than the Yiddish he spoke at home."[38]

Although Yash as listener is set apart from the rest of the passengers, he is at the same time depicted as one of them, belonging to the same immigrant generation of split personalities. Upon arrival in France, Yash reflects on the nature of travel for a generation of immigrants: "I look at the gloomy faces, and it occurs to me that twenty-five years from now, this kind of traveler will disappear completely. The last remnants of the old generation travel now to visit their ancestors' graves [*keyver-oves*]. All fathers and grandfathers have already died out, and the sons are already beginning to die out. When the grandsons will travel to the Soviet Union, Poland, Lithuania, Rumania, it will also be for pleasure; Poland will for them be like a summer trip to Paris, Switzerland, Italy; nobody will travel back home. People will travel out into the world in order to cover their suitcases with foreign stickers; nobody will travel to search for their own roots" (206).[39] All the characters Yash encounters on the ship are struggling with their uprooted identities; they are looking for some kind of ideological or personal solution to their crisis. Only in transition on aboard the ship are they (for a short time) fully alive in short-lived social and sexual encounters. This is a generation that has tried to transform itself in the name of an ideology or belief in the American dream, but it has been sorely disappointed and disillusioned.

Yash's most intimate and painful reminiscence takes place on the train from Warsaw to Lublin and relates to the death of his brother Hetske and his mother's desperate prayers: "my mother kept throwing complaints at God [*bavorfn got mit taynes*]" (265). This is the only place in the book where Yash remembers an interaction with his mother. Initially Yash internalized his mother's despair. Then, he provided her with the argument that although a religious Jew is obligated to tithe a certain part of his fortune, God had already taken more than His share. The more his mother cried out to God, the more "I cooled down." The human tragedy is beyond religious consolation; death has no justification or remedy. Returning twenty years later to face his dying mother, Yash is as unprepared and defenseless as he was as a child witnessing his mother's prayers to the silent *polep* (ceiling). The teacher from Wisconsin tells Yash about visiting her relatives in a Swedish town where she was raped by a family member who later wanted to marry her. This story demonstrates the hollowness of the dream of reclaiming one's cultural roots. Yash's trip back to visit his dying mother cannot reverse his personal history or liberate him from his rootless existence. But it can reconnect him with that part of his self originating in Lublin and later repressed in America.

Music plays an important role in *Ven yash iz gekumen*, particularly in the way the book opens and closes. The first sentence of the book is a quote from a Hasidic *nign* (wordless melody) in which the act of singing to God is presented as a redeeming force that transcends *blote* (dirt, mud).

This sets the narrative in motion and introduces Shteynman as a secular *rebbe* (Hasidic rabbi) who conducts a *tish* (a Hasidic rabbi's table and gathering place for his followers) with guests from the hotel. The word *blote* is used in various settings throughout the book as an important metaphor that crystallizes different layers of meaning. In the description of the barefoot *shikse* (pejorative term for a non-Jewish woman) who works in the hotel, her feet are described as *bashpritst mit blote* (15, sprinkled with mud). Later, at the end of Shteynman's story of his return to Poland where he becomes a fervent Zionist, he mentions that the artisans who listened to his Zionist speeches realized that *mir zukhn zi oystsushlepn fun blote* (96, we seek to drag them out of the dirt). The final use of the word is in connection with Shteynman's walk with the narrator in the vicinity of the hotel, which he describes in this way: "You are apparently not familiar with our muddy areas [*mit di blotes in undzere vonvozn*]. They consist of the moisture from the first six days of Creation" (216). Here, *blote* is described as a primordial element of universal chaos, remaining from the original Creation. This myth also relates to the Gentile woman, who lacks any sense of shame and sexual inhibition. (The narrator gets a glimpse of her frivolous *rendez-vous* with Brodski's Gentile bodyguard [209].) The element of *blote* is also related to the Polish-Jewish exile from which the Zionists hope to rescue the Jews. Thus, *blote* synthesizes biblical, historical and sexual meanings which have to do with chaos and exile, removed from the purpose and meaning that suffuse the universe with order and spirituality in poetry and music (the *nign*).

Sentimental dance music is connected with *di farkalekhte* (the calcified), as the guests in the hotel are called. Another type of music is represented by the nightingale, the *kop zinger* (head singer), who sings to the narrator on his way to Kuzmir. Two modes of music, or perceptions of the nightingale as the symbol of poetry, are contrasted here: "There was no sign of degrading sweetness in the nightingale's song, of pandering to the conventional taste. On the contrary—it was perfection of expression. It simply tore at the heart that this bird had been so insulted, over sweetened and licoriced to the world while it represented such an unpopular and wise musical Hebrew [*muzikalishe ivre*]" (249). Here Glatshteyn presents his poetic credo, wherein authentic artistic expression originates in the silence of the woods, associated with the origin of the world (*ur-likht, ur-shtilkeyt* [original light, original silence]). Like the bird's singing, this creative impulse belongs outside a cultural realm and is the very opposite of sentimental poetry. This image of the nightingale characterizes Glatshteyn's poetics as independent of any ulterior motive save the artistic refinement of poetic musicality, the sounds and rhythms of words. In other words, three types of music—the Hasidic *nign*, a frivolous dance band, and the nightingale's musical *ivre* (Hebrew) related to Jewish liturgical music—are used to characterize three different worlds: Shteynman, *di farkalekhte*, and Yash.

The sickness of *di farkalekhte* originally had to do with sclerosis, later with the calcification of the brain, and now applies to people with nervous syndromes or simply complete idiots of the quiet and tranquil kind. At the beginning of the book, Shteynman's high spirited *tish* is interrupted by Brodski, a rich assimilated Jew who interrupts the cozy atmosphere when he shouts: "In ancient Egypt the mummies made a terrible noise" (11). Although the guests reject this comment as the ravings of a madman, it nevertheless touches them to the core. This remark alludes to their disease caused by neither physical nor psychological conditions, but must be seen as a reflection of their *goles* (diaspora) existence. They are like mummies, already dead, and their singing and noise are a desperate outcry of slaves in exile. According to Shteynman's neo-Hasidic gospel, it is only through song, story-telling and religious devotion that *di farkalekhte* can be redeemed from exile and be temporarily brought back to life. Shteynman points toward Zionism as a radical remedy against the process of calcification that threatens madness, chaos and death. But he views Zionism only as a way to redeem the Polish Jews from their historical exile, not as redemption in a spiritual-religious sense.

In Thomas Mann's novel *The Magic Mountain* (1924), the hotel sanatorium becomes a microcosm of the universal human condition and the deathly disease, tuberculosis, a metaphor for life as "sickness to death." After seven years in the sanatorium, the only hope that the protagonist, Hans Castorp, has for escape is to enlist in the army at the outbreak of World War I. The novel depicts a lost generation unable to create the spiritual basis for a new life. Glatshteyn creates a similar symbolic universe in his focus on the hotel as a microcosm of Polish Jewry stuck in an exile of increasing anti-Semitism, unable to recover from their diaspora existence except through artistic and religious means. Unlike in *The Magic Mountain*, death and sickness are never delved into in *Ven yash iz gekumen*; rather, they are described as an inexplicable end, in the case of Yash's mother's death; *di farkalekhte's* slowly mummification, or as the negation of meaning and spirit. An example of this latter image of death is the narrator's reminiscence of how Reb Levi (the *tsadek*, the holy man as genius) and Zelig (reduced to an animal-like human being) become spiritual twins in the face of death. They actually die at the same time, and the narrator remembers their deaths as interconnected. After Reb Levi's death, his manuscripts are unintelligible to the scholars and what remains are "corporeal words [*gufike verter*] but lacking soul and clarity" (203). Unlike Hans Castorp who escapes the sanatorium likely to meet death in the war, Yash in the end regains his rightful place as the successor of the secular *rebbe,* Shteynman. What he inherits is a "dead language" and a *nign* saved from Shteynman's mouth before he dies: "I relayed it to the audience like I would have read an unbelievable text for them, or translated from a dead language which already had ceased to exist" (293). When the dying Shteynman begins to sing, his face looks like a sheet of music to Yash, and the guests around his bed are momentarily carried away, joining in with the *nign* as in the beginning of the book. A little later, shame and embarrassment make the guests stop singing. What remains of the *nign* after Shteynman's death is its potentiality in the hand of Yash who has been entrusted with its melody. The similarity between this episode and Peretz's short story "A klezmer toyt" (A Musician Dies)[40] underscores the distance between Peretz's proud secular *yidishkeyt* and the hotel guests' shame and alienation from the *umgloyblekhn tekst* (unbelievable text). In Peretz's story, the dying *klezmer* (musician), surrounded by his wife and his musician sons, summons them defiantly to play his *ani maamin* (article of faith) without assembling the traditionally required quorum of ten men. Yash, on the other hand, is required to serve as the interpreter of Shteynman's *toyte shprakh* (dead language) for the guests.

Another reference to music that connects the theme of *goles* (diaspora) with linear (autobiographical) and cyclical (seasonal) time occurs when Yash, on returning from Kuzmir, reflects on a novel by the Spanish writer Ramon Valle-Inclan (1866–1936). This book is divided into four sonatas, after the seasons of the year. This classical form is associated with leisure and with the regular flow of life through seasonal changes belonging to a Gentile world far removed from the frantic desperation of Polish Jews. In contrast, a Jewish life is in the case of Shteynman, played to the tune of a *nign* repeated over and over again and transmitted from one generation to the next. Yash is on his way back from the "art market" in Kuzmir, moving toward death as darkness increases in the world around him in the form of pogroms and threats of war. His visit to the hotel outside Lublin takes place at the end of August, the period of *slikhes* (penitential prayers), in which a religious Jew makes *khezhbn hanefesh* (stocktaking of the soul) and looks back upon his life. Jewish ritual time is not mentioned at all. The notion of time is shaped by the alarming urgency felt by the hotel guests representing Polish Jewry as moving toward its exit from history.

The book's first and most important autobiographical reminiscence (33–55) is a *tour de force* of retrospective prose. Here the narrator talks about himself in the third person as a *kleyn yingele* (a little boy), *dos oyg fun a yungerman* (the eye of a young man), and a *dritn* (a third). He then shifts to a more intimate approach addressing his self in the second person singular *du* (you). This autobiographical section is framed by the narrator's encounter with Shteynman. Glatshteyn's own name is not mentioned in the book except for the name Yash in the title. Yash is first introduced by Shteynman after Brodsky's remark about the Egyptians mummies: "Come along, young man! My name is Shteynman. What is your name? You just arrived today at noon. And he took me by the arm and led me to the garden gate, a few steps from the hotel" (17). Henceforth, it is through Yash's eyes and ears that the reader is given a report of what happens to him during his stay at the hotel. The narrator's name is not revealed; he is presented in general terms as a *yungerman* (young man). The other term used to describe Yash, "the American son," completes his characteristics as defined by his American origin and role as a son. His identity has not crystallized yet through the attachment of a name. Shteynman, on the other hand, has both a name and a concrete history, specified in his childhood memories from the 1860s, parents' names, and rabbinical ancestry. Later, this is emphasized further through his encounters with historical figures such as Rabbi Hildesheimer, Theodor Herzl, Herman Graetz and Jacob Gordin. Shteynman is described in real historical terms, while Yash's identity is fluid, hidden behind general qualities. This anonymous quality of the I-narrator is peeled away layer by layer throughout the book, culminating in the carriage ride back from Kuzmir. During this ride historical time, the darkened pre-war period of the late 1930s, is transcendentally unified with Yash's middle aged "I." Although Yash is never named, he nonetheless becomes part of an historical chain as Shteynman's rightful son and successor.

As his name signifies, Shteynman is that linking together of *man*hood, the establishment of an adult identity, with *shteyn* (stone), the rock-like quality that represents an unbreakable core. His is the developmental goal that Yash, the *yungerman*, is striving toward, and finally succeeds in becoming at the end of the book. At the same time, as Richard Fein points out, Shteynman and Glatshteyn share one syllable.[41] Although Shteynman is depicted as an historical character, he is also fictional, an idealized alter-ego. Glatshteyn uses this play on names to emphasize its ambiguous fictional character. The solid core of Glatstheyn's identity, its "stone" quality, is represented in the surrogate father Shteynman, while the slippery fluid quality of his identity, its *glat* (smooth) part, remains as a nameless potentiality represented in Yash. The episode with Finkl, who insists that only a coincidence prevented him from becoming the narrator's father, dismisses the question of biological fatherhood as insignificant. Glatshteyn's father, who was alive when he visited Lublin in 1934 (and was killed in Maidanek at the age of seventy-six), plays no significant role in the book and is only mentioned a few times.

The *yungerman* also appears in the first autobiographical section in connection with *dos shtik nishterndike oyg* (45, a piece of searching eye) closely related to the narrator's American identity, *der istseyder forsher* (44, the East Side scholar). Was it not for the *yungerman*'s eye, *dos yingele* (the little boy), the narrator's childhood identity, would have disappeared. This eye possesses the ability to remember not only passively but actively, through the creation of a childhood past. It is this eye that keeps the narrator in touch with his memories from Lublin during his alienating years on the Lower East Side of New York. Yash's ability to listen and record other peoples' talk, his "golden ear," is complemented with a visionary eye. The eye signifies Yash's historical awareness of himself and his search for autobiographical coherence. Through his analytical, retrospective eye, which directs him toward a fuller identity, Yash is connected to a deeper historical awareness of his own destiny.

The act of recall is triggered by the death of Yash's mother depicted as the end of time, catapulting him back to his first conscious moment: "There is nothing to lease from the stop, not a hair—it is the end. Let it mean a hundred or thousand, or a trillion, but now it is over. I wanted to think about nothing other than one, about the very beginning, about the first one, about the first step" (36). The first autobiographical section takes place in a twilight zone in which Yash is half asleep and without the usual censors of subconscious memories. This makes it possible for him to let the inner eye's process of recall transcend linear time and bring him in touch with the first conscious moment of his life "the first point of memory [*dermon-punkt*] on the horizon of barely remembering [*koym-koym gedenken*]" (44). Significantly, Yash's first memory is of going with his aunt to bring food to his father serving in the *kazarmes* (the tsar's army). This walk is depicted as an adventurous, never-ending

journey. The father figure is out of reach, exiled in his army service both
as a Pole and a Jew who cannot eat the army's *treyf* food and is therefore
dependent on his family's care packages. The main theme of the following American reminiscences is the sudden death of the Lower East Side
yungerman's high school teacher and the suicide of his unknown neigh-
bor. This confrontation with death brings the narrator to reminiscence
about the death of his mother, specifically his consultation with Dr.
Tenenbaum who tells him his mother "is on her death bed. Death is the
very opposite of life" (53).

In the last part of this autobiographical section (53–55), time is linked
to the multiplication of Yash's selves, which increases his sense of
plonter [confusion]. He realizes that neither the *yingele* nor the *forshndikn
oyg*, but instead a *shpogl-dritn* (brand-new third) (53) is talking to the
doctor. The *shpogl-dritn* is named as a quantifiable number and associated with the memory of the American Richard Corey. This internal
multiplication of selves is replaced by the unquestionable clarity with
which the doctor spoke to Yash, immediately after his carriage ride to
his father's house to visit his dying mother. Here the style of the reminiscences changes into an intimate, imploring, poetic outcry about in-
exorable time as the narrator rides in a carriage that never reaches its
destination. In the face of his mother's death, the narrator's eyes are
closed. He is not able to arrive in time to see and fully experience what
has happened: "A dream can last a full twenty years and the message of
the dream is a moment, barely caught and seen in the flight of time's
momentum" (55). A period of Yash's life, his first twenty years in America, is over. He has been transformed into somebody else without having been fully able to experience this cosmic transformation in which
"the sky actually cracked open" (54). He is like a character in a dream
driven forwards by unconscious forces beyond his control. Time as
waste *farshvenderishkeyt; fartakhleveter tsayt* (54, waste; squandering
time), which eats away relentlessly at life and limb, in the process of
aging, does not lead to clarity. The internal *plonter* resulting from Yash's
inner autobiographical search can be seen as an image of the *inzikhist*'s
introspection; a road which only exacerbates confusion in endless self-
multiplication. The self is sunken like Atlantis into a dream landscape.
In it, linear and cyclical time has been replaced by the contraction and
expansion of dream time, preventing the self from truthfully seeing itself except through a distorted prism.

The image of Yash in the carriage is repeated at crucial moments
throughout the narrative. This is one more example of the work's

travelogue character. The reminiscence of Yash's walk to his father in the *kazarme,* the ride to his dying mother, and the trip to and from Kuzmir can all be viewed as the continuation of his trip across the ocean in *Ven yash iz geforn.* Like a traveler searching out new areas to explore and delineate in order to come to terms with his inner world, the image of Yash in the carriage crystallizes his self-exploration through time and movement. This image is repeated at the end of the book, when the coachman wakes Yash and convinces him to go to Kuzmir. Yash had not planned a trip to Kuzmir but nevertheless accepts. There is a kind of destined inevitability in this final part of his journey. On the way back from Kuzmir, once more *durkh a driml* (through a dream), the narrator experiences an episode during which "half of the carriage in which I sat moved away from me, as did the horse, and I remained alone [*eyner aleyn*]" (283). In this moment he is disconnected from the carriage and transported into another reality, a timeless state that can be characterized as an epiphany. At the end of Peretz's *Mayne zikhroynes,* the shepherd's whistle in the Swiss mountains transcends the dichotomy between feeling and thought, truth and falsehood, life and death. In this transcendental moment Peretz's alter ego experiences an epiphany in which he is unified with the surrounding world. Similarly, on his way back from Kuzmir, Yash experiences a breakdown of time and place, and the unification of his self and the world. Peretz's epiphany grows out of a nature experience and comes to him from without. Glatshteyn's epiphany, on the other hand, grows out of a self-reflective process *durkh a driml* (through a dream), a half conscious state of introspective clarity which takes place independently of the natural scenery around him.

During this time Yash arrives at an inner clarity and harmony allowing him to momentarily transcend his alienation and belatedness, finally bringing him in touch with the essence of his being. He sees himself as on the way to the *rayon fun harbst* (region of autumn), in the context of the seasonal four part sonata form of the Spanish novel. He realizes that he is traveling in an allegorical carriage. Through this metaphor, his life and his mother's death become, like a musical variation on a main theme, representative as part and parcel of Jewish life, and the historical movement in the world at large. This vision of an organic wholeness between the "I" and the world breaks his traveling mode for a moment. Yash has finally arrived home to a destiny that is organically linked to mythical, historical and autobiographical time (middle age). He is also moving towards the ultimate timeless state, death, where his right hand's creativity will wither away like an *opgeshosn hant* (hand that has been shot off). Similarly to *Ven yash iz geforn* in which the narrator swears loyalty to Jewish-Poland, he repeats the scriptural oath to Jerusalem (Psalm 137). This time, however, he does so with an awareness of his own mortality: "We will, all of us—me and all my remembrance and forgetfulness—travel quickly to winter with a shot-off hand. May that be the hand by which I swore that it should dry out, if I will forget you, and everything which has been reflected in my eyes and in my consciousness" (284). Something is added to the oath from the first Yash book: at the end of the trip, Yash swears that he will never forget what he saw and learned during his life, including the trip he is about to conclude.

In analyzing the ways in which Glatshteyn explores the various aspects of time, one must keep a simple fact in mind. An autobiographical work is never the recollection of a past life existing independently of the writer's present moment and waiting to be retrieved. Rather, it is a reflection on the writer's life patterned in the moment of writing. Glatshteyn's choice of *geforn* (movement) and *gekumen* (homecoming) as the leitmotifs of the two Yash books summarizes the period of 1934–1940 in his creative career. It is characterized by crisis and a breakdown of values, leading to clarity and a renewed artistic and ideological foundation for him as writer. This was accomplished through the Yash books' autobiographical quest into the past, the present and his own mortality. The autobiographer is always addressing his own mortality when he sets out to once-and-for-all (for only rarely does a writer write a second autobiography) give an account of his life. That is precisely why childhood plays such a crucial role in the autobiography: it is a phase of life in which timelessness and eternity transcends the adult's ego-oriented devotion to linear clock-time. In many ways, the childhood encapsulates the Romantics' obsession with transcending time and space altogether (Novalis) or anchoring eternity in the individual consciousness (Wordsworth). But this fascination with childhood is at the same time "a deep fascination with death itself, the ultimate timeless state."[42]

As in *Ven yash iz geforn*, Glatshteyn employs two types of literary styles in *Ven yash iz gekumen*. A good example of these styles, alternating between the characters' own monologues and Yash's report of their life stories, is his encounter with Sabe. Glatshteyn utilizes his narrator-on-the-spot, like a reporter, to bear witness to the factual accuracy of his impressions. At the same time, he also presents the characters' monologues, with their twist and turns of spoken Yiddish, in order to make them fully alive as individuals and heighten the emotional impact of their narratives. The following is an example of the shift between these two literary styles: first Sabe's own monologue, and then Yash's third person account which begins in the last sentence of the quote: "'Sabe,' he argued with me, 'I am afraid of you. You have such hungry eyes, a hungry mouth. Even your words are hungry.' He often spoke to her about the poetry of Jewishness and for her it was a new world" (111). In the autobiographical sections, the prose becomes more flexible and complex. Glatshteyn uses an associative prose style with poetic features such as metaphors, descriptive adjectives and meter shifts. The rhythm of the prose changes constantly, alternating long winding sentences with short staccato ones. The flexibility of the prose highlights the inner monologue quality of the reminiscences.

The shift in time between the narrator's present moment of recall in the hotel and his youth on the Lower East Side is emphasized through the use of words of English origin (e.g., *pushkart, tomeytos, a nikl* [push carts, tomatoes, a nickel], 40). Additionally, Glatshteyn utilizes one of his favorite stylistic devices, the coinage of new words (e.g., *vayt-avekkayt, fremd-veltikeyt* [faraway-ness, foreign worldliness], 40),[43] along with language folklore,[44] song titles or whole verses, in order to create a certain poetic air around a particular memory. The following is an example of what the Yiddish critic Shmuel Niger characterized as Glatshteyn's "free prose"[45:] a long sentence in an associative style, followed by ultra short sentences locating the memory in time and space, including a piece of language folklore: "Then arrived cold, ice-covered windows, long nights blooming apart, silent shutters, muddy rains and milder days. A warm house. Father is already home. No one can even remember when he returned from his military service. Mother embroiders singing "In the Temple, In the Corner of the Classroom" (42).

The meta-poetic aspect of the book is subtly expressed in the different styles used to describe Yash's encounter with the other characters. In his encounter with Sabe, she characterizes her story as a *roman* about love and jealousy, and Yash suspects that her story is all made up. This blurring of the boundary between fiction and reality triggers Yash's memory of his first sexual attraction to Yokhtshe characterized as a "a growing world without language, with red smeared on yellow memories" (115). The yellow memories are associated with *di gele prese* (the yellow press) in which *di shund romanen* (the pulp novels) were serialized; that is, a literary universe in which all distinctions are blurred in an outpouring of sentimental emotion, depicting reality in glaring, plain colors. Contrasting Sabe's *roman,* the next encounters, divided into small chapters, consist of inquiries by visitors who bemoan their poverty in front of Yash, asking him to intercede for them on his return to America. These various requests have the appearance of one "voice representing a whole social class," pleading with Yash as the messenger from America, the land of "legendary bread." This section brings to mind Peretz's *Bilder fun a provints-rayze* (Pictures from a Journey in the Provinces), whose main theme similarly is a traveling intellectual's confrontation with the poverty and backwardness of the *shtetl*.[46] Glatshteyn contrasts Saba's *roman* with the social realism of the poverty-stricken visitors in order to outline the social-economic extremes of Polish Jewry.

Between these two encounters, Glatshteyn inserts a section about theater which includes a brief play. We are again led into an unreal dream world with grotesque images and reminiscences about Yash's first Purim-play and his experiences as a prompter in the Yiddish theatre. Suddenly, Yash finds himself with Sabe and his parents watching a Yiddish play. His father wants to see a Yiddish play in the Goldfaden tradition, with popular songs such as "Koldunye," "Heyse babkelekh" (Hot Cakes), and "In the Temple in the Corner of the Class Room." The play actually begins with a traditional Sabbath scene, but the idyll is broken when the sexuality of the dialogue becomes explicit and Yash finds himself in bed with Sabe on stage. This dream section in which Yash's bare feet symbolize his feeling exposed and ashamed, "the shame of my naked feet" (135), relates to his ambiguous relationship to his poetry as a Yiddish writer.[47] Peretz, representing high Yiddish literature geared towards intellectuals with refined European aesthetic taste, is contrasted with the sexual vulgarity and folklorist cliché of the Yiddish popular theater in America. The aesthetic dichotomy between Europe and the USA is highlighted by the distinction between Sabe's upper class status and the vulgar masses', including Yash's parents, tastelessness and explicit sexual desires. When Saba shows literary erudition by quoting critical articles about theater, the people in the audience begin shouting at her: "Shut up! Shut up [*Sharap*]! Shut your mouth [*Farmakh s'lokh*]. Phooey, the vulgarity of the translation shocked me, to apply such crudeness to this kind of warm and small and talkative creature. I was ready to tear everyone apart for her sake, but she played indifferently with her tongue. I obey them like cats, she said, the whole yellow press with its 'shut up.' This is Europe" (122). The dilemma between *shund* and art-theater is also at the heart of the metapoetic difference between Shteynman and Yash. Shteynman writes popular Hasidic tales for the Yiddish newspaper. His populist philosophy of giving the masses entertainment and moral enlightenment expresses a fundamentally different literary credo than Yash's modernist aestheticism exemplified in the nightingale episode. Yash seeks to refine and explore the poetic medium for its own sake without attempt to "pander to the conventional taste" (249).[48]

In the encounter between Yash and the young Hasid, another literary style is introduced. It combines religiousness and artistic expression and thus transcends the secular world of *shund,* as well as social realism and art theater for *di hekhere fenshter* (high society) as represented by Peretz. The Hasid rejects Peretz's Hasidic tales as moralistic parables and envisions a creative encyclopedia which would include all genres and styles in a renewal of Jewish thought: "First of all, you must understand, we have to get rid of the Gentile forms. Our creation must include everything: poetry, philosophy, drama, psychology, astronomy, epigrams—everything" (159). The Hasid's hero and literary role model is Nachman of Bratslav, an artistic innovator and a lover of Yiddish. His literary credo connects Hasidic beliefs and fervor with the deepest resources of the Yiddish literary medium in Nachman of Bratslav's tales.[49] This *nigndike yidishkeyt* (melodious Jewishness), as Glatstheyn described Peretz's literary heritage, is Yash's legacy from Shteynman: a realization that "religiosity and art are the same" and that the superficial distinction between the secular and the religious only limits the Yiddish writer.[50] This artistic credo is made complete with the final literary style employed in the book: the biblical. This style is initially presented in the autobiographical section when the narrator buys a burial plot for his mother. He is suddenly a part of a *shtikl khumesh* (piece of the Bible), and plays the role of Abraham negotiating with the Hittites for a burial plot for his deceased wife Sarah (34–35, Genesis 23–25:19). Later, Shteynman refers to himself as *yankev avinu erev ptire* (our ancestor Jacob on his death bed) and actually reenacts Jacob's death bed scene with his blessing of the twelve tribes (221–22).[51] Echoing Peretz, Shteynman mentions the Bible as the primary source for the Jewish writer and speaks of prophecy *mit an ayen nisht mit a yud* (*profetizm* not *profitizm*) (223, with the letter *e,* not with the letter *i* [prophet not profit]).[52] This biblical foundation will turn Jewish literature into "a mirror of our concept of Jewishness" (224), a modern *midrash.*

Finally, in the Kuzmir section, the narrator meets Jewish artists who are on pilgrimage to the picturesque *shtetl* in order to recreate it in painted images. The legend of Esterke gives the *shtetl* its distinct folklorist character and indicates the problematic relationships between

Polish Gentiles and Polish Jews.[53] Visitors can watch artifacts that are supposedly left from the historical period from which the legend originated. The *sthetl* landscape and the castle ruin on the top of the hill facing the river Vistulla, where King Casimir the Great (1310–1370) allegedly took the Jewish Esther as his wife, is transformed into a mythical landscape. Yash has finally arrived home to the quintessential Jewish *shtetl* transformed into an artist colony and art fair.[54] He meets Jewish artists who are unable to combine their artistic creativity with the economic necessity of selling their skills as craftsmen. This refers back to the episode in *Ven yash iz geforn* where the narrator, after working eight years as a journalist, asks his newspaper editor for a leave of absence in order to go on his trip to Poland. Yash, like the Jewish artists in Kuzmir, cannot find a way to fuse his creativity with the reality of earning a living and thus create art without any self-censorship or commercial purpose. In many ways the Yash books are the answer to this dilemma in their fusion of high and low literary genres. They signify a new artistic direction in Glatshteyn's literary career, toward a more accessible way of writing. Yash's meta-poetic journey through various historical periods and literary styles is brought to an end in Kuzmir, the quintessential Jewish *shtetl*-as-artist-colony. Only the mythical and artistic images of the *shtetl* remain as evidence of an outer reality. The literary images of his memories belong to a legendary artistic ivory tower in Kuzmir's art fair. They are far removed from the social and political reality of Polish Jewry, haunted in 1934 by economical boycott and anti-Semitism.

Throughout the Yash books, the Gentile world is depicted as either an anti-Semitic threat to Jewish existence, or as the threatening "outside world" which "steals" Jewish souls through assimilation. The hopeful note of coexistence between a new generation of young Poles and Jews in the end of *Ven yash iz geforn* is repudiated in *Ven yash iz gekumen*, where Jews are depicted as under siege from a hostile, anti-Semitic environment. The failure of the positivist vision of Polish intellectuals such as Marya Konopnicka (1860s–1870s) has become blatantly clear. In the end, the relationship between Yash and Shteynman, in which the latter talks and the former listens, is momentarily reversed when Shteynman asks Yash to tell him something. At first, Yash is inclined to say something he considers trivial: he wants to describe the encounter on the trip with a Jewish playwright who proudly shows the indoor plumbing in his house as an example of how modern and Americanized his lifestyle has become. At the same time, the Jewish playwright acknowledges that his art is dying out because only a few people are interested in Jewish plays. However, instead of telling this story, Yash describes his visit to a sanatorium for Jewish children, where he finds himself eating *borsht* next to an anti-Semitic doctor who firmly believes that science will conquer all diseases. The red *borsht* suddenly turns into a blood tie between Yash and his potential mortal enemy: "We removed the spoons from our mouths and dipped them into the common bowl, concluding a red alliance [*a roytn bund*] over the bloody beet soup'" (233). In the juxtaposition of these two stories, Glatshteyn poignantly addressed the question of co-existence between Jews and Poles: enlightenment (science, economical progress, socialism) has not led to the obliteration of anti-Semitism, but instead to assimilation and spiritual mummification, the abandonment of Jewish culture and identity.

In the Yash books Glatshteyn staged his visit to Lublin as an autobiographical quest through the use of literary styles from the novel, travelogue and memoir. This innovative fusion of styles and genres made it possible for Glatshteyn to reflect the complexity of his fragmented self and life story by avoiding nostalgic approaches to the Old World as either the lost paradise of his childhood or an authentic Yiddish-land. Glatshteyn turned his personal pain at losing his mother and his search of a father surrogate into a representative metaphor for a whole generation of immigrant Americans displaced from their origin in the Old World. At the same time, Yash's personal journey home to reclaim his family and national origin in Jewish Poland was meant to reverse his acculturation. According to the Yash books, the political and ideological answer to the impending national catastrophe of assimilation and the anti-Semitic threat to Jewish existence had to grow out of a restoration of the self, leading to a strengthening of Jewish identity. Glatshteyn returned home to Jewish Poland in the Yash books, while simultaneously remaining solidly anchored in an American-Yiddish context. The latter, particularly through Anglo-American modernism and the *inzikh* movement, provided him with the artistic freedom and inspiration to experiment with the fictive nature of self-representation and fusion of literary genres and styles. Glatstheyn's homecoming in *Ven yash iz gekumen* took place in New York. It closed the first period of his creative career (1920–1937), which was characterized by radical modernist experimentation. It also signified the beginning of a more explicit identification as a Jewish poet by providing Glatshteyn with some of the artistic and ideological means of responding to the destruction of Eastern European Jewry in the Holocaust.

Part III

After the Holocaust

5

Of a World That Is No More

A gramafon in varshe
veynt ariber keyn amerike,
bet zikh in gramen:
a brivele der mamen
zoltstu nisht farzamen;
shrayb, mayn kind,
shrayb geshvind
a brivele der mamen.
Varshever gramafon fun nayntsn hundert tsvelf,
vos dayn geveyn hot zikh tsu mir dertrogn
in nayntsn hundert fertsik finf!
Ikh ken dir zogn
fun danen, fun nuy york,
az s'iz gornisht mer geblibn.
Ale voltn mir geshribn
a brivele iber yamen,
a brivele der mamen
ober—
vu iz di mame? . . .

A gramophone in Warsaw
cries all the way to America,
implores in rhymes:
a letter to mother
you should not delay;
write, my child,
write quickly
a letter to mother.
Warsaw gramophone in nineteen hundred twelve,
your cry was carried to me
in nineteen hundred forty five!
I can tell you
from here, from New York,

that nothing has remained.
We would all have written
a letter over the ocean,
a letter to mother
but—
where is mother? . . .

Aaron Zeitlin, "Warsaw in 1912" (December 1945)[1]

Yiddish life-writing after the Holocaust nearly effaced the writer's self and turned his life narrative into a parable of survival of the destruction of Eastern European Jewry. Like Marcel Proust's *In Search of Lost Time* (1913–1927), the Yiddish writers Y. Y. Trunk, Chaim Grade, I. B. Singer and Joseph Buloff sought to retrieve and actualize their past's infinite possibilities. They intended to compensate through storytelling and dialogical imagination for what had been tragically cut short in historical reality. They created "a world that is no more" (the title of I. J. Singer's 1946 autobiography)—a world that never existed in historical reality anyway—with an artistic urgency similar to Walter Benjamin's description of Proust's method: "Proust's method is actualization, not reflection. He is filled with the insight that none of us has time to live the true dramas of the life that we are destined for. . . . The wrinkles and creases in our faces are the registration of the great passions, vices, insights that called on us; but we, the masters, were not home."[2] Their guilt at having survived made Trunk and Grade even more determined to avoid exploring their artistic selves as part of the radically changed world after the Holocaust. Singer, however, had no such loyalties that would interfere with his self-posturing in his extensive life-writing.

The great Yiddish poet Abraham Sutzkever possessed an almost magical belief in the life-sustaining powers of poetry and began wrestling artistically with the meaning of the Holocaust in the Vilna ghetto (1941–1943). It was in the Vilna ghetto that Sutzkever first experienced poetry as a way of defying death, literally believing that it had the power to keep him alive: "The whole power and wonder of the Yiddish language . . . revealed itself to me in the Vilna Ghetto. There I truthfully could say that life and death were in the hand of the Yiddish language. My language, my poem was my magic protection on which the arrows of death were repelled. In poetry, I even became a free person in the ghetto and would under no circumstances have switched places with my torturer, the ostensibly free people."[3] In *Griner akvarium* (1953–54, Green Aquarium), Sutzkever would turn this experience into a literary credo that made his life dependent on his ability to create lasting art. However, even Sutzkever, who shared the fate of the Vilna Jews until their systematic murder in Ponar (a resort area in the vicinity of Vilna), was caught in the same quandary as the Yiddish writers in New York. For Yiddish writers after the Holocaust, the very act of writing became a way of defying the death sentence carried out with such systematic cruelty by the Germans. Regardless of artistic method, Yiddish writers felt an obligation to those who were murdered, and they commemorated them in life-writing that insisted on art's ultimate victory over death. By summoning the colloquial voices of Eastern European Jews, Yiddish writers created wholeness out of their memory shards. Yiddish literature had always excelled in depicting Jews talking to each other and to the reader as a metaphor of literary authenticity. The inscription of life-writing in an infinite web of *shmues* (talking) confirmed Yiddish writers' ties to their primary artistic source: the historical and cultural memory stored in the Yiddish language.

The third phase of Yiddish life-writing can be precisely dated to March 1941, when Y. Y. Trunk, fleeing Warsaw at the outbreak of World War II in September 1939, started to write his seven volume memoir *Poyln: zihroynes un bilder* (1944–1953, Poland: Memoirs and Pictures). He began writing two days after he arrived in New York City after his flight via Vilna, Central-Asia, Japan, and San Francisco.[4] It took him one decade to complete the work, which became a model for Yiddish life-writing after the Holocaust in its focus on the collective ethos of an obliterated community. Trunk's response to the destruction of his people was to create a grand epic about the decline of the upper strata of Polish Jewish society and the rise of a new secular Jewishness embodied in folklore, Yiddish literature, and the Jewish socialist Bund. In contrast to Abraham Joshua Heschel, who focused on the scholarly elite in his 1945 lecture on the Eastern European Era in Jewish History at YIVO, Trunk's memoirs included the whole religious, social and cultural pyramid of Polish Jewry.[5] Both Heschel and Trunk summarized the Eastern European Era in Jewish history in a narrative form that drew on Yiddish literary models. These two authors sought to erect a literary *matseyve* (gravestone) over a destroyed community. With the absence of gravestones to which people could return and recite the Kaddish, Yiddish life-writing provided imaginary, portable gravestones. On them were

carved the collective histories of Jewish communities otherwise condemned to oblivion. For the primarily secular audience for Heschel's
1945 YIVO lecture and Trunk's multi-volume epos, these eloquent trib-
utes to a world they had left as children or knew only indirectly through
Yiddish theater, film and literature became an important way of commemorating Jewish cultural achievement and continuity. Another form
of commemoration were the hundreds of memorial *(yizker)* books as-
sembled and edited by a collective of writers affiliated with the *lands-
manshaftn* (society of immigrants from the same town or region in the
old country) in America and Israel, the remnants of the destroyed communities.[6] In his tribute to the democratization of Jewish education in
Eastern Europe, summarized in the Yiddish proverb *toyre iz di beste
skhroyre* (Torah is the best merchandise), Heschel chose not to quote
from the rabbinical sources or from historical accounts. Instead he ex-
cerpted a paragraph from Abramovitsh's *Shloyme reb khayims*.[7]

The success of *Poyln* among Yiddish readers, evident from its many
reprints, was, to a large extent, a result of Trunk's use of small chapters
with captions modeled on the Yiddish chapbook. Like the chapbook,
Poyln depicted a colorful externalized reality full of dramatic events
and personalities. Peretz's neo-Romantic credo in *Mayne zikhroynes* provided Trunk with the model for his artistic method in *Poyln*. This is evident from his response to critics who criticized him for overstating the
grotesque in Polish-Jewish life: "Every fact that happened is no more
than a shell in which are hidden many possibilities. Possibilities simply
lacking the circumstances in which they could be activated and expressed. The task of the artistic expression is, therefore, to create illu-
sory conditions for all the hidden psychological possibilities and realize
them in act and character. First in this aspect is the complete shape of
both a human being and a historical period revealed to us. To give one's
imagination free rein [*fabulirn*] is really the same thing as creating conditions for hidden possibilities. The possibilities inherent in a fact are
often more characteristic of a person and a period than the real events."[8]

Peretz had introduced Trunk to Yiddish literature in 1908, and, like a
whole generation of other Yiddish writers, encouraged him to switch
from Hebrew to Yiddish. In his own writing, Peretz demonstrated that
it was possible to express lofty ideas as a Yiddish essayist and literary
critic and simultaneously reach a wider readership through Yiddish
storytelling. By declaring, as quoted by Trunk in volume five of *Poyln*
(entitled "Peretz"), that he was only envious of two writers, Sholem
Aleichem and Shakespeare, Peretz perceptively expressed his "anxiety

of influence" by equating the Jewish Mark Twain and the British bard.[9] This inspired Trunk to reevaluate Sholem Aleichem from that of a light hearted humorist, the dominant view among the Jewish intelligentsia before the 1920s, to that of a world-class writer. Although it took Trunk more than two decades to publish his first book about Sholem Aleichem, the seed planted by Peretz led to the publication of short stories and two critical works in 1927 and 1930.[10]

Trunk's two books about Sholem Aleichem introduced a Freudian and Jungian approach in Yiddish criticism. This view transcended what he called "a schematic-academic method of criticism"[11] in an attempt to analyze "Sholem Aleichem's work as a key to the Jewish collective psychology in its full historical context."[12] Trunk's appraisal of Sholem Aleichem's work as the "psychological and historical base of Yiddish literature" without which Peretz's work would have been a "building hanging in the air,"[13] contributed to the general critical reappraisal of Sholem Aleichem in the 1930s. Trunk viewed his Sholem Aleichem books as his most important, without which, as he mentioned in a 1953 interview, "it would have been impossible for him to write *Poyln*."[14]

Trunk's memoirs emphasize the humorous and the grotesque, thus creating a distance between his writing and the historical trauma to which it bears witness. This was poignantly expressed by the Yiddish poet Aaron Glants-Leyeles in his reminiscences about his friend Trunk in New York during the spring of 1943: "I asked him about the grotesque which can be found in his descriptions [in *Poyln*]. Sometimes it even seemed like he was mocking.—What do you mean?—said Trunk.—If I hadn't created an objective distance to the pictures and characters in my memoirs I wouldn't have been able to write at all. Only a sea of tears would have come out." I understood it very well. I personally have had such experiences. I had seen people laugh in hospital rooms at the bedside of very sick people—laugh in order to overcome the big wail stuck inside them."[15] After his wife's death in 1944, and until his own death in 1961, Trunk lived by himself in an apartment in the Washington Heights area of Manhattan. In order to support himself "Trunk began churning out a library of Yiddish folk classics rewritten in super idiomatic Yiddish. . . . Not even Dik, writing under contract for the Widow Rom, produced as much in one decade as Trunk."[16] All in all, eight works were published between 1951 and 1960. These were based on popular folk tales and Jewish folklore such as the stories of Chelm and Hershele Ostropolier, The Bove–Mayse, Sabbatai Zvi, Tales of Ba'al Shem Tov and Joseph della Reina. The transformation of Trunk from an essayist and literary critic in inter-war Poland to old-world Yiddish storyteller in America was begun with *Poyln*.

Unlike most other Yiddish writers, Trunk's life experiences—which included owning real estate, distinguished rabbinical *yikhes*, marriage into one of the richest Polish Jewish families (the Prives family), and wide knowledge of European literature—would seem to make him the ideal chronicler of the Polish Jewish community. I. B. Singer characterized his friend Trunk as a man of contradictions: a capitalist and a Bundist, a preacher of collectivism and an extreme individualist, an elitist writer about Plato and Seneca and a fervent supporter of the working class. These contradictions gave Trunk the broad perspective that made *Poyln* such an entertaining memoir. However, Trunk's identification with the Polish Jewish collective resulted in a nearly complete erasure of his own inner journey. The literary critic Shmuel Niger pointed out that Trunk's choice of perspective and style in *Poyln* excluded any self-reflection about his refugee status as an exiled Yiddish writer in New York: "This is a book which enabled a very sensitive writer to speak about being deeply rooted [*ayngevortsltkayt*] in Jewish Poland and thus avoid speaking about his displacement [*oysgevortslt vern*]."[17]

Another Polish Yiddish writer in America, Isaac Bashevis Singer, emerged in 1943 from a seven-year-long writer's block with two articles about Yiddish literature. In these articles he opposed any Yiddish literary experimentation with European trends and political "isms" and favored a return to Jewish themes, myths and styles. He pointed out that many social, cultural and political sectors in Polish society were beyond the pale of Yiddish writers' life experiences. The unique character of Yiddish as a minority language situated in a multilingual, often hostile Eastern European context reinforced its close ties to *derekh hashas* (the way of the Talmud; orthodox Jewish practice). As a result, Singer characterized Yiddish as unfit for artistic use outside a richly textured, traditional Jewish world. Singer argued that the best Yiddish writers naturally sought out "the grand, the deeply Jewish, the eternal," a view originally pioneered by Peretz. Singer's article, published in *Tsukunft* in 1943 (coinciding with the Warsaw Ghetto Uprising), was a literary call to arms among Yiddish writers in America. It ended with the sobering statement that what "remained for him [the Yiddish writer] was only to draw from his memories."[18] This observation turned out to be an accurate prediction of the artistic output by Yiddish writers who survived the Nazis such as Chava Rosenfarb, Chaim Grade and Y. Y. Trunk. They would primarily base their work on memories of the old world, and, except for Singer, would rarely depict their new North American home.

Yiddish life-writing after the Holocaust emphasized the theatrical, humorous, and entertaining qualities exemplified by Sholem Aleichem's *Funem yarid*. Another type of life-writing, Holocaust memoirs, proliferated in survivor accounts such as those in Mark Turkov's series Dos poylishe yidntum (Polish Jewry) published in Buenos Aires, which included Elie Wiesel's *Un di velt hot geshvign* (1955, And the World Was Silent), later published in French and English as *Night*.[19] An accomplished corpus of Yiddish works originated in the ghettos. They included the works of Abraham Sutzkever, Isaiah Shpiegl, Yitskhok Katzenelson and diaries by Herman Kruk and others.[20] Finally, there were the *kines* (dirges) of Yankev Glatshteyn, Kadya Molodovsky, Aaron Zeitlin, and Chaim Grade, lamenting the tragedy in elegiac verse.[21] Yiddish literature in 1940s and 1950s America maintained a delicate balance between poetic lamentations, Holocaust memoirs, and *yizker* books, on the one hand, and a deliberate distancing from the horrors in fiction and life-writing, on the other.[22]

In his 1982 autobiography, Irving Howe described his New York Yiddish writer friends during the early 1950s. He had met these writers while working on the first English anthology of Yiddish literature in translation: "What, I used to wonder, could be the unspoken feelings of these Yiddish literary friends? In their private talks, how did they cope with the certainty that the literature to which they had devoted their lives was approaching its end? I was a loyal ally, but still at least half an outsider. I did not share their memories and could not reach to the floor of their emotions. There was a limit beyond which they would not go, even with me; they refused, as a gesture of both honor and will, to acknowledge the bleakness of their future. Undeluded, no doubt inwardly desperate, they still felt an obligation to confront the world with a complete firmness of posture. One of the arts of life is to know how to end."[23] This emotional complex did not find a voice in Yiddish life-writing in America, except for Singer's works such as *Enemies: A Love Story* (1972), *Lost in America* (1976–1981) and *Shadows on the Hudson* (1998).[24] Instead, Yiddish writers in America went into inner exile, where they immersed themselves in an imaginary pre-Holocaust Jewish world or lamented the annihilation of their people.[25] One of the Yiddish writers in inner exile in the 1950s was Chaim Grade, who "resided in the North Bronx ... but in the deepest part of his self he was still back in the shadowy brilliance of Vilna during the late twenties."[26] Unlike other Eastern European exiles in America such as Vladimir Nabokov, Czeslaw Milosz and I. B. Singer, Grade never tried to explore his new American home. Instead, Grade devoted all his creative energy to bearing witness to the lost world of Vilna, the Jerusalem of Lithuania.

Grade and Singer, the most important Yiddish prose writers after the Holocaust, held very different views regarding how to write about the heritage of Eastern European Jewry. Singer felt no particular loyalty to the Jewish martyrs of the Holocaust. The Holocaust confirmed his bleak view of history and human nature as ruled by irrational forces, a view that he had delineated in his first novel about the 1648 Chmelnicki pogroms, *Sotn in Goray* (1933, Satan in Goray). If anything, the Holocaust fortified Singer's nihilism and emphasis on literature as entertainment and storytelling. Grade, on the other hand, was "left shouldering a mountainous guilt"[27] at having escaped the fate of his destroyed community and, in particular, his murdered mother and wife. Grade came out of the cataclysm of the Holocaust even more committed to create literature as a memorial to his Jewish Vilna. At the same time, Singer and Grade's backgrounds could not have been more different. Grade was a *litvak*, poet, and his mother's loyal literary biographer. In contrast, Singer was a *galitsianer*, storyteller, and the rebellious son who obsessively mined his autobiography to fit his artistic needs. While Singer lived more than fifty years of his life on the Upper West Side of Manhattan, Grade was a newly arrived refugee in New York in 1948.

As pointed out by the historian Lucy Davidowicz, "Grade's life and writing were shaped by two dominant influences—his mother and the yeshiva."[28] Orphaned in his late teens, he spent a decade studying in the *muser yeshive* in Navarednok, a town 150 kilometers south of Vilna, until he broke away from the religious world in 1932.[29] In the 1930s he was associated with the literary group Yung vilne (Young Vilna) and published two collections of poetry, *Yo* (1936, Yes) and *Musernikes* (1939). These focused respectively on his mother who had a fruit stall at the Vilna market and on the inner world of the *muser yeshive*. In a speech given upon receiving a Yiddish literary prize in Vilna in March 1939, Grade pointed out that his poetic goal was to fulfill his responsibility to his community by writing about its collective predicament. As a result, he was not interested in his personal life story of "terror and fear from an unprotected childhood and lonely youth. . . . To these nightmares and feelings I am not allowed to return. My road leads to society, to its problems and goals. That is my responsibility."[30]

In contrast, Singer's years of deprivation in Warsaw and the *shtetl* Bilgoray during World War I became his most direct experience of Jewish collective disaster. Later, he lived through the Holocaust from a safe distance in New York and decided to keep silent about what had happened to his family during the war.[31] As Janet Hadda concludes her reading of Singer's novel *Di familye Mushkat* (1945–1948, *The Family Moskat*), "it underscores both Bashevis' distance from the physical suffering of World War II and the depth of his identification with the victims."[32] In contrast, the Holocaust witnessed by Grade and Abraham Sutzkever respectively as a refugee in the Soviet Union and incarcerated in the Vilna Ghetto 1941–1943, became the defining event of their artistic careers. As is evident in *Der mames shabosim* (1955, *My Mother's Sabbath Days*), Grade's loss of his mother and wife and, in particular, the guilt of having left them a few days after the German invasion of Vilna in June 1941, still haunted him many years later.

Grade's breakthrough as a prose writer was the story "Mayn krig mit hersh raseyner" (My Quarrel with Hersh Raseyner). In this story Chaim Vilner, a secular Yiddish writer, is confronted with his former friend from the *muser yeshive*, Hersh Rasayner, on one hot summer day in Paris in 1947.[33] Their argument about God, art and the meaning of life is carried out in a densely textured Hebraized Yiddish with learned references to religious sources. The story's central stylistic device is the rhetoric of *pilpul* characteristic of Biblical and the Talmudic text study in the *yeshive*. Grade explored and questioned the most basic tenets of Judaism in the aftermath of the Holocaust through the passionate debate of his alter egos. In the early 1950s Grade began to serialize prose fiction in the Yiddish daily *Tog morgn zshurnal* and later in *Forverts*, beginning with *Di agune* (The Agunah) and part of his grand epic about the *muser yeshive* world, *Tsemakh atlas*. Similar to the poet Yankev Glatshteyn, Grade's first major prose work was an autobiographical novel, *Der mames shabosim*. Thereafter, he devoted most of his creative energy to writing novels. The following year, I. B. Singer published his memoir *Mayn tatns bezdn shtub* (1956, *In My Father's Court*), similarly focusing on the religious features of traditional Jewish life associated with the writer's parents. Grade's depiction of his mother reflected through her pious Sabbath observance is fundamentally different from Singer's theatrical display of subversive and extreme behavior in his father's rabbinical court.

Cynthia Ozick's short story "Envy; or Yiddish in America" (1969) depicts a thinly disguised version of Singer in the character Ostrover. His

Slavic sounding name suggests the vulgarity *(prostkeyt)* of somebody who had become a literary success in America by playing by *di goyim's* rules. His opponent, Edelshteyn, whose name evokes associations with the ethically refined *(edl)* writer of European extraction (modeled on Grade and Glatshteyn), feels trapped in the provincial narrowing circle of Yiddish in America. In order to reach readers outside the Yiddish world, both look constantly for a translator. In real life, Grade was the loyal son trained in the *muser yeshive* in ethical introspection and deeply devoted to his destroyed Vilna Jewish heritage. Singer, in contrast, was the rebellious reactionary with rabbinical *yikhes* (ancestry) and a solid dose of *misnaged* (opponent of the Hasidim) skepticism inherited from his mother. Like that of the false messiah Sabbatai Zvi who inspired him to write *Sotn in Goray,* his work was motivated by extreme sexual and religious behavior. Janet Hadda mentions that Singer used a pig doodle as his signature both in Yiddish and in English. The choice of this signature indicated that he equated his work, as if seen through his orthodox father's eyes, with blasphemy and pornography.[34] This is effectively captured in Ozick's "Envy; or, Yiddish in America" in which Ostrover is called repeatedly a *khazer* (pig) by his Yiddish writer opponents. Ostrover becomes a crude antidote to the glorification of the Eastern European Jewish heritage propagated in anthologies of Yiddish literature and studies of the Jewish *shtetl* in the 1950s.[35] Eliezer Greenberg, a Yiddish poet and editor (with Irving Howe) of Yiddish literature in English translation, was appalled by Ozick's merciless depiction of the petty squabbles of Yiddish writers in America. As depicted by Ozick, they desired only one thing: fame and money to be gained through translation of their work into English. Only Singer succeeded in this venture, to the great chagrin of Grade. Upon hearing that Singer had received the Nobel Prize in literature in 1978, Grade purportedly said that is was "a great tragedy for the Jewish people."[36] Less dramatic, and more succinct, was Greenberg's response to Irving Howe, who defended Ozick's story when it came out: "He turned on me with anger and said, 'Some things are more important than writing a good story!' Too late, I agree."[37] Grade's work exemplified what was more important for a Yiddish writer than writing a good story in the aftermath of the Holocaust. Nowhere was this more evident than in his autobiographical novel *Der mames shabosim.*

Greenberg's review of the book in the literary journal *Di goldene keyt* in 1955 described it as "an artistic autobiographical novel, and not a book of stories as it is labeled."[38] The book is structured on a broad, tripartite narrative canvas that transcends the fragmentary character of the individual chapters. Each chapter is a self-sustained unit that fits the weekly installment of the Yiddish press (where it was first serialized) and contains a poignant description of an episode or a character. The main temporal and spatial focus in the first and longest part (more than half the work), entitled "Der mames shabosim," is the narrator's encounter with his mother on the Sabbath in her cellar apartment in Vilna. In the first section we learn that the narrator attended a *yeshive* from which he later broke away in order to become a writer. He dates several women, finally getting married to Frumme-Liebtshe. This event is followed by his mother's marriage to her second husband at the end of part one. In the second part, "Ek velt" ("The End of the World"), the narrator is depicted during the nearly two years of Soviet and, later, Lithuanian rule in Vilna. This is followed by his flight and parting from his mother and wife at the German invasion of the Soviet Union in June 1941. Separated from his Vilna community, the narrator survives as a refugee in Kazakhstan. The third part, "The Seven Little Lanes," depicts his return to the ruined Vilna ghetto and his encounters there with Jewish survivors. In the final climactic scene, he enters his mother's apartment during Neilah, the closing prayer at the end of Yom Kippur, her *yortsayt*, the day when she was murdered in 1941.

   The book does not address the complex social, political and religious issues in inter-war Poland during Grade's *yeshive* years or his later involvement with socialist and literary circles in Vilna.[39] The author excluded everything that might divert attention from his artistic vision of his mother as the embodiment of self-sacrificing piety. Unlike Abramovitsh, Grade is not interested in recording the cultural geography and history of a threatened or destroyed Jewish community. Abramovitsh sought to expose Jewish poverty with the purpose of educating his readers about the crippling effect of the *shtetl*'s wretched socio-economic conditions.[40] Grade, in contrast, has been severed from the destroyed Vilna Jewish community forever. There were no remaining Jews to enlighten or educate; all Jewish institutions and buildings had been destroyed. During the same year that Chaim Grade published *Der mames shabosim* he also edited a volume of short stories by Jonah Rosenfeld. These stories about the abuse, brutality and violent conflicts among the poorest strata of Jewish society resonated with Grade's artistic method and themes.[41] The main thrust of Grade's book, however, was its focus on a Jewish female universe through his portrait of his mother. As noted by the Yiddish critics Eliezer Greenberg and Yankev

Glatshteyn, no Yiddish writer before Grade had given such a sensitive, intimate portrait of the Jewish mother in all her endearing, archetypical qualities. Grade's devotion to his mother had already found poetic expression in his first collection of poems, *Yo,* whose two first poems were titled "Mayn mame" (My Mother) and "Mame un zun" (Mother and Son). In his review of Grade's poetry, Glatshteyn pointed out the two major risks confronting a Yiddish writer in this particular endeavor: "the theatrical [*teatralishkayt*]—in regard to the language and music of the Yiddish theater—and the wedding jester populism of 'A Letter to My Mother'."[42] The Yiddish popular theater's exploitation of Yiddish folk songs exemplified in the tear-jerking hit "A brivele der mamen" (A Letter to My Mother) obviously worked against a serious literary depiction of the mother figure. At the same time, the Freudian discourse of sexuality and violence so prevalent in Rosenfeld's work was not relevant to Grade's. According to Glatshteyn, it would "have been inappropriate to let the Jewish doctor from Vienna into the atmosphere of Vilna's poverty."[43] Instead, Grade turned his mother into an allegory of traditional Jewish female virtues that transcended the particularity of the autobiographer's psycho-history. For Glatshteyn, Grade's poetry about his mother was his most authentic because of its absence of eroticism and the "naked" details of his autobiographical past. Grade succeeded in sublimating his oedipal mother relationship by avoiding anything that would defile her idealized, spiritualized image. Unlike Anglo-Jewish writers in the 1950s such as Saul Bellow and Philip Roth who made the Jewish mother an important locus of power, sexual fantasy and ambivalence, Grade presented a mother figure who, in Anita Norich's words, "serves not as a microcosm of a nation, society, or people but rather as a substitute for such larger constructs."[44]

The book was dedicated to Grade's half brothers, the sons of his father's first wife who immigrated to Chicago before the war. In the English translation published some thirty years later, this original dedication was replaced by another taken from *Der mames tsvoe* (My Mother's Will), a collection of poetry from 1949: "To the memory of my mother, daughter of Rabbi Rafael Blumenthal, Vella Grade, Martyred in Vilna on Yom Kippur 5702–1941. To the memory of her neighbors, the mothers of our Jewish street, who lived together in holy poverty and together went to their deaths." This change of dedication shifts the book's perspective to that of a Holocaust memoir, even though, strictly speaking, only the third part of the book falls into this category. This part's account of Grade's encounters with Jewish survivors after his return to Vilna in

1944, along with his direct expression of grief, vengeance and hatred of the German murderers, might have been one reason why the book was not immediately translated into English. Expressions of Jewish feelings of revenge was toned down or altogether erased in Holocaust memoirs in non-Jewish languages in the 1950s.[45] An English translation of the "Seven Little Lanes," the book's last part, was published by the Bergen-Belsen Memorial Press in 1972. Not until 1985, however, after the resurgence of interest in Holocaust memoirs became the norm, was the book finally published in a complete English translation.

Evidently, Grade's origin as a Yiddish writer was closely tied to his relationship to his mother. This is elaborated in a section midway through the first part of *Der shabes shabosim*. The goose-dealer Alterke conducts romantic affairs with several women, driving his wife Lisa, who is unable to conceive a child, to attempt suicide. After hearing about the marital problems between Alterka and Lisa from the other market women, Grade's mother Vella returns home where she encounter her son, Chaimke. Vella admonishes her son not to "write about this, as you wrote about me sitting with my baskets at the gate. That's all you need—for Alterke to find out you're making poems of him."[46] Grade's mother is referring to his poetic portraits of her in his first collection *Yo*. Lisa then appears in order to unburden herself and seek advice from Vella about her husband's romantic affairs. At this point we are unexpectedly presented with a portrait of the artist as a young man through the conversation between his mother and a deeply distressed woman. Rather than being proud of her son's literary fame in Vilna, Vella tells Lisa that she is extremely uncomfortable with his depiction of her dozing off in the market, and tells him not to write about her again. However, he insists that he must continue to do so because, as she explains to Lisa: "He says that he doesn't mean only me; he means all the mothers like me, all the women of my kind, all women of my class. I ask him: 'Why did you have to choose me?' So he answers that he chose me because he feels guilty toward me. 'I gave you a lot of trouble when I was little. And even now I can't make your life any easier,' he says. I ask you, Lisa—does that make any sense? God is my witness that I'm not angry at him for not helping me with my livelihood. May I only have the strength to keep on working! 'You don't owe me anything,' I say to him. 'It's the Almighty to Whom you're in debt. Don't sit down to eat without first washing your hands and pronouncing the blessing.'"[47] In this passage Grade creates a startling portrait of himself as a young man viewed from his mother's perspective. The passage also outlines his artistic method, by depicting his mother as a representative of her class and gender, typifying the poorest strata of Vilna Jews. Grade's alienation from his mother and her environment is evident in his mother's incomprehension of what she characterizes as his "mania" *(meshigas)*. This "mania" of writing is related to his feelings of guilt towards her.

In a 1945 article the literary critic Nachman Mayzel reminisces about a meeting with Grade in a Vilna hotel in 1936. When Mayzel asks Grade to introduce him to his mother, to whom "he has devoted such wonderful, sensitive poems," Grade turns the conservation in a different direction, avoiding the subject. The next day Grade shows up with a bag of frozen apples, which is a gift to Mayzel from his mother: "With special admiration we took out the apples which were already falling apart because of frost; they looked dark brown. We ate them eagerly with great appetite like a rare fruit and, as was customary, we threw ourselves into a long conversation about eternal questions, a conversation which had no beginning and no end."[48] Grade's mother's position at the bottom of the social ladder is transformed into a literary icon of poverty in the form of the forbidden, frostbitten fruit, which the two Yiddish literati eat with great delight while discussing spiritual matters. Mayzel's satirical observation about the young Grade's distance from his mother's social world confirms Avrom Novershtern's point that "the indissoluble bond between Yung Vilne and Jewish Vilna was mainly forged after the Holocaust."[49] It was only after the Holocaust and the death of his mother that Grade overcame his romanticizing relationship to the poor Jews in his mother's courtyard and was able to give a stark, realistic portrait of them in *Der shabes shabosim*.

In the third part of *Der mames shabosim*, entitled the "Seven Little Lanes" (where the ghetto was located), Grade encounters the pediatrician Anna Itkin, who survived along with one of her twin sons. It is through her that Grade learns about the life of his wife and mother in the Vilna ghetto. Grade's choice of a pediatrician calls to mind an observation that Shoshana Felman makes in her analysis of Albert Camus' *The Plague:* "the doctor's testimonial stance is, of necessity, at once one of resistance (to the Plague) and one of preservation (of life, as well as of its memory)."[50] In a conversation with Itkin, Grade passionately argues that the survivor must take revenge or forget everything. Itkin responds that to value human life is even more crucial in the wake of the catastrophe because "so few of us are left alive that we must not, even for the sake of executing a murderer risk our own lives."[51] The relationship between Itkin and her son parallels that of the first part's primary relationship between Grade and his mother. And just as the cyclical character of the narrative, which begins and ends on Yom Kippur, evokes the continuity of Jewish sacred time, so does the continuity of the most basic human relationship, that of a mother and her son, become a literary trope of hope.

The Seven Little Lanes are equated with an eternal accursed Sabbath, "but the Sabbath here is from the chapter of curses in the Bible." This reference to the curses in Leviticus and Deuteronomy indicates that the sacred temporal dimension of the Sabbath has lost its meaning and the relationship between sacred and profane in Jewish tradition has been severed. Grade inscribes the Seven Little Lanes in a biblical discourse of divine retribution. Related to this complex are two episodes at the beginning and the end of the second part which crystallize Grade's literary response to the Holocaust. In the first episode, Grade is denounced as a potential German spy by a *kolkhoznik* (a member of a Soviet collective farm) during his flight from the front. As a result, he is escorted by Red Army soldiers to be shot. The soldiers find a Hebrew bible in Grade's pocket which confirms their suspicion that he is a German pastor disguised as a Jew. On the way ostensibly to be executed, the soldiers and their prisoner suddenly meet a rider on a horse, a Red Army officer. Having checked the passport and noticing the bible, the officer immediately orders the soldiers to release Grade, who is left alone in the middle of a meadow. He glances at the open bible and sees a verse from Jeremiah in its original Hebrew: "For I am with thee, saith the Lord, to save thee: though I make a full end of all nations whither I have scattered thee, yet I will not make a full end of you: but I will correct thee in measure, and I will not leave thee altogether unpunished."[52] Grade is convinced that the officer is Jewish and wonders if he meant this quote from Jeremiah to be a form of secret communication. The miraculous rescue of Grade associated with the redemptive message of Jeremiah points to a Biblical discourse of sin, retribution and redemption. This discourse unites the two male Jews for whom Hebrew has become, in this highly charged situation of national and individual life-and-death, the secret redemptive language.[53] A parallel episode with no biblical reverberations occurs at the end of part two. A Jewish refugee Moyshe Troyman, his girlfriend, and Grade are run over by a truck driver in a hit-and-run accident. Moyshe Troyman dies shortly thereafter whereas Grade survives the accident unharmed. Again, Grade has miraculously been spared a meaningless death in a foreign place: "Ever since I ran away from home, I have always thought that the worst fate of all must be to close your eyes for the last time knowing that you are surrounded by strangers who won't mourn for you or even remember your name after they have buried you."[54]

The importance of staying alive to bear witness and leave a testimony became the primary motivation behind Grade's work. Grade wrote some of the best Yiddish prose works after the Holocaust, when he re-created the Yiddish voices of his mother and other women in Jewish Vilna. However, when he stretched his mother Vilna metaphor too far by trying to expunge his guilt for having abandoned her, Grade's work turned into elegy, which "rather than keeping that past alive, helps lay it softly to rest."[55] In *Der mames shabosim* Grade gives a convincing account of his artistic origins as the prodigal son of mother Vilna in her poverty-stricken misery and Sabbath glory. Moreover, he bears witness to the destruction of this world and its transformation into autobiographical memory and literary artifice. This is achieved through the finely crafted voices of the female characters in his mother's poor section of Jewish Vilna and the few survivors in the Seven Little Lanes.

Several critics have noticed the discrepancy between I. B. Singer's successful literary career in America and his self-portrait as a failure, a loser in life as well as in art.[56] These critics have argued that Singer's life-writing is coloured by his guilt at having succeeded artistically in America while the Polish-Jewish culture, which served as his creative inspiration, was destroyed in the Holocaust. This reading of Singer's life-writing as a means of negotiating between his loyalty to his murdered people and his own egotistical needs for literary success has been most succinctly expressed by Janet Hadda: "He, like his narrators, feels guilty—and also somewhat left out—about having avoided the catastrophe that has become a pivotal event in Jewish life. These unhappy responses are without question severely exacerbated by the fact that Singer's own ascent as a popular writer cannot be separated from the very fact of his having lived to describe the perished heritage of Jewish Eastern Europe."[57] This "guilt as subtext"[58] relates to the transformation of the relatively unknown Yitskhok Bashevis in interwar Poland (1925–1935) into the internationally acclaimed Isaac Bashevis Singer (mid-1950s onwards), culminating in his being awarded the Nobel Prize for Literature in 1978. This view convincingly portrays the psychological background for Singer's work but does not account for its artistic qualities, which are particularly evident in *Mayn tatns bezdn shtub*. This work was written with an awareness of earlier Yiddish autobiographies whose artistic assumptions and techniques Singer elaborated and redefined.

From the beginning of his literary career in 1925 Singer rejected the Yiddish literary ethos of ideological involvement, historical progress and psychological development. Life-writing was particularly well suited for this ethos because it depicted individual development on the premise that the self was an entity that could be constructed and deconstructed through an autobiographical quest. Imagining one's childhood self and describing its metamorphosis as a movement forward in time endowed this quest with a purpose: to demonstrate the possibility of change through the child's development from his limited origins in the *shtetl* towards a truer, more authentic self represented by the mature writer in the metropolis. Singer rejected this ethos as illusionary and false and wrote instead a memoir *Mayn tatns bezdn shtub* that replaced historical development with a variety of spaces as backdrop for a polyphony of life stories. These stories showed the individual's character and destiny to be governed by historical and instinctual (particularly sexual) forces beyond his control. Singer focussed on the individual as he responded to the terrifying and unpredictable currents of life by employing a pre-novelistic discourse that transcends any quest for meaning or self-understanding.[59] He depicted the individual as a passive being pulled in different directions by historical and demonic forces. This artistic vision was successfully expressed in the book's sixty story-vignettes, each of which was crafted as a miniature epic universe.

As cultural leaders representing humanism and cultural progress, the three classical Yiddish writers' life-writing became exemplary of the Yiddish literary renaissance. Singer rejected this approach and turned instead to two of the most original Yiddish autobiographers of the second generation. Glatshteyn's self-portrait as observer to other people's stories in the Yash books was similar to that of Singer's child protagonist in *Mayn tatns bezdn shtub*. But unlike Yash's role as confidante, the one who is directly addressed by other people, Singer's child-protagonist listens secretly to the theatrical performances and the intricate stories of the people in his father's rabbinical court. It is through the child that we witness these characters' conflicts and extreme emotional reactions. Singer describes his beginnings in childhood as defined by a fully developed world-view, which precludes any self-transformation or belief in human progress.[60] Singer's approach in *Mayn tatns bezdn shtub* was related to Rosenfeld's use in *Eyner aleyn* of the Jewish family as the setting for his depiction of Jewish moral depravity.[61] Singer, however, was not interested in exploring psychological conflicts and emotional complexes that he viewed as belonging to the Yiddish literary ethos of world betterment and rational analysis—something he rejected.[62] Unlike most Yiddish literary autobiographies written after the Holocaust, the creative impetus for *Mayn tatns bezdn shtub* was not triggered by an overwhelming sense of loyalty to the heritage of Eastern European Jewry. Although Singer mentions several times that a particular character was later martyred in German death camps, his work did not seek to commemorate a world which had been physically destroyed.[63] Instead, the rabbinical court was made into a stage on which Singer brilliantly exposed human follies and illusions in order to create his own original vision of an unredeemable humanity. Singer's exquisite use of the rich theatricality of literary Yiddish made the book Singer's most popular among his Yiddish readership. Peretz-farlag in Tel Aviv republished *Mayn tatns bezdn shtub* in 1979 as a tribute to Singer after he was awarded the Nobel Prize in literature. In 1957, the book was also successfully made into a Yiddish play: Dovid Likht's stage production ran in New York for fourteen weeks.[64]

Given the enormous quantity of autobiographical material written by I. B. Singer during the last thirty-five years of his life (1956–1991), which Khone Shmeruk characterized as "the author's autobiographical obsession,"[65] it would be impossible to examine it all in this study. A significant part of Singer's life-writing, including at least five memoirs and several thinly disguised autobiographical novels, has not been published in book form.[66] Singer's "autobiographical obsession" indicated his constant need to rewrite his personal history during the last three decades of his life. Only two memoirs were published in book form: *Mayn tatns bezdn shtub* depicting the author's childhood and early adolescence in Warsaw and Bilgoray between 1907 and 1917, and *Gloybn un tsveyfl oder di filosofye fun protest* (1974–1978, Faith and Doubt or the Philosophy of Protest) which only appeared in book form in English translation.[67] The locus of Singer's childhood memoir is the rabbinical court over which his father, a unlicensed rabbi, presided between 1907 and 1917. This court was on Krochmalna Street, a poor section of Jewish Warsaw. *Mayn tatns bezdn shtub* was originally published in the *Forverts* under Singer's journalistic pseudonym, Yitskhok Varshavski.[68] However, as Singer notes in the introduction, he finally decided to publish them under his literary name, Yitskhok Bashevis because "this series gives a picture of a life and an environment which appeared once and therefore is unique." Apparently Singer needed to legitimize his choice of the Yiddish memoir by emphasizing its commemorative aspect, although his method was very different from that of Y. Y. Trunk and Chaim Grade.

Several chapters are introduced by the passive construction: *a tir hot zikh geefnt* (a door opened).[69] Thus, people from the outer world enter into the rabbinical family's introspective, religious life. The dichotomy between inside and outside the family is elaborated in a series of oppositions: the family is characterized by puritanism, bookishness, and otherworldliness; and the outside world is *treyf*, chaotic and threatening. People from the outside world have stories to tell, *tshikave mayses* (spicy stories) that are more *oysterlish* (bizarre)—the first word in the book—than any stories in books. These story-tellers are the distressed people who come to ask Singer's father for religious advice. As a child Singer is fascinated by the adult world, with its passions and complications that he does not fully comprehend. His father's *bezdn shtub* gives him direct access to the richness and diversity of people's stories, whereas his mother's stories present him with his *yikhes*, the family chronicle. People cease being individuals and become channels for stories passed on through generations: "I sat and swallowed every word. This was not only talk, but what my brother called 'literature.' From these words grew characters. Bilgoraj, Tomashov, Rakhev became near to me from my mother's talk. People came to life. I sensed that from her mouth spoke generations" (265).

The first section of the book (chapters 1–23) presents its basic narrative pattern: the religious life of the Singer family is interrupted by the people who ask the rabbi for advice or need him to preside over a *dintoyre* (a Jewish law suit). The Singer family consists of the parents and Isaac without any mention of his two older siblings, Hinde Ester and Joshua. Isaac's curiosity propels him to sneak into the *bezdn shtub*, or listen at the door. These stories allow him a glimpse into a chaotic and grotesque adult world which transgresses the normative religious system represented by his father's rabbinical authority. The first story, "A Sacrifice" depicts a woman who seeks a divorce after a long marriage so that her husband can marry a younger woman who can bear children. Everything turns out differently than planned: the young woman does not conceive, and the old man dies. The child's fascination with this story is due to its fusion of "life, death, lust, devotion and love without limit" (13). To Isaac this "real life" story is far more fascinating than the stories that appear in the newspaper or on the stage. In the final episode of the first section (chapter 23), the narrative pattern is momentarily reversed. In order to replace the corruptible *gabes* (rabbi's assistants) who steal the money they are supposed to collect for Singer's father, Isaac himself volunteers to become a *gabe*. Walking through Krochmalna Street and entering peoples' homes, he is directly confronted with their poverty, physical deformity and insanity. After glimpsing a corpse on the floor with a grieving woman next to it, Isaac leaves in shock, traumatized by the experience: "I had a bizarre feeling [*an oysterlish gefil*]: just like I suddenly became many years older in one day" (138).[70] The child protagonist's fascination with the hopeless poverty of Krochmalna Street is a recurrent theme in the book.

The second section (chapters 28–53) shifts the focus from the Singer family to Isaac's brother's studio. This is the second important location in the book in which the autobiographer's older brother, Joshua, an up-coming painter, spends his time with other artists. The studio is the diametric opposite of the *bezdn shtub;* in it, the graven image has replaced the Torah; nakedness, puritanism; worldliness, *derekh hashas* (the way of the Talmud). This way of life is no less fascinating to Singer than the *bezdn shtub*. It provides him with a modern narrative perspective that enables the future story-teller to utilize the polarity between Orthodox Judaism and modernity as an artistic arena of self-invention and self-exposure: "What a sudden transition from my father's rabbinical court to this studio. It occurs sometimes to me that this transition complies with my character, with my destiny, with my creativity. In my stories there also is only one step from the rabbinical court to nakedness and from nakedness to the rabbinical court. I remained interested with life and soul in both stages of humanity" (288). With the outbreak of World War I, the rabbinical court rapidly declines. This development, caused by the religious and moral disintegration on Krochmalna Street, under-mines the livelihood of Singer's father. The Singer family is literally starving, struggling for survival, and only a few people come to ask for rabbinical advice. In 1917, Singer and his mother leave Warsaw in order to seek shelter in the *shtetl* Bilgoray where Singer's grandparents reside (depicted in the third section, chapters 53–60). As late as the eve of World War I, this *shtetl* is an anachronism, with no trace of Haskalah. This is exemplified by the fact that nobody there has heard of Y. L. Peretz who used to live in neighbouring Zamosc. The spirit of the town encapsulated by Singer's rabbinical family "was deeply rooted in the Middle Ages."[71] This traditional Jewishness provides Singer with the material for his stories. These are "slices of traditional life" that have been arrested in time beyond the modern upheaval of Jewish life in the early twentieth century.[72] In Bilgoray, the adolescent Singer experiences the last remnants of old *yidishkeyt* as a connection to his people's past, through which he is introduced to a picturesque gallery of pre-modern characters and superstitious beliefs: "I entered a piece of old Jewishness, and somewhere I knew that this was for me a spiritual treasure. Everything inside of me said: This must be described."[73]

In "Strong Ones" (chapter 45), Singer shows more directly how his childhood experiences prepared him for his future role as story-teller. Singer describes his *kheyder* experience as yet another example of how the human condition is characterized by the law of the jungle, the survival of the fittest. Singer points out that the children are not defenseless victims of the *melamed*'s brutality, but rather victims of their own struggle for power, each with his distinct character: the bully, the schemer, the liar, and the victim. Initially, Singer himself has no distinctive traits to show off among the other children. Most of them are against him, and he feels like an outcast. However, the situation suddenly changes as the result of new power constellations among the children. Everybody flocks around him, until this too suddenly ends. Then Singer realizes that he can only avoid the constant flux between the children's loyalty and disloyalty by remaining aloof. He devotes himself to religious studies and starts to write, while retreating into his own inner world. One day the children approach him with a letter of consolation, and as a result Singer feels like the biblical Joseph when he was approached by his brothers in Egypt. Singer has become a latter-day Joseph, endowed with a unique story-telling talent that sets him apart and gives him power over the others kids, his future readers.

The second vignette "Why the Geese Shrieked" highlights the book's thematic and stylistic character as well as crystallizes the basic dynamics in the family triad: father, mother and the child protagonist. The first paragraph introduces a story about supernatural forces such as *dibukim . . . gilgulim, letsim . . . nisht-gute* (15, dibbuks . . . transmigrated souls, pranksters . . . demons), all of which form a daily topic of conversation in the Singer family. The story about a woman who comes to the rabbi to seek advice about two dead shrieking geese is narrated from the child's perspective in short descriptive sentences including dialogues between the woman and his parents. Only when the geese shriek does the child-observer relate his own reactions to their frightening sound. Terrified, he seeks protection by grabbing his mother's shirt like "a three year old child." His father, as frightened as his son, views the dead, shrieking geese as proof of a supernatural realm, an omen from heaven—or, at least from the Evil One. When the geese shriek the second time, the father presents this as proof of God's existence. Singer describes his father's reaction as being motivated by a passionate, irrational belief; he is *tseflamt* (blazing, aflame), and Isaac feels that someone has struck him with all his might. Father and son are united in instinctual fear, surrendering all common sense, whereas his mother exudes anger and shame. With arms covered in blood like a surgeon, she removes the geese's windpipes. The third time the dead geese are expected to shriek, they are silent "as only two dead geese without windpipes can be silent." The two positions, represented by his father's belief and his mother's scepticism, graphically outlined through their opposite reactions to the shrieking geese, have been transformed into a human and cosmic drama—"the mighty drama which unfolded here-in front of our eyes." What initially seems a rather trivial story about a woman and her shrieking geese has become a drama about the existence of God, life and death, man and woman. Although the outcome of the story indicates the mother's rationalistic triumph over the father's religious superstition, Singer successfully recreates his father's and his own childish desire to be carried away into a supernatural realm which, for a brief moment, suspends the reader's disbelief as well.[74]

A central Singer theme, presented in many variations throughout the book, is the human capacity to interpret reality so that it fits into an ultimately fixed belief system. This is poignantly depicted in the vignette "The Magical Sign" in which a group of Raziminer Hasidim are suddenly faced with facts that totally undermine their belief in a *moyfes* (magical sign). On the advice of her doctors, a prominent Raziminer hasid's daughter who has had problems conceiving goes abroad for an operation. Believing that she has actually given birth without the intervention of a surgeon, the Raziminer hasidim start to celebrate the miracle. In the midst of the joyous celebration her father receives a letter saying that it was an operation that saved both mother and child from mortal danger. After a moment's confusion, the father shouts: "Jews, if that is the case, the miracle is even greater" and the celebration resumes. Singer laconically concludes the episode by comparing the Raziminers' stubborn faith to that of political activists: "Years later I saw party activists do the same by twisting the facts and corrupting the logic in order to turn the defeat into a victory." Later, the Raziminer *rebbe* dies because he stubbornly refuses to have an operation.

At the end of the vignette, Isaac retreats to the balcony where he, all alone, can conduct his inner monologue about the eternal questions. The balcony, which is suspended between the public space of the rabbinical court and Krochmalna Street, becomes the only place where Isaac can give free rein to introspection. But his introspection does not address his individuality or personal life. Instead he ponders abstract, eternal questions, which recur in a somewhat formulaic form throughout the book: "I don't at all exaggerate when I say that the eternal questions, the paradox of time, space, infinity obsessed me before I learned to pray, or how to write." There is no development or change in the child's perspective throughout the book. Unlike other Yiddish autobiographers, Singer's self is defined once and for all as a static, hollow entity. Its only redeeming quality is its ability to observe and create stories about people in his father's rabbinical court. He is suspended between the rabbinical court's crumbling belief system and Krochmalna Street's terrifying world that produces human calamities. The family which is viewed as a safe haven of nurture and *heymishkeyt* (homelike warmth)—at least ideally—in life-writing by the classical Yiddish trio, is explicitly rejected by Singer: "The homelike warmth of a family was lacking." The writer's origin and home becomes instead a public space through which people pass with their chaotic lives. There is no way for Isaac to hide or cultivate an inner world except for the brief moments on the balcony. This lack of any private introspective realm originates in a pre-modern autobiographical discourse: "In ancient times the autobiographical and biographical self-consciousness of an individual and his life was first laid bare and shaped in the public square. . . . But the square in earlier (ancient) times itself constituted a state (and more—it constituted the entire state apparatus, with all its official organs), it was the highest court, the whole of science, the whole of art, the entire people participated in it. In following epochs, man's image was distorted by his increasing participation in the mute and invisible spheres of existence. He was literally drenched in muteness and invisibility. And with them entered lonelinesss. The personal and detached human being—'the man who exists for himself'—lost the unity and wholeness that had been a product of his public origin."[75]

The rabbinical court becomes a complete public universe, a separate Jewish state, both spiritually and physically, which defines Singer's artistic imagination and self-perception. Singer's rejection of humanism and modernism is highlighted in the way he portrays himself in *Mayn tatns bezdn shtub*. Here he is depicted without introspection except for the traditional, inner monologue about "eternal questions." The psycho-sexual make-up of Singer's family is particularly interesting because his brother, I. J. Singer and his sister, Ester Kreytman, both Yiddish

writers, wrote their own autobiographical accounts portraying the
same family in different ways and periods.[76] Singer explicitly acknowledges his brother's autobiography as covering the earliest period of his
childhood in the town Leontshin: "I will not write about Leontshin, because my older brother has written thoroughly about it in his work *Of A
World That Is No More*." Singer was the last surviving writer of the three
siblings when he began *Mayn tatns bezdn shtub* in 1955. (I. J. Singer died
in 1944, and Esther Kreitman in 1954.) He could now freely recreate his
own version of the family mythology.[77] Devoting a chapter to his sister
("My Sister"), Singer acknowledges that she was actually the first in the
family to demonstrate "a literary spark." But Ester Kreytman is relegated to a marginal role in Singer's childhood, and her literary work is
never mentioned. She is discarded as a troubled, emotional woman
who never outgrew her hysteria and lack of self-esteem in relationship
to her dominant mother.[78] Singer and his older brother both portray
their father with similar characteristics: the father was a *batlen* (imprac-
tical person) married to a practical, rationalist, and sceptical wife. It is
striking, though, that Singer paints an adoring, beautified image of his
father, while his brother describes him with critical distance.[79] In their
respective portraits of the same father, the two writers reveal their different artistic agendas. Singer refashions his family story so it becomes
a mythical tale of "faith and doubt," as represented by his two parents.
I. J. Singer, on the other hand, rejects his parents' religious life with a
critical post-Maskilic stance that reveals their incompatibility and inability to create a *heymish* (homelike) atmosphere for him as a child.

Singer developed a simple narrative style which he used for his own
deeply pessimistic purposes by creating an artistic vision out of everyday life as he had first experienced it in his father's rabbinical court.
Mayn tatns bezdn shtub were not scenes from a lost world, trying to resur-
rect in imaginary literature what had been destroyed in historical reality. They were instead a kaleidoscope of Jewish life, carefully crafted to
present a particularly bleak mythological view of the human condition.
A chaotic, terrifying universe, different from anything else in modern
Yiddish literature, can be discerned behind the simple, straightforward
narrative flow of Singer's stories. Singer's modernism did not express
itself in complex language, elaborate metaphors, or in the fusion of
styles and genres as was the case of Glatshteyn. Instead it was expressed through black, nihilist tales that depicted extreme and supernatural realities.[80] Singer's international literary success from the mid-
1950s until his death in 1991 made him rich and famous but did not

alter his artistic views.[81] In his "spiritual autobiography" *Globn un tsveyfl*, published in book form in English as *Love and Exile* at the peak of his international fame between 1976 and 1981, Singer depicted his struggle to maintain his autonomy and avoid being entangled in cultural or political ideologies. To isolate one-self and to remain apart from the modern world—these were the goals Singer's alter ego inherited from his father. He rejected the faith of his father, but was unwilling to assimilate into the modern world of culture and politics as his brother had. As a result, Singer was rooted neither here nor there in a self-chosen no man's land of individual exile. Accordingly, the crux of Singer's life story in *Globn un tsveyfl* became his loss of faith in both his father's God and his brother's modernity.

In *Globn un tsveyfl*, Singer presented his "philosophy of protest," which appears in the Yiddish title of the work, *Gloybn un tsveyfl oder di filosofye fun protest*.[82] "The philosophy of protest" is a fantasy about temples where people could study and protest "the various misfortunes God had sent to humans and animals." In this temple, The Book of Job will be used as the new Torah, except for the final segment in which Job's suffering is mitigated through divine intervention. The protesting prophets of the temple are writers and philosophers such as Otto Weininger, Edgar Allan Poe and Schopenhauer, "who rejected life and considered death the only messiah," echoing the last words of the English translation of Singer's family saga *Di familye Mushkat*.[83] What keeps Singer from committing suicide, the most logical consequence of his "philosophy of protest," are "the idol of literature and the idol of love." Yet his love life, as Singer depicted it in *Globn un tsveyfl*, was characterized by promiscuity and lack of true satisfaction. His sexual encounters which took place in secret, occurred in a social vacuum and were primarily played out as bodily exercises without any deeper affection or spiritual meaning. As for his writings, Singer considered them a contribution of falsehoods to "the world of lies/falsehood" (the material world; *oylem-ho'sheker*) removed from "the world of truth" (*oylem-ho'emes*) the realm of death. Focussing on his coming of age as a writer in Warsaw and subsequent emigration to America concluding on the eve of World War II, *Gloybn un tsveyfl* presented an immature and puerile self-portrait of the writer as a young man. In *Mayn tatns bezdn shtub*, on the other hand, Singer showed how his story-teller origins grew directly out of childhood experiences in his father's *bezdn shtub*. His loyalty to his father's and brother's opposing world views served him well when he portrayed Krochmalna Street as being torn between traditional religious beliefs and modern secularism. The story-vignette enabled Singer to condense his world view and artistic credo in a formulaic, simple story-telling style that made his work highly popular among his Yiddish readers.

Singer mentioned several times in *Mayn tatns bezdn shtub* that the fifty year old narrator and the child were more or less the same person. This static world view, along with Singer's refusal to depict himself as influenced by historical, social and psychological conditions, was perhaps his most distinctly reactionary artistic mark. Faithful to his 1932 literary manifesto "On the Question of Poetry and Politics,"[84] Singer did not employ the autobiographical genre as a means of serving extra-literary ends, such as commemorating a destroyed world. On the other hand, neither did he write a Rousseauian autobiography in search of his "true" self. Rather, he depicted his artistic origins as the unchangeable child observer in his father's *bezdn shtub* destined to become a story-teller.

In closing, I will examine *Fun altn markplats* (1985–1988, *From the Old Marketplace*), which brilliantly summarizes the generic characteristics of the Yiddish literary autobiography. It was written by the Yiddish actor Joseph Buloff (1899–1985) who like Sutzkever and Grade recreated Vilna, Jerusalem of Lithuania as his spiritual and artistic origins. *Fun altn markplats*, serialized in Sutzkever's journal *Di goldene keyt* in 1985, the year of Buloff's death, ran in ten consecutive issues through 1988.[85] The author envisioned the Vilna marketplace during a period of great social and political upheaval by focusing on his coming of age during the failed 1905 revolution, the outbreak of World War I and the subsequent occupation by Russia, Germany and Poland. Unlike Grade's emphasis on the *yeshive* and his mother's traditional world, Buloff made the marketplace, the center of Jewish social and economic life in Eastern Europe, the locus of his memoir. Except for the one chapter in which he paid tribute to traditional religious devotion on Yom Kippur (chapter 22), Buloff depicted Jewish existence in multi-cultural Vilna in political, socio-economic, and theatrical terms.[86] In this setting, Buloff fashioned a magical universe similar to childhood accounts such as I. B. Singer's *Mayn tatns bezdn shtub* and Sholem Aleichem's *Motl peyse dem khazns*.

Buloff's guilt over surviving the cataclysms of the two world wars which completely obliterated Vilna provided his main impetus for writing the book. As described in the epilogue, the old actor Buloff coincidently meets his childhood friend Berchik the Orphan on one of his frequent theater tours to Brazil. Berchik, who now goes by Boris and has made a career as a popular violinist, reminds him about their childhood adventures in the Vilna marketplace half a century earlier. Boris mentions the four buttons he lent to him while playing in the marketplace, and adds that Buloff owes him four additional buttons for teaching him to play "Perpetum Mobile" on the violin. Instead of sharing these memories, Buloff turns him away. On the ocean liner back to America he is suddenly overwhelmed by guilt because of his indifference to his old friend: "Span the ocean and half a globe, run to the old marketplace and find the boy that I was and demand buttons from him who had once borrowed from someone who was now also someone else? And where was the marketplace? The bloody Holocaust had swept not only the people and the market but even the ground on which it stood off the face of the earth. Not even a trace, a sign had remained. It was as if it had never existed, not even in a dream. That's true, I agreed, but what would have harmed me if, standing there in the dressing room, I had torn some buttons off my jacket and jokingly handed them to him—here, good brother, the payment on my debt."[87] As Ruth R. Wisse points out, this episode relates to a similar crisis of guilt and resistance to delve into the past in Reb Shloyme's agonizing monologue which introduces *Shloyme reb khayims*. Reb Shloyme refuses to let the young *yeshive bokher* from Lithuania stay in his Talmud Torah, but then is tormented by remorse.[88] Then, Reb Shloyme retrieves the buttons of his caftan which he has kept for forty years and which he wore through his years as wandering *yeshive bokher*. As a result, Reb Shloyme decides to write his autobiography in order to expunge his sense of guilt and to reconnect with the Lithuanian *yeshive bokher* he used to be. In a slightly different fashion Buloff decides to write a long letter explaining himself to Boris. After several unsuccessful attempts at locating Boris, and after the letter has been transformed into "a thousand multi-sized unnumbered pages," Buloff decides to publish this "odd, lengthy letter with which I wanted to repay the eight buttons to my partner Berchik from the old marketplace."[89] There is a crucial difference between the famous writer Reb Shloyme's feeling of alienation from the Jewish *shtetl* and his younger self, and Buloff's desperate attempt to reach out to his childhood friend in a letter that never reaches its destination. While Abramovitsh addressed a readership that shared his memories from bygone days, Buloff has lost most of his readers to the cataclysmic events of the Holocaust. Buloff pays homage to Abramovitsh as the first in an illustrious line of reluctant Yiddish autobiographers. As a result, Buloff decides to write his childhood memoir as a way of paying a debt to his people whose humiliation and annihilation provide the backdrop for his artistic fame. With *Fun altn markplats*, the Yiddish literary autobiography comes full circle by reaching back to Abramovitsh's autobiographical quest in *Shloyme reb khayims* almost a century earlier.

The book's epigram encapsulates Buloff's view of childhood as the origin of artistic creativity: "One lives only once, in his childhood and adolescence—the rest is just a repetition." The wise person quoted in the epigram is Barve's Son who, in traditional Jewish practice, is named as the son of his father. The father, in this case, is an insignificant tailor with no great deeds or learning to his name. Barve's Son, in contrast, is the learned *apikoyres* (heretic) of the market place, Buloff's spiritual twin. He serves as a well-informed authority among the poor shop owners and beggars in the marketplace. As a kind of political and scholarly commentator, he provides them with explanations and perspectives on the constant stream of events that keeps the marketplace in a state of crisis in its attempt to adapt to the constant change of rulers. His anti-religious stand places him firmly within the camp of the socialists, while his visions turn him into a prophetic voice who warns the market people of the tragedies ahead. He functions as a Greek chorus, standing apart from the mundane action in the marketplace similar to the Jester in Peretz's drama *Bay nakht afn altn mark* (1907, At Night on the Old Market Place).[90] From this position, he castigates and gives meaning to the chaotic events that continues to descend on the market people.

The market people view Yosik (Buloff's autobiographical alter ego) as a charlatan, a useless element out of touch with reality. Barve's Son on the other hand, has the ability to see beyond daily survival in a rejection of the market people's religious beliefs which he characterizes as self-destructive in a period of war and pogroms. Barve's Son's rationalism and disillusioned view of history originates with the Marxist ideology which, personified in the Russian Communist rulers, embodies the coming of a new age. The contrast between Barve's Son and Yosik is highlighted in a former member of the municipal Yiddish theater in Vilna, Tanya's characterization of Yosik during World War I: "Just now, when you danced through the whole tragic carnival of wars and revolutions with its bands and banners, its marches, its songs, its killings and murders—its hunger and deaths . . . I recognized in your eyes the eyes of the midget in the little sideshow at the horse market. You were and you've remained the ridiculous *lampedusser* who looks at world-shaking events as merely a new installment of 'The Conqueror of

Death' with yourself in the starting role of Chantille Jeantaigne Delacroix. . . . Shall I say that you belong to the very last category of the
useless unnecessary elements."[91] Here, Tanya who becomes a commis-
sar in the short lived Soviet regime in Vilna at the end of World War I
anticipates the increasing enmity of the Soviet Union for the kind of
artistic independence that Yosik represents.

Childhood and adolescence are the periods of life featured by the
classical trio who rarely ventured beyond the late teens in their autobiographical novels. Their romanticist version of childhood as a magical time of endless opportunity and creativity, as portrayed from the
perspective of the adult writer, also characterized some of their best
Yiddish fiction. The paradigmatic example is Sholem Aleichem's *Motl
peyse dem khazns* which provided a literary model for Buloff's work.
Like Buloff's dramatic art as actor and director on the Yiddish stage, his
magical realism in *Fun altn markplats* originated in his childhood. The
first play which Buloff's directed, Osip Dimov's *Singer of His Sorrow,*
was presented from a child's perspective which enabled him to turn the
improbable narrative into pure fantasy.[92] Similarly, in *Fun altn markplats,* Buloff created a fantastic universe told from a young person's perspective, with himself as both director and star. Buloff's mastery of the
written word owes a great deal to his apprenticeship as a Yiddish actor
in the Vilna Troupe from its inception in 1918 through the 1920s. The
Vilna Troupe first great success, Sh. Anski's *Der dibek* (The Dybbuk), encapsulated the group's commitment to literary quality as part of a Yiddish cultural renaissance in Eastern Europe. The Vilna Troupe intended
to give dramatic shape and voice to the emergence of serious Yiddish
literature.[93]

Without warning, Yosik learns that his father has fled to America in
order to avoid conscription. When he returns as a millionaire, Yosik's
life is again turned upside down. From being a poor kid playing around
the garbage bins of the old market place he is suddenly a rich man's son
attending a gymnasium. Then the father loses all his wealth on doctors'
bills when he contracts tuberculosis and must travel abroad for medical
treatment. What ultimately saves him from dying is his conversion
from free-thinker, chaser of material goods and women to becoming a
bal-tshuve (a return to orthodox observance). This newfound faith has a
healing effect on Yosik's father, and results in a transformation that is
just as miraculous as the wonders of the fictional Delacroix, the main
character in the penny novel "Conqueror of Death." In contrast, another sick person, Barve's Son lacks the ability to believe. While dying

of tuberculosis, his prophetic ability reaches new heights in its anticipation of the coming destruction of the marketplace. In Sholem Aleichem's novel *Motl peyse dem khazns,* there is a clear movement from the old to the new world, from traditional Judaism to the Golden Land of opportunities, from the death of the father to Motl's rebirth in spring. Motl is the life-affirming, unchangeable spirit of childhood renewal reflecting Sholem Aleichem's artistic optimism in the possibility of a new beginning for Jews in America. Buloff gives a both less mythological and more fantastic depiction of his child protagonist. In the beginning Yosik befriends one of the Cossacks patrolling the marketplace. He admires his manly appearance as the antithesis of the powerless Jews in the marketplace. Yosik changes his allegiances during the 1905 pogroms which makes it clear to him that his friendship with the Cossack is just as illusionary as his other dreams of achieving inexhaustible strength.[94] Yosik becomes the quintessential Jewish survivor who, like his hero Delocroix, is characterized by the ability to escape the forces of destruction and death. Unlike Motl, his ingenuity is not rooted in a naive belief in the progressive improvement of the world but in his talent for dramatization. *Motl peyse dem khazns*'s linear narrative progress from the old to the new world, from death to rebirth has been replaced by small segments of fateful encounters and intrigues that suddenly and, in most cases, inexplicably, can make a person rich or poor, sick or healthy, dead or alive. The Yiddish stage and the penny novel's fascination with the fantastic deeds and dreamlike fulfillment provide the artistic models for Buloff's *Fun altn markplats.* The driving force behind Yosik's dramatic talent for disguise and manipulation is his desire to stay alive rather than accept the increasing absurdity of a reality defined by war, totalitarianism and anti-Semitism.

In an episode taken right out of the Yiddish theater, Yosik courts the non-Jewish girl Niura by faking knowledge of English. Later, when he intends to play "Perpetum Mobile" on the violin to prove that he is worthy of his artist name Paganini the Third, he instead plays the sheet music which he imagines is written on her face.[95] This sheet music on her face reveals her fascination with the mysterious, Jewish character of Yosik who seems to have stepped out of a melodrama on the Yiddish stage. Reality has suddenly been cracked open and reveals an infinite array of poetic, psychological and erotic possibilities.[96] The climactic moment at this private performance of "soul music" is Niuri's erotic surrender to Yosik's dramatic talent. In another episode, Yosik through sheer *chutspe* and dramatic eloquence convinces the board of teachers at the final examination that he must be admitted to the Gymnasium in spite of his lack of academic credentials. Buloff depicts the final examination as the crucial rite of passage, and coveted door to professional status allowed to the Jews in the last years of the tsarist reign. As Jews in the age of Enlightenment, his classmates take full advantage of this opportunity for breaking out of the circumscribed Jewish ghetto life. Yosik, on the other hand, breaks all rules by appealing to his examiners' empathy, through *chutspe* and dramatic talent achieving the same goal as his classmates: admission to the Gymnasium. In a response to a question from the feared examiner from St. Petersburg with the nickname "The Dragon from St. Petersburg" in front of his classmates and teachers, Yosik confronts them with his life of Jewish misery, *tsores*, they believe that they can escape through education and assimilation in Russian society: "'What is your problem, my little friend?' And I blasted out, 'Not one, your Excellency, but ten—an impoverished millionaire. One mother sick after a Caesarian delivery, the second forced to leave the house because of an illegitimate pregnancy, a father in the grip of death, a couple of grandparents who died simultaneously, and if all that is not enough there are two students in the gymnasium who are after me—to kill me only because, as your excellency has heard it, I'm a *lampedusser* and a Jewish *lampedusser* to boot.'"[97] As a result of this performance, a litany of his life's miseries, which plays on the assimilated Jewish examiner's suppressed compassion for a fellow Jew, he is admitted to the Gymnasium with high recommendations.

The book is a typical example of the Yiddish literary autobiography. First of all, we learn very little about the man behind the actor's mask. The focus is on the entertaining aspects of his external life, his activities and adventures, and the work does not reflect or analyze his inner world. Secondly, Buloff elaborates on the comic aspects of his life, and how he survived his dysfunctional family, the war and the short lived Communist regime in Vilna. The book stresses the life-affirming, artistic creativity of Buloff's younger alter ego, and brings to artistic fulfillment the dramatic possibilities from the Vilna marketplace as he recalls it seventy years later. Thirdly, Buloff has inscribed the book among some of the classical Yiddish literary works such as Peretz's *Bay nakht afn altn mark* and Sholem Aleichem's *Motl peyse dem khazns* by rewriting their themes, styles and narrative forms. Additionally, Buloff's fondness for depicting vulgar speech, immorality and sexuality is influenced by I. B. Singer unsentimental, comical vignettes in *Mayn tatns bezdn shtub*. Finally, as Curt Leviant points out, the book's war section equals the hilarious absurdity of Jaroslav Hasek's *The Good Soldier Schwejk* (1921–1923) combined with Charlie Chaplin and the Marx Brothers.[98] Buloff created a master piece of Yiddish literature, a lasting testimony to the lost world of Jewish Vilna. In the book's last paragraph, the image of Vilna retreats into the Eastern European landscape with its characteristic national and Christian symbols: a Polish flag and a white cross. There is, however, no human trace left in the Yiddish autobiographer's memory of paradise lost: "I looked for the last time at the sleeping city, which lay draped in a foggy, dirty sheet. Several green roofs lacking houses floated in the air along with a Polish flag without a pole and a white cross without a church. At the foot of the mountain was the river, a water snake harnessed to a bridge."[99]

Conclusion

All this must be considered as if spoken by a character in a novel—or rather by several characters.

 Roland Barthes, *Roland Barthes by Roland Barthes*[1]

It is now possible to delineate the main characteristics of the Yiddish literary autobiography and make some comparisons with the genre as it appears in Hebrew and Jewish-American literature. Two main influences intersected in the Yiddish literary autobiography: the Rousseauian quest for truthfulness and the externalized drama of Yiddish fiction. The discourse of self-analysis in Rousseau's *Confessions* and, from the beginning of the twentieth century, Freud's psychoanalysis informs very few examples of the Yiddish literary autobiography. The most important exception, Peretz's *Mayne zikhroynes,* departed from Abramovitsh's and Sholem Aleichem's novelistic lives narrated in chronological progression by employing a fragmented, introspective style. *Mayne zikhroynes* presented meta-poetic, psychological and philosophical perspectives on the disparate units of Peretz's autobiographical narrative. This set Peretz's work apart from the two other classical writers and introduced psychoanalytic concepts and modernism in Yiddish literature.

The main trend in Yiddish literature, exemplified by Mendele Moykher Sforim and Sholem Aleichem, dominated the Yiddish readership's horizon of expectations. By employing these writers' colloquial style, the next generations of Yiddish life-writers succeeded in maintaining a hold on their readership. New artistic solutions to the question of autobiographical truthfulness were developed in Glatshteyn's Yash books, and I. B. Singer and Grade's life-writing. Only Jonah Rosenfeld's *Eyner aleyn,* more closely resembled the Rousseauian prototype in its self-reflective style and pathological apologetics. Still, Rosenfeld's work was crafted as a suspenseful *roman* intended to lure the reader into the complex elaboration of his autobiographical hero's twisted inner world. The seven Yiddish writers' return to their origins in Jewish Eastern Europe in the form of life-writing was conceived during the cataclysmic upheavals of Eastern European Jewry in the first half of the twentieth century resulting from acculturation, immigration, pogroms, and the Holocaust. These threats to the Jewish people further compelled Yiddish life-writers to focus on collective destiny as a template on which they inscribed their self-portraits.

The Yiddish literary autobiography emphasized the textual aspects of the autobiographical act *(graphe)* and the life narrative *(bios),* and mostly effaced the self *(autos).* Typical in this regard was Sholem Aleichem's epigram from the introduction to *Funem yarid:* "Why novels when life is a novel?" ("Tsu vos romanen ven dos lebn iz a roman?") stressing the work's novelistic and fictional character. The French post-structuralist Roland Barthes similarly highlighted this feature in the epigram to his autobiography *Roland Barthes about Roland Barthes* (1975): "It must all be considered as if spoken by a character in a novel." However, long before Roland Barthes introduced semiotic criticism in the 1970s, Yiddish writers had developed their own "semiotics," which drew on folklore, colloquial speech and irony.[2] Moreover, as Paul John Eakin points out, "language remains inescapably central as the medium in which inner states are culturally negotiated and expressed."[3] To negotiate "inner states" in Yiddish, a language rooted in a traditional mindset and collective ethos, heightened the ironic clashes between the Yiddish writer's modernity and his medium's artistic potential. Yiddish writers became masters of comic relief, irony, meta-discourse and wordplay inscribed in a literary discourse that was highly ambivalent about modern concepts such as "privacy", "inwardness" and "self."

A typical example of this artistic strategy is presented in the beginning of the second volume of Sholem Aleichem's *Funem yarid* entitled "A mayne-loshn fun a shtifmame" (A Step-Mother's Invective). In the aftermath of his mother's sudden death, the thirteen-year-old year Sholem and his siblings await their father's return from Berdichev with a new wife. The children express their stereotypical expectations of the "evil" stepmother by imagining the terrible things she will do. After a short "honey-moon", the stepmother's true hotheaded temperament expresses itself in "her authentic Berdichev step-motherly vocabulary — glib, juicy, blooming."[4] After Sholem Aleichem has presented several examples of his stepmother's curses, he interrupts the narrative with a brief reflection on the significance of his stepmother for his future literary career: "The hero of this biography must admit that many of the curses and maledictions in his works came straight from his stepmother's invective. Very early on, before Sholem knew anything about writing, he wanted to jot down all of his 'stepmother's curses just for the fun of it and collect them in a little dictionary."[5] As a result, the young Sholem decides to write an alphabetic list of his step-mother's curses entitled "A Stepmother's Invective" which becomes his first literary work. When his father discovers the little booklet which Sholem has toiled over for several days, he gives it to his wife. To the boy's great surprise, his stepmother breaks out in a frenzied laughter reading it: "She almost got apoplexy from the shrieking."[6] This remarkable episode depicting the genesis of Sholem Aleichem as a young artist, crystallizes several important features of the Yiddish literary autobiography. First, the episode is presented in dramatic terms in the form of a detailed account told from the boy's point of view sprinkled with reflections by the fifty-odd year autobiographer. Its comic potential is graphically displayed in the hilarious alphabetical catalogue of curses inserted in the text. Secondly, the power of the boy's comical creation to change his stepmother's mood is manifested as a victory of art over the bleak circumstances of life. The devastating death of Sholem's mother in a cholera epidemic followed by the "evil" stepmother's arrival have been transcended through a comic catharsis that makes even the stepmother break down in laughter. The loss of the mother (tongue), *mameloshn*, has been compensated for by a language of invectives (*mayneloshn*) that turns reality upside down. The orphan's sense of being cursed by destiny has been transformed into an aesthetic principle of pleasure and laughter.

This principle is repeated in various forms from Abramovitsh's loss of his father in *Shloyme reb khayims* to Grade's tribute to his murdered mother in *Der mames shabosim*. The language of invectives is wonderfully evoked in Jonah Rosenfeld's *Eyner aleyn* where it is used to express the autobiographer's anger against his boss and stepfather. At the same time it enables Rosenfeld to settle the scores with his powerful editor at the *Forverts*, Abe Cahan. Grade, Singer and Buloff similarly present a rich catalogue of Yiddish curses and idioms in their depiction of Jewish life in the poor sections of Warsaw and Vilna. An important part of the aesthetic delight of these works is the intricate way in which colloquial speech, proverbs and curses are woven into the narrative fabric. The English translation can only approximate the original Yiddish expressions which often allude to Jewish religious sources. Moreover, what Benjamin Harshav calls "a second level of language . . . the language of communication accepted by the speakers of a community"[7] is a central feature of Yiddish literary discourse. The semiotics of Yiddish communication is characterized by a particularly rich system of "signals, rules of conversation, encapsulated formulas and labels, allusions to codified and richly connotative life situations."[8] In most cases, the Yiddish writer does not attempt to distance himself from the semiotics of communication in his community that, to a large extent, determines his artistic origins and self-perception. Instead he draws on its "psycho-semantic" potentials by transposing his own sense of self through the speech and mentality of "regular" Jews.

The Yiddish writer's artistic origins were predicated on the loss of the mother (language), and this separation became a precondition for the development of his artistic individuality. As such, the Yiddish literary autobiography exemplifies an important universal feature of the genre: "The logic of individuation, presumably a gain in the ethos of individualism, is predicated on loss," Paul John Eakin writes: "language and the other, language taught by the (m)other, enable the articulation of self that, conceptually, is by definition founded on the recognition of its separation from the other, its division from plenitude. The language of autobiography is a further naming of the self, a further re-enactment of this primal partition."[9] In the Yiddish literary autobiography, the loss of the mother and the naming of the self take place across the abyss of the tragic demise of Eastern European Jewry. Moreover, the naming of the self is intrinsically linked to the naming of a people decimated by external historical forces. This feature is already apparent in Abramovitsh and Sholem Aleichem's portrayal of their parents as representative of a way of life doomed to extinction. The absence of the mother and the creation of an ideal father figure provide the backdrop for the Yash books' description of a collective gallery of characters. His two parent figures become substitutes for the cultural heritage of Eastern European Jewry, confronting the autobiographer with the double loss of his mother (tongue) and his "ideal" father figure (Shteynman/Peretz). Grade and Singer's works similarly focus on their parents' traditional world observed from the point of view of their autobiographical selves as voyeurs.

The Yiddish literary autobiography became a highly influential model for life-writing by Jewish-American writers. Particularly those Jewish-American writers with a more direct connection to Eastern European Jewish culture displayed the complex of loss, return and retrieval characteristic of Yiddish life-writing. The motif of return to Jewishness runs like a red thread through Jewish-American autobiographies from Ludwig Lewisohn's *Up Stream: An American Chronicle* (1922) to the recollections of Kate Simon, Alfred Kazin and Irving Howe about their working class, socialist, and Yiddishist roots in Brooklyn, the Bronx, and the Lower East Side.[10] The loss of culture, language, and homeland is indicated in the titles of some of these works such as Eva Hoffman's *Lost in Translation: A Life in A New Language* (1989) and I. B. Singer's *Lost in America* (1981). Yiddish life-writing's main theme of "delineating the specifics of . . . retrieval"[11] is exemplified in a return to Israel in Saul Bellow's *To Jerusalem and Back: A Personal Account* (1976), and the historian Lucy Dawidowiz's *From That Place and Time: A Memoir 1938–1947* (1967) about her one year sojourn in Vilna in 1938–1939. Even the paradigmatic success story of Americanization, Mary Antin's *The Promised Land* (1912), updated more than half a century later in the embrace of the American dream in Norman Podhoretz's *Making It* (1967), consists of compelling descriptions of the *shtetl* left behind be it in Lithuania or Brooklyn. However, a more penetrating exposition of cultural loss in the individual lives of Jewish-American writers are presented in the Yiddish literary autobiographies of I. B. Singer, Yankev Glatshteyn, and in Ephraim Lisitzky's Hebrew memoir *In the Grip of Cross Current* (1959). These works surpass most life-writing by Jewish-American writers in the ways in which they "dramatize the acute strain of Americanization and the tragic sense of isolation and loss that were its by-products."[12] This characterization also applies to Philip Roth's work that combines life-writing and fiction in highly innovative ways, for example, *Counterlife* (1986), *Patrimony: A True Story* (1991), and most recently *The Plot Against America* (2004).

The American Jewish diaspora has provided a more stimulating cultural environment for life-writing than Israel because of America's prosperity and relative security, which loosened the collective constraints on the self. In recent decades there has been a resurgence of Hebrew life-writing, most recently Amoz Oz's *Sippur Al Ahavah V'hoshekh*

(2001, *A Tale of Love and Darkness*), which tells of the writer's coming of age during the Israeli War of Independence in 1948. However, Alan Mintz's point about the "surprisingly prolonged absence" of Hebrew life-writing in the first half of the twentieth century still essentially holds: "With the exception of Agnon and Lisitzky, there are few if any significant examples of autobiographical writing in Hebrew literature from before World War One until Pinhas Sadeh's *Life As a Parable* (1954)."[13] In contrast, the American ethos of individualism and self-invention has been highly conducive to life-writing. American Jews' exceptional role as the first Jewish community in two millennia to live in a diaspora along with a Jewish homeland that "they have chosen not to be gathered in,"[14] propelled some Jewish-American writers' return to an imaginary Old World. An unsurpassed proof-text for the Old World, the Yiddish literary autobiography has greatly influenced the genre in Jewish-American literature. With the complete destruction of Yiddish culture in Eastern Europe, and the withering of its branches in America, Israel and Russia, Yiddish life-writing remains a compelling artistic expression of the inner life of Eastern European Jewry.

Chronology

Glossary

Notes

Bibliography

Index

Chronology

Sholem Yankev Abramovitsh (Mendele Moykher Sforim)

1836	Born in Kapulye, Minsk province. Some confusion exists regarding Abramovitsh's date of birth, which is listed variously as December 20 of either 1835 or 1836, or January 2, 1836.
c. 1842	Begins studying the Bible with his first teacher, Yossi Reubens
c. 1848	Leaves *kheyder* to study Talmud and rabbinic literature with his father, Khayim-Moyshe Broyde.
c. 1850	Father dies at age forty; Abramovitsh sent to study in the *yeshive* in Timkevitsh.
1850–52	Studies in *yeshives* in Slutsk and Vilna.
c. 1853	Moves back to his mother's and new stepfather's home near Kapulye, in the village Melnicki. Begins to write for the first time. Composes a series of nature poems in Hebrew and a verse adaptation of Moshe Luzzato's *Leyesharim tehila* (Praise for the Righteous).
1854	Travels to southern Russia with Avreml der Hinkediker (Abraham the Lame). They go through Volhynia, Podolia, and Ukraine. In Kamenets-Podolsk, Podolia, Abramovitsh meets Abraham-Ber Gottlober and learns Russian, German, and mathematics from his daughters.
c. 1854	Marries his first wife.
1856	Passes his teacher's examinations and takes a teaching position in the Kamenets-Podolsk Jewish government school.
1857	Gottlober publishes Abramovitsh's first Hebrew article, "Mikhtav al dvar hakhinukh" (A Letter on Education), in his journal *Hamagid*. The article explains the necessity of educating Jewish children in secular subjects, a popular theme of the *maskilim*.

c. 1857	Divorces his first wife. Their two children both died.
1858	Marries Pessie Levin. Moves to Berditchev.
1859	Abramovitsh's son Mikhail is born.
1860	Publishes a collection of critical articles in Hebrew titled *Mishpat shalom* (The Judgment of Peace).
1862	Publishes his first Hebrew story, "Limdu hetev" (Learn to Do Good), and the first volume of *Sefer toldot hateva* (Book of Natural History), based on a German work by Harald Othmar Lenz.
1864–65	Publishes his first Yiddish work, *Dos kleyne mentshele* (The Little Man). The novel is serialized in *Kol mevaser*, the Yiddish supplement to the Hebrew journal *Hamelits*, edited by Alexander Tsederboym. This is the first time Abramovitsh uses the pen name Mendele Moykher Sforim.
1865	Publishes the novel *Dos vintshfingerl* (The Magic Ring).
1866	*Dos kleyne mentshele* is issued in book form.
1867	Publishes the second volume of *Sefer toldot hateva* and a collection of critical articles in Hebrew titled *Eyn Mishpat* (The Well of Judgment).
1868	Publishes *Ha'avot vehabanim* in Hebrew.
1869	Publishes *Di takse* (The Tax), a five-act drama and his first play, and the novel *Fishke der krumer* (Fishke the Lame). Forced to leave Berditchev because of public resentment over his satirical exposure of the wealthy Jews of Berditchev in *Di takse*. Moves to Zhitomir. Translates Jules Verne's *Cinques semaines en ballon* into Yiddish as *Der luftbalon* (The Balloon). Passes his exams at the Rabbinical Institute in Zhitomir. As a result of delivering a radical sermon he is not ordained.
1870	Publishes "Der fish" (The Fish) in *Kol mevaser*, an attempt to spread knowledge of the natural sciences.
1871	Publishes "Et ledaber" (A Time to Speak), a polemic against the Hebrew writer M. L. Lilyenblum, in *Hamelits*.
1872	Publishes the third volume of *Sefer toldot hateva*.
1873	Publishes the novel *Di kliatshe* (The Nag).
1875	Publishes "Dos yidl" (The Little Jew), a story in poems; *Zmires yisroel* (Songs of Israel), a Yiddish translation of shabes songs in verse; and *Peyrek shire* (A Sequence of Hymns), a Yiddish verse adaptation of the Hasidic *Perek shira*.
1878	Publishes the novel *Kitser masoes binyomin hashlishi* (The Travels of Benjamin the Third).
1881	Moves to Odessa to become director of a Reform Talmud Torah (Jewish school). Keeps this position to the end of his life.
c. 1882	Abramovitsh's daughter Rachel dies. His son Mikhail is exiled for political activities. Soon after, Abramovitsh stops writing for a prolonged period.

1884	Publishes the play *Der priziv* (The Draft) and a Russian translation of his play *Di takse*.
1885	Publishes *Kitser masoes binyomin hashlishi* in Polish translation.
1886	Publishes *Di kliatshe* in Polish translation. Returns to writing in Hebrew with the story "Beseter ra'am" (In the Secret Place of Thunder). This is the first time Abramovitsh uses his pen name, Mendele, on a Hebrew work.
1888	Publishes expanded versions of *Fishke der krumer* and *Dos vintshfingerl*.
1889	Publishes an expanded version of *Di kliatshe* and his first autobiographical essay in Hebrew.
1894	Begins to publish the autobiographical novel *Ba-yamim ha-hem* (*Of Bygone Days*) in Hebrew.
1896	Publishes his Hebrew translation of his Yiddish novel *Kitser masoes binyomin hashlishi*. Begins translating a number of his Yiddish works into Hebrew
1899	Publishes a sequel to his autobiographical novel *Ba-yamim ha-hem* titled *Shloyme reb khayims* (Solomon, the Son of Chaim) in Yiddish. Abramovitsh's Yiddish adaptation of Leo Pinsker's *Auto-emancipation* appears in Gershom Bader's *Yidisher folkskalendar*.
1901–5	Continues to publish revised material in Yiddish and Hebrew.
1905	Leaves Russia after the October pogrom in Odessa. Settles in Geneva, Switzerland.
1908	Returns to Odessa and to his position in the Talmud Torah.
1909–13	Publishes Jubilee collection of his Hebrew works. Within the same period, a 17 volume collection of his Yiddish work is published.
1910	Abramovitsh's seventy-fifth birthday. Celebrations all over the Jewish world.
1913	Publishes a Yiddish translation of Genesis, *Bereyshis*, with Kh. N. Bialik and Y. Kh. Ravnitsky.
1916	Abramovitsh's last publication, a chapter of his memoirs, appears in *Undzer lebn*.
1917	Abramovitsh dies on December 8 in the Jewish hospital in Odessa. On December 10, thousands attend his funeral.

S. Y. Abramovitsh, "Shtrikhtn tsu mayn biografye," in *Dos mendele bukh*, ed. Nachman Mayzel (New York: Yidisher kultur farband, 1959); Dan Miron, *A Traveler Disguised* (New York: Schocken, 1973); Fishl Lakhover, *Toldot ha-sifrut ha-ivrit ha-khadashah*, vol. 3 (1937); Shmuel Niger and Yankev Shatski, *Leksikon fun der nayer yidisher literatur*, vol. 6 (1981); Zalman Reyzen, *Leksikon fun der yidisher literatur, prese un filologye*, vol. 1 (1926); Ken Frieden, *Classic Yiddish Fiction* (Albany: State University of New York Press, 1995).

Yankev Glatshteyn

1896	Born on August 20 in Lublin, Poland. Receives a traditional education.
1909	Travels to Warsaw to meet with Y. L. Peretz, Nomberg, and Prilutski and show them some of his writing. Composes his own sermon for his *bar-mitsve,* which is published by the community.
1914	Immigrates to America to escape anti-Semitism in Poland. His first published story, "Di geferlekhe froy" (The Dangerous Woman), appears in the fifteenth-anniversary issue of *Fraye arbeter shtime.*
1918	Begins studying law at New York University.
1919	Publishes his first poems, *1919, In roykh* (1919, In Smoke) and *Tirtl-toybn* (Turtle-doves), in the New York journal *Poezye.* Marries his first wife, Nettie.
1920	With N. B. Minkov and A. Leyeles, publishes a modernist manifesto about Introspectivism, which will lay the groundwork for the Inzikh movement in poetry.
1921	Publishes his first book of poetry, *Yankev glatshteyn.*
1923	Nettie becomes pregnant with their first child; Glatshteyn takes a job teaching at the Sholem Aleichem school in the Catskills but leaves after becoming romantically involved with one of his students.
1925	Begins his newspaper career as a columnist and editor of *Di naye varheyt.*
1926	Becomes a regular contributor to the daily *Morgn zshurnal;* publishes his journalistic writing under various pseudonyms. Becomes co-editor of the monthly journal *Loglen.* Publishes his second volume of poetry, *Fraye ferzn* (Free Verse).
1928–29	Edits the journal of the Introspectivists, *Inzikh.*
1929	Publishes *Kredos* (Credos), a third book of poems.
1933	Meets Fanny Mazel, a painter and sculptor, who later becomes his second wife.
1934–38	Serves on the editorial board of *Inzikh.*
1934	Travels to Europe to visit his dying mother. This journey inspires two books of prose: *Ven yash iz geforn* and *Ven yash iz gekumen.*
1937	Publishes his fourth book of poetry, *Yidishtaytshn* (Yiddish Meanings).
1938	Begins writing the column *Prost un poshet* (Plain and Simple) under his own name. Writes his famous poem "A gute nakht, velt" (Good Night, World).
1940	Wins the Lamed prize for *Ven yash iz gekumen.*
1943	Publishes *Gedenklider* (Memorial Poems), which includes "A

gute nakht, velt" and a cycle of poems about the Hasidic master Nachman of Bratslav.

1945   Begins writing a column in the journal *Yidisher kemfer* titled "In tokh genumen, arum bikher, mentshn, un zakhn" (In Essence: About Books, People, and Things). Co-edits the collection *Finf un zibetsik yor yidishe prese in amerike* (Seventy-five Years of the Yiddish Press in America).

1946   Publishes the book *Shtralndike yidn* (Radiant Jews), in which many of the poems address the Holocaust.

1947   Publishes his first book of criticism, *In tokh genumen: eseyen 1945–1947* (In Essence: Essays 1945–1947)

1952   Leaves his first wife and moves in with Fanny Mazel.

1953   Publishes a collection of poetry, *Dem tatns shotn* (My Father's Shadow).

1954–55   Co-edits the journal *Yidisher kemfer.*

1956   Receives a second Lamed prize for his collected poems *mayn gantser mi* (From All My Toil).

1957   His sixtieth birthday is celebrated in New York.

1960   A two-volume collection of his newspaper colum. lished titled *In tokh genumen.*

1961   Publishes a volume of poetry, *Di freyd fun yidishn vort* (The Jᵤ of the Yiddish Word).

1966   Receives the H. Leivick Prize and the Kessel Prize; is awarded an honorary doctorate from Baltimore Hebrew College. Publishes another volume of poetry, *A yid fun lublin* (A Jew from Lublin).

1967   Receives the Kovner award for *A yid fun lublin.*

1971   Dies suddenly on November 19 during the celebration of his seventy-fifth birthday. His last volume of poetry, *Gezangen fun rekhts tsu links* (Songs from Left to Right), is published just before his death.

Leksikon fun der nayer yidisher literatur, vol. 2 (1981); Janet Hadda, *Yankev Glatshteyn* (Boston: Twayne Publishers, 1980); Ruth Whitman, "The Man and His Work," in *The Selected Poems of Jacob Glatstein* (New York: October House, 1972); Jan Schwarz, "Yankev Glatshteyn," in *Dictionary of Literary Biography,* ed. Joseph Sherman (forthcoming).

Chaim Grade

1910   Born on April 4 in Vilna.

c. 1918–32   Studies in *yeshives* in Vilna, Bielsk, Olkenik, and Bialystok, and with the Navaredok *muser* movement. Spends seven years

	studying with the rabbi Hazon Ish. On his own, studies Hebrew, Yiddish, and world literature.
1932	Leaves the *yeshive* and publishes his first poems in *Vilner tog,* a daily newspaper edited by Zalman Reyzen. Becomes a member of the literary group Young Vilna.
1936	Publishes his first book of poems, *Yo* (Yes).
1939	Publishes his long poem *Musernikes.*
1941	Grade and his wife Frume-Liebe flee the Nazi advance. His wife returns to Vilna while he continues into the Soviet Union.
1941–46	Lives as a refugee in the southern provinces of Russia. His wife and mother perish in the Holocaust.
1945	Publishes a volume of poems, *Doyres* (Generations).
1946	Moves to Poland for six months; moves to France and becomes involved in Jewish cultural work in Paris.
1947	Publishes a book of poems, *Pleytim* (Refugees), written during the war.
1948	Comes to New York as a delegate to the Jewish Culture Congress. Travels and lectures in all the major Jewish communities in North America. Settles in New York and begins to work for the daily newspaper *Morgn zshurnal.* Publishes poems in *Tsukunft* and *Yidisher kemfer.*
1949	Publishes a book of poems, *Der mames tsvoe* (My Mother's Will).
1950	Publishes a book of poems, *Sheyn fun farloshene shtern* (Beauty of Extinguished Stars). Receives the Bimko prize from the Jewish Culture Congress for *Der mames tsvoe.*
1953	*My Quarrel with Hersh Rasseyner,* an English translation of his novella *Mayn krig mit hersh raseyner,* is published in *Commentary.*
1955	Publishes his autobiographical novel *Der mames shabosim (My Mother's Sabbath Days).*
1956	Wins the Lamed prize for *Der mames shabosim.*
1958	Publishes the prose collection *Der Shulhoyf* (The Synagogue Courtyard), which includes the novel *Der Brunem (The Well).*
1961	Publishes a novel, *Di agune* (The Abandoned Wife).
1962	Publishes a book of poetry, *Der mentsh fun fayer* (The Man of Fire).
1967	His novella *The Well* is published in English translation.
1967–68	Publishes his two-volume novel of *yeshive* life, *Tsemakh atlas.*
1969	Publishes a volume of poetry, *Oyf mayn veg tsu dir* (On My Way to You).
1970	Receives the Leivick and the Manger prizes.
1972	Publishes *The Seven Little Lanes,* an English translation of the third part of *Der mames shabosim.*

1974   Publishes *The Agunah* in English translation. A new book of stories, *Di kloyz and di gas: dertseylungen*, is published.

1976   *The Yeshiva* (2 vols.), an English translation of *Tsemakh atlas*, is published. Publishes *Der shtumer minyen*, a book of stories.

1980   Begins to serialize *Fun unter der erd*, a novel about the Vilna ghetto, in the *Forverts*. The publication of this work is interrupted by the author's death.

1982   *Rabbis and Wives*, a collection of stories in English translation, is published. Grade dies on June 26.

Leksikon fun der nayer yidisher literatur, vol. 2 (1981); "Chaim Grade," in *Encyclopedia Judaica* (Jerusalem: Macmillan, 1971); Inna Hecker Grade, foreword to *My Mother's Sabbath Days: A Memoir* (Northvale, N.J.: Jason Aronson, Inc., 1997); Curt Leviant, introduction to *The Agunah* (New York: Bobbs-Merrill, 1974); *Leksikon fun yidish-shraybers*, ed. Berl Kagan (New York: R. Ilman-Kohen, 1986).

Yitskhok-Leybush Peretz

1852   Born on May 18 in Zamosc, Lublin province.

1864–1967   Studies in *yeshives* in Zamosc and Shevershin.

1867   Peretz begins to read secular literature including novels, history, natural history, and physics in Polish, Russian, French, and German.

c. 1871   Marries Sarah Lichtenfeld, the daughter of a well-known *maskil* and Hebrew poet, Gabriel Yehuda Lichtenfeld. Moves to Sandomir, Radom province. Has a son who dies.

1871   Begins to write poetry in Hebrew.

c. 1873   Peretz's son Lucian is born.

1874   Compiles a handwritten volume of his Polish poetry titled "Wiersze różnej treści" (Poems on a Variety of Topics).

1875   Publishes his first Hebrew poem in Peretz Smolenskin's journal *Hashakhar*.

1876   Divorces his first wife, moves to Warsaw, and begins teaching Hebrew. Publishes more Hebrew poems in *Hashakhar*. Takes exams to become lawyer and begins practicing law.

1877   Publishes, with his former father-in-law, a collection of their Hebrew poems, *Sippurim bashir veshirim shonim* (Stories in Verse and Other Poems).

1878   Returns to Zamosc and marries Helena Ringelheim. Busy practicing law, Peretz begins an eight-year publishing hiatus.

1886   Briefly moves back to Warsaw in order to be closer to the community of Hebrew writers. Begins to publish Hebrew sketches and poetry in Nakhum Sokolov's *Ha'asif* and other Hebrew journals.

1887   Publishes the poem "Le'almah ha'ivryah vehi misnakrah" (To the Jewish Girl Who Renounces Judaism) in Sh. P. Rabinovitsh's *Knesset yisrael.*

1888   Publishes his groundbreaking long poem *Monish,* his first Yiddish work, in Sholem Aleichem's *Di yidishe folks-bibliotek.* Peretz's license to practice law is revoked after he is accused of revolutionary activities.

1889   Settles permanently in Warsaw.

1890   Publishes his first book of Yiddish stories, *Bakante bilder* (Familiar Scenes) as well as stories in the second volume of Sholem Aleichem's *Di yidishe folks-bibliotek.* Participates in a statistical and ethnographic expedition to small towns in the Tomashev region of Poland, organized by Jan Bloch, a Jewish Polish millionaire and convert to Catholicism.

1891   Edits and publishes the first volume of *Di yidishe bibliotek* (The Jewish Library), which is comprised of articles, novellas, poems, feuilletons, and criticism by contemporary Yiddish writers including Peretz himself. With the help of friends, secures a job as a record-keeper for the Warsaw Jewish Community Council, a post he will keep until the end of his life.

1892   The second volume of *Di yidishe bibliotek* includes his *Bilder fun a provints-rayze in tomashover paviat* (Pictures from a Journey in the Provinces), based on his participation in Jan Bloch's expedition. Writes a brochure titled *Ver es vil nisht, shtarbt nisht af kholere* (He Who Does Not Want to Need Not Die of Cholera) to educate Jews about hygiene and health issues during the cholera epidemic in Poland.

1893   Begins to publish stories in the American Socialist journals *Arbeter tsaytung* and *Tsukunft.*

1894   Begins editing and publishing *Yontev bletlekh* (Holiday Pages), a monthly Yiddish periodical with Dovid Pinski and Mordecai Spektor. In Hebrew, he publishes a book of love poems, *Haugav: shirei ahavah* (The Harp: Love Poems), and several stories. In Yiddish, he edits a collection titled *Literatur un lebn* (Literature and Life), in which his stories "Dos shtreyml" (The Fur Hat) and "Bontshe shvayg" (Bontshe the Silent) appear.

1895   Publishes the third volume of *Di yidishe bibliotek.*

1896   Due to financial constraints and threat of censorship, his journal *Yontev bletlekh* ceases publication.

1898   Peretz's father dies. Peretz publishes Jewish folk songs in the Viennese journal *Der Urquell.*

1899	Arrested in August at a lecture organized to benefit workers' causes. Spends two months in prison in the Warsaw Citadel. After his release, publishes his first neo-Hasidic tales in the Zionist weekly *Der yid* and the journal *Di yidishe familye*.
1901	Peretz celebrates his fiftieth year (according to another version of his birth date, May 25, 1851). The first collected editions of his Hebrew and Yiddish works are published in honor of his twentieth year of literary activity.
1903	Resumes writing in Hebrew. Publishes a Hebrew drama, *Khurban beit tsadik* (Destruction of a Hasidic Dynasty), which he later rewrites in Yiddish as *Di goldene keyt* (The Golden Chain).
1904	Begins writing *Folkstimlekhe geshikhtn* (Stories in the Manner of the People).
1905–1907	Writes reviews of the Yiddish theater productions in Warsaw, including plays by Dovid Pinski and Sholem Ash.
1906	One of Peretz's plays, *Der nisoyen* (The Temptation), an early variation of *Di goldene keyt,* is performed on stage. Peretz becomes the literary editor of the daily Yiddish newspaper *Der veg.*
1907	Publishes the first version of his famous play *Bay nakht afn altn mark* (Night in the Old Marketplace).
1908	Delivers the keynote address at the Czernowitz Conference on the status of Yiddish as a Jewish national language.
1909	Establishes a Yiddish theater studio.
1908–13	Ten volumes of his collected Yiddish works are published.
1913–14	Serializes his autobiography *Mayne zikhroynes* (My Memoirs) in the journal *Di yidishe velt*. Works for the Yiddish newspapers *Fraynd* and *Haynt*.
1914	After the outbreak of World War I, works on behalf of the Jewish refugees by establishing soup kitchens and an orphanage in Warsaw.
1915	Publishes his last story "Ne'ilah in gehenem" (Yom Kippur in Hell) in *Di yidishe velt*. In the last months of his life, he composes over one hundred childrens poems. Dies on April 3.

Nachman Mayzel, *Y. L. Perets: zayn lebn un shafn* (New York: IKUF, 1945); Shmuel Niger, *Yitskhok leybush perets* (Buenos Aires: Argentiner opteyl fun altveltlekhn kultur-kongres, 1952); Shmuel Niger and Yankev Shatski, *Leksikon fun der nayer yidisher literatur,* vol. 8 (1981); Zalman Reyzen, *Leksikon fun der yidisher literatur, prese un filologye,* vol. 2 (1926); Ruth Wisse, *I. L. Peretz and the Making of Modern Jewish Culture* (Seattle: University of Washington Press, 1991); Ken Frieden, *Classic Yiddish Fiction* (Albany: State University of New York Press, 1995).

Jonah Rosenfeld

1880	Born in Tshartorisk, Volin. Studies in *kheyder* until the age of twelve.
1893	Both his father and mother die of cholera. Interrupts his education at the Pohost *yeshive* and moves to Odessa, where his older brothers have arranged an apprenticeship for him with a turner.
1902	Shows some of his early writing to Y. L. Peretz who visits Odessa.
1904	With Peretz's help, publishes his first writing, "Dos lernyingl" (The Apprentice), in the St. Petersburg journal *Fraynd*.
1905	Leaves his work as a turner and devotes himself to writing literature.
1909	Publishes his first collection of stories, *Shriftn* (Writings), in which Rosenfeld's story "Konkurentn" (Competitors) appears.
1910	Publishes a book of short stories, *In di shmole geselekh* (In the Narrow Alleys).
1912	Publishes his first novel of working class life in the Odessa daily *Sholem-aleykhem* and a collection of novellas and stories, *Nakht un toyt* (Night and Death).
1914	Moves to Kovel. Settles in Kiev after the outbreak of World War I.
1919	Publishes a volume of stories and novellas, *Froyen* (Women). Moves back to Kovel.
1921	Immigrates to America, settles in New York.
1922	Publishes his first dramatic work, *Der shvartser shleyer* (The Black Veil), in the Yiddish daily *Forverts*. Over the next ten years writes several plays.
1924	Six volumes of his collected works are published in New York under the title *Gezamlte shriftn* (Collected Writings).
1927	Publishes the autobiographical *Er un zi* (He and She), which is subtitled "The Diary of a Former Writer."
1929	A collection of his writing titled *Geklibene verk* (Collected Work) is published in Vilna.
1935	A conflict arises between Rosenfeld and Abraham Cahan, the chief editor of the *Forverts*. The *Forverts* ceases to publish any of Rosenfeld's work.
1937	Is diagnosed with the stomach cancer that will eventually kill him and undergoes surgery; begins to write the autobiographical novel *Eyner aleyn* (All Alone).
1940	Publishes *Eyner aleyn*.
1944	Dies in New York on July 9.

Leksikon fun der nayer yidisher literatur, vol. 8 (1981); Nachman Mayzel, *Forgeyer un mittsaytler* (New York: IKUF, 1946); Shmuel Niger, introduction to Rosenfeld's *Geklibene verk* (New York: CYCO-bikher farlag, 1955); Jan Schwarz, "The Trials of a Yiddish Writer in America: Jonah Rosenfeld's Autobiographical Novel," *Prooftexts* 18, no. 2 (May 1998).

Sholem Aleichem (Sholem Rabinovitsh)

1859	Born March 3 in Pereyaslav, Poltav province (Ukraine). Grows up in Voronkov, which he later fictionalizes as Kasrilevke.
1872	Mother dies. Goes to live with his grandparents in Bohslov, Kiev province. Returns to live with his father and stepmother in Pereyashlav.
1873	Begins studying in the Pereyaslav Russian school.
1876	Graduates with distinction and gives lessons in Russian.
1877–79	Works as a private tutor in Sofiovka, Kiev province, for the daughter of a wealthy Jewish landowner, Elimelekh Loyev.
1879	Returns to Pereyaslav. Publishes his first Hebrew writing in *Hatsfira.*
1880	Begins working as the government rabbi in Luben, Poltav province.
1881	Publishes his first early Hebrew articles in *Hamelits.*
1883	Marries Olga Loyev, his former student, on May 12 in Kiev. Publishes his first Yiddish stories in Alexander Tsederboym's *Yidishes folksblat* and uses the pseudonym Sholem Aleichem for the first time. Loses his position as rabbi due to the influence of his father-in-law, who opposes his marriage. Moves for a short time to Belotserkov, Kiev province.
1884	Works briefly for the Kiev millionaire Brodsky. Publishes stories, feuilletons, articles, and poems in the Russian Yiddish press.
1885	Inherits a fortune after his father-in-law dies. Starts business ventures in Kiev. Spends summers in Boyarka, Kiev province, later fictionalized as Boyberik in *Tevye der milkhiker.*
1886	Publishes *Bilder fun der berditshever gas* (Street Scenes from Berditchev).
1887	Settles in Kiev. Publishes *Dos meserl* (The Pen-Knife), which earns him the critical attention of Simon Dubnov in the Russian Jewish journal *Voskhod.*
1888	Publishes the first volume of *Di yidishe folks-bibliotek* (The Jewish Popular Library), which includes some of the best Yiddish writing of the time, such as Y. L. Peretz's debut poem, *Monish,* and Mendele's *Dos vintshfingerl.* The volume also includes his

first novel, *Stempenyu*. Publishes his novel *Sender blank* in the *Yidishes folksblat* as well as *Shomer's mishpet* (The Trial of Shomer). Travels to Odessa to meet with Jewish writers Ravnitsky, Abramovitsh, and Dubnov. Father dies, and Sholem Aleichem publishes a small volume of poems in his memory.

1889   Publishes the novel *Yosele solovey* (Yosele the Nightingale) in the second volume of *Di yidishe folks-bibliotek*.

1890–91 Loses his fortune in the Kiev stock market and travels to Odessa, Paris, Vienna, and Czernowitz. Returns to Odessa after his mother-in-law settles his debts.

1892   Under various pseudonyms, publishes a number of stories, including *London,* the first in a series of letters between his characters Menakhem-Mendl and Sheyne-Sheyndl.

1893   Returns to Kiev and becomes involved in business on the stock exchange.

1894   Publishes for the first time in American journals, *Di toyb* (Pittsburgh) and *Filadelfyer shtot tsaytung* (Philadelphia). Writes a satirical drama about the Kiev stock exchange, which is confiscated by the Russian censor.

1895   Publishes his first story about Tevye the Dairyman in Mordecai Spektor's journal *Der hoyz-fraynd*.

1896   Publishes the second installment of letters between Menakhem-Mendl and Sheyne-Sheyndl in *Der hoyz-fraynd*.

1898   Publishes several Zionist essays and fiction including "Oyf vos bedarfn yidn a land?" (Why Do the Jews Need a Land?).

1899   Publishes the second and third stories about Tevye and the third series of Menakhem-Mendl letters in the weekly *Der yid* (The Jew).

1902   Begins writing and publishing his *Ayznban-geshikhtes* (Railroad Stories).

1903   Becomes a regular contributor to *Der fraynd,* the first daily Yiddish newspaper in Russia. Publishes the play *Tseseyt un tseshpreyt* (Scattered to the Winds), the novel *Moshkele ganev* (Moses the Thief), as well as a number of stories. The first collection of his Yiddish works appears. Edits a collection, *Hilf* (Help), to benefit survivors of the Kishinev pogrom. Translates three Tolstoy stories from Russian into Yiddish for the book.

1904   Publishes a brochure on the life and work of Theodor Herzl. Meets the Russian writer Maxim Gorky and, for the first time, meets I. L. Peretz in Warsaw. Continues to publish Tevye and Menakhem-Mendl stories.

1905   Travels to Vilna, Kovno, Riga, Lodz, and other cities to give readings of his work. *Tseseyt un tseshpreyt* is performed for the first time by a Warsaw Polish theater company. Establishes a Yiddish theater company in Odessa. Meets Y. D. Berkovitsh, his future son-in-law, in Vilna, with whom he will collaborate for the rest of his life. Leaves Russia with his family (wife, four daughters, and two sons) after surviving the Kiev pogrom, never to return to Eastern Europe, except for two trips to Russia in 1908 and 1914.

1906   Begins a period of wandering that will continue until the end of his life. Lives in Lemberg, Geneva, and London; travels to Galicia, Bukovina, Vienna, Romania, Switzerland, Belgium, and Paris to give public readings of his work. Arrives in New York in October.

1907   Returns to Geneva after failing as a writer and dramaturge in New York. Publishes the first part of *Motl peyse dem khazns* (Motl the Son of Cantor Peyse), and adapts some of his earlier fiction for the theater. Acts as a delegate to the Zionist Congress in The Hague, and publishes his reflections *Kongres bilder* (Congress Scenes). Meets with Kh. N. Bialik in Geneva.

1908   Celebrates his twenty-fifth anniversary as a Yiddish writer. Writes his comedy *Der oytser* (The Treasure). Goes on a lecture tour of Russia. While touring, becomes severely ill with tuberculosis and goes to Italy to recuperate.

1909   Celebrates his fiftieth birthday. His major Yiddish works are collected in three volumes, including Menakhem-Mendl's letters and Tevye's monologues. His writing begins to appear in Russian translation.

1910   Y. D. Berkovitsh begins to translate his work into Hebrew.

1910–13   Lives in Italy, Switzerland, and Germany. An eight-volume Russian translation of his work is published in Moscow.

1913   Publishes a complete volume of Menakhem-Mendl letters. An English translation of *Stempenyu* is published.

1914   Dramatizes *Tevye der milkhiker.* A German translation of his collected stories appears. Goes on his last lecture tour of Russia. After the outbreak of World War I, flees with his family to Copenhagen. A few months later he travels to New York. He is received enthusiastically at Cooper Union and Carnegie Hall. His oldest son Misha dies in Copenhagen.

1915   Lives in New York and contributes to the New York Yiddish press. Writes the comedy *Dos groyse gevins* (The Grand Prize). Publishes *Funem yarid (From the Fair)*, his autobiographical novel.

1916   Dies on May 13 in New York. Hundreds of thousands attend his funeral.

Sholem aleykhem bukh, ed. Y. D. Berkovitsh (New York: Farlag ikuf, 1926); Nach-
man Mayzel, *Undzer sholem-aleykhem* (Warsaw: Yidish Bukh, 1959); Dan Miron,
"Shalom Aleichem," in *Encyclopedia Judaica* (Jerusalem: Macmillan, 1971);
David Roskies, "Mythologist of the Mundane: Sholem Aleichem," in *A Bridge of
Longing* (Cambridge, Mass.: Harvard University Press, 1995); *Leksikon fun der
nayer yidisher literatur,* vol. 8 (1981); Ken Frieden, *Classic Yiddish Fiction* (Albany:
State University of New York Press, 1995).

Isaac Bashevis Singer

1904	Born on July 14 in Leoncin, Poland.
1908	Family moves to number 10 Krochmalna Street, Warsaw, where his father serves as rabbi.
1917	Moves with his mother and younger brother Moyshele to the town of Bilgoray in southern Poland, his mother's hometown.
1918	Becomes a Hebrew teacher at a secular school for boys and girls in Bilgoray.
1921	Enrolls at a rabbinical seminary in Warsaw; returns to Bilgoray after a year.
1923	Moves back to Warsaw permanently and is introduced for the first time to the Yiddish Writers' Club in Tlomatske 13, Warsaw.
1924	Becomes a proofreader for the journal *Literarishe bleter.* Publishes his first critical article under the pseudonym Yitskhok Tsvi.
1925	Publishes his first work of fiction, the short story *Af der elter* (In Old Age), in *Literarishe bleter,* for which he wins a prize. Adopts his mother's name Bashevis (Batsheva) as his pen name on the story "Vayber" (Women). Publishes two Hebrew stories in *Ha-yom.*
1925–32	Publishes short stories and novellas in the Warsaw Yiddish press.
1927	Publishes a manifesto on literary realism, *Verter oder bilder* (Words or Pictures).
1928	Translates two Knut Hamsun novels into Yiddish.
1929	Translates a German translation of Gabriele D'Annunzio's *Il piacere* (Pleasure) into Yiddish.
1930	Rokhl Shapira (Ronye) gives birth to his only son, Israel. Translates Erich Maria Remarque's *Im Westen nichts Neues (All Quiet on the Western Front)* and Thomas Mann's *Der Zauberberg (The Magic Mountain)* into Yiddish.
1932	Launches the Yiddish journal *Globus* with the Yiddish poet Aaron Tseytlin. Publishes the critical article "Tsu der frage fun dikhtung un politik" (On the Question of Poetry and Politics).
1935	The Warsaw Yiddish Pen Club publishes his first novel, *Sotn in*

goray (Satan in Goray), which had originally been serialized in *Globus* (1933). Emigrates to America and begins writing for the Yiddish daily *Forverts*.

1935–36   Serializes his second novel, *Der zindiker meshiekh* (The Sinful Messiah), in the *Forverts*. He stops writing fiction for seven years.

1936–43   Publishes critical articles, interviews with writers, and popular science pieces in the *Forverts* under the pseudonyms D. Segal and Yitskhok Varshavski.

1937   Meets his future wife, Alma Wassermann, while working on a theater project in the Catskills.

1940   Marries Alma.

1943   Emerges again as Bashevis with two articles: in *Di tsukunft* titled "Arum der yidisher proze in poyln" (Concerning Yiddish Literature in Poland) and in *Svive* titled "Problemen fun der yidisher proze in amerike" (Problems of Yiddish Prose in America). Publishes four new short stories together with a re-issue of his novella *Sotn in Goray*. The book is introduced by Aaron Tseytlin.

1944   His brother, the Yiddish writer Israel Joshua Singer, dies suddenly.

1945   Publishes the famous story "Gimpl tam" ("Gimpel the Fool") in *Yidisher kemfer*.

1945–48   Publishes his third novel, the family chronicle *Di familye mushkat (The Family Moskat)*, in serialized form in the *Forverts*.

1950   *The Family Moskat* is published in English by Knopf, the first of his works to be translated into English.

1953   "Gimpel the Fool," Saul Bellow's translation of "Gimpl tam," is published in *Partisan Review*.

1954   His sister, the Yiddish writer Hinde Esther Kreitman, dies in London.

1955   Reunites with his son, Israel Zamir, whom he has not seen in twenty years.

1955–56   Serializes his autobiographical work *Mayn tatns bezdn shtub (In My Father's Court)* in the *Forverts*. It is also published in book form.

1957   The New York Yiddish Folksbine performs a successful stage adaptation of *Mayn tatns bezdn shtub*.

1958   *In My Father's Court* is published in English translation.

1960   Publishes the historical novel *Der knekht* (The Slave) in the *Forverts*.

1962   Publishes the story "Taybele un Humizah" (Taybele and Her Demon).

1963	Publishes the book of short stories *Gimpl tam un andere dertsey-lungen* (Gimpel Tam and Other Stories).
1963–65	Serializes his autobiographical work *Fun der alter un nayer heym* (On My Old and New Home) in the *Forverts*.
1966	Publishes the novel *Sonim: a geshikhte fun libe (Enemies: A Love Story)* in the *Forverts*.
1968	Publishes the story "Di kafeterye" (The Cafeteria) in *Di tsukunft*.
1970	Wins his first National Book Award, for the short story collection *A Day of Pleasure*.
1971	Publishes a book of short stories *Mayses fun hintern oyvn* (Tales from Behind the Stove).
1972	Publishes an English version of *Enemies: A Love Story*.
1973	A stage adaptation of *Yentl the Yeshiva Boy* is performed at the Brooklyn Academy of Music.
1974	Wins a second National Book Award, for the short story collection *A Crown of Feathers*. Publishes the autobiographical novel *Neshome-ekspeditsyes* (Soul-searching) in the *Forverts* and in English translation as *Shosha*.
1974–76	Serializes his autobiographical work *Gloybn un tsveyfl* (Faith and Doubt) in the *Forverts*.
1975	Is awarded an honorary doctorate from the Hebrew University in Jerusalem. Publishes a book of short stories, *Der shpigl un andere dertseylungen* (The Mirror and Other Stories).
1976	*A Little Boy in Search of God*, a translation of the first part of his autobiographical work, is published in English.
1978	Wins the Nobel Prize for Literature and delivers his acceptance speech in Yiddish. *A Young Man in Search of Love*, a translation of the second part of his autobiographical work, is published in English.
1979	*Lost in America*, the final translation of his autobiographical work, is published in English.
1979–80	Publishes *Figurn un epizodn fun literatn-fareyn* (Figures and Episodes from the Writers' Club), another autobiographical work, in the *Forverts*.
1982	Publishes *Di mishpokhe* (My Family) in the *Forverts*. Forty-seven of his stories, translated into English, are published as *The Collected Stories of Isaac Bashevis Singer*.
1984	Becomes a member of the Jewish-American Hall of Fame.
1985	A collection of his childrens stories is published in English as *Stories for Children*.
1986	Receives the Handel Medallion, New York City's highest award.
1990	Is elected to the American Academy of Arts, becoming the only writer in a non-English language to be a member.
1991	Dies on July 24.

Edward Alexander, *Isaac Bashevis Singer* (Boston: Twayne, 1980); Janet Hadda, *Isaac Bashevis Singer* (Oxford: Oxford University Press, 1997); David Neal Miller, *Bibliography of Isaac Bashevis Singer, 1924–1949* (New York: Peter Lang, 1983); David Roskies, "The Demon as Storyteller: Isaac Bashevis Singer," in *A Bridge of Longing: The Lost Art of Yiddish Storytelling* (Cambridge, Mass.: Harvard University Press, 1996); Khone Shmeruk, "Yitskhok Bashevis-Singer," in *Leksikon fun yidish-shraybers*, ed. Berl Kagan (New York: R. Ilman-Kohen, 1986).

Glossary

akeyde	the binding of Isaac in Genesis 22:1–24
ani maamin	article of faith
apikoyres	a heritic
balebos	master; the head of the household
bal-melokhe	craftsman
bal-tshuve	a Jew who chooses to become Orthodox
bar-mitsve	Bar Mitzvah, a celebration of a Jewish boy's reaching the age of obligation (thirteen years) to uphold Jewish law
bashert	destined
batlen	an idle and impractical person
besmedresh	*Beit Midrash,* house of study
beys-avodim	house of bondage
blote	mud; dirt
chutspe	impertinence, nerve
cohen	descendent of the High Priest who receives special honours in the synagogue
derekh hashas	the way of the Talmud; Orthodox Jewish practice
din-toyre	a court of Jewish law
divre-toyre	a sermon about the Torah
drash	an interpretation of a sacred text
edlkeyt	refined; noble
emese shikse	a genuine non-Jewish woman
fayf	whistle
gabe	*gabbai,* trustee or warden of a public institution, especially a synagogue
galitsianer	a Jew from Galicia
gazln	a thief
goles	diaspora
halakha	Jewish law

hasid	a member of various ultra-orthodox Jewish dynasties originating in Central and Eastern Europe in the late eighteenth century
haskalah	the Jewish enlightenment
hefker-yung	a lawless, wanton young person
hekhere fenshter	high society
heymish	homey, intimate
ile	a prodigy, a precocious child
inzikhist	introspectivist; a modernist poetic movement in Yiddish literature in the 1920s and 1930s
kaddish	a prayer said by a mourner
keyver-oves	the grave of ancestors
khazer	a pig
kheyder	a traditional Jewish school for children
khezhbn hanefesh	religious and spiritual stock-taking
khevre	friends; society; a gang
khumesh	the five books of Moses
khupe	wedding
kines	dirges
kise hakoved	the throne of God
kleyn yingele	a little boy
klezmer	musician
kolboynik	rascal
landsmanshaftn	a society of Jews from the same town in Central and Eastern Europe
lebnsbashraybung	life writing
lebnsgeshikhte	life history
lern yingl	apprentice
litvak	a Jew from the Baltic States, Lithuania and White Russia
loshn koydesh	the Holy tongue, Hebrew
makher	an important person
malekh hamoves	the angel of death
mame-loshn	the mother tongue, Yiddish
maskil	an exponent of the Jewish enlightenment
matseyve	a gravestone
mayne-loshn	language of invectives
melamed	a teacher in the traditional Jewish school for children (*kheyder*)
melokhe	a craft
meshugas	a crazy obsession
dos meydele	the girl
mikve	a ritual bath
misnaged	an opponent of the Hasidim

mizbeakh	an altar
moyfes	a sign
muser	ethical instruction
nign	wordless melody
nusekh	version, style
opfal	trash
oylem-ho'sheker	the world of lies
oylem-ho'emes	the world of truth
oytser	treasure
pardes	garden *(pshat, remez, drash, sod)*
parnes	an elected head of the community
parnose	livelihood
pilpul	hair splitting argument, particularly in Talmudic discourse
plonter	confusion
poeme	long poem
proster yid	vulgar, uneducated Jew
pshat	the literal meaning of a text
rebbe	a Hasidic rabbi
remez	the symbolic meaning of a text
roman	a novel; a romantic involvement
sabobones	superstition
shabesdik	Sabbath-like
sheygets	pejorative term for a non-Jewish male
shikse	pejorative term for a non-Jewish woman
shive	the seven days of mourning after the death of a person
shmues	a conversation
shrayber	a writer
shterntikhl	a decorated head covering for a woman
shtetl	a town with a Jewish community
shund	trashy literature
slikhes	the days of repentance before the Jewish new year, Rosh Hashana
sod	secret
soyfer	a scribe
takhles	practical matters
talmid-khokhem	a scholar of Jewish sacred texts
talmetoyre	Talmud Torah
tfiln	phylacteries
tikn	improvement
tish	a Hasidic rabbi's table and gathering place for his followers
ti'shebov	the ninth day of Av commemorating the destruction of the first and second Temples
tkhine	a penitential prayer in Yiddish for women

tohuvevohu	primordial chaos
tsadek	a holy man
tsore	trouble; plight
tsvoe	a will
vide	a confession
yeshive	Yeshiva; Talmud Academy
yeshive bokher	an unmarried yeshivah student.
yeytser-hore	the evil inclination
yidishkeyt	Jewishness
yikhes	ancestral origin
yizker	commemoration
yortsayt	anniversary of the death of family member
zeyde	grandfather
zikorn	memory
zkhus oves	the merit of ancestors
zogn vide	confessing

Notes

Introduction

1. David G. Roskies, "Yiddish Studies and the Jewish Search for a Usable Past," in *Yiddish in the Contemporary World: Papers of the First Mendel Friedman International Conference on Yiddish,* ed. Gennady Estraikh and Mikhail Krutikov (Oxford: European Humanities Research Center, University of Oxford, 1999), 30.

2. Edward W. Said, "Reflections on Exile," in *Reflections on Exile and Other Essays* (Cambridge, Mass.: Harvard University Press, 2000), 173.

3. Ruth Wisse, "The Yiddish and American-Jewish Beat," *Prooftexts* 21, no. 1 (Winter 2001): 137.

4. See Bal-Makhshoves (Isidor Eliashev), "Memuarn-literatur," in *Geklibene shriftn* 3 (1929), 58–70; Yankev Shatski, "Yidishe memuarn literatur," *Di tsukunft* 30 (August 1925): 483–88; Nachman Mayzel, "Di yidishe geshikhte un di yidishe literatur," in *Tsurikblikn un perspektivn* (Tel-Aviv: Perets farlag, 1962), 107; Yitskhok Rontsh, "Amerike in der memuarn-literatur," in *Amerike in der yidisher literatur* (New York: Rontsh bukh-komitet, 1945), 175–202. On critical works about the Jewish autobiography in English and Hebrew, see Marcus Moseley, "Jewish Autobiography in Eastern Europe: The Extent and Significance of the Phenomenon," chapter 7 in "Jewish Autobiographies in Eastern Europe: The Prehistory of a Literary Genre" (D. Phil. dissertation, Trinity College, Oxford 1990), 492–540; David G. Roskies, "The Forms of Jewish Autobiography" (Unpublished paper, 1987); Anita Norich, "The Family Singer and the Autobiographical Imagination," *Prooftexts* 10 (1990): 91–107; and David Assaf's introduction in *Journey to a Nineteenth-Century Shtetl: The Memoirs of Yekhezkel Kotik* (Detroit: Wayne State University Press, 2002).

5. Chana Kronfeld characterizes "Confessional literature" (diaries, letters, and autobiographies) as marginally canonical in her chart on the formation of modern Hebrew literature. See Chana Kronfeld, *On the Margins of Modernism: Decentering Literary Dynamics* (Berkeley: University of California Press, 1996), 228.

6. See Anita Norich, "Yiddish Literary Studies," *Modern Judaism* 10, no. 3 (Oct. 1990): 297–309.

7. See Benjamin Harshav, *Language in Times of Revolution* (Berkeley: University of California Press, 1993), for a definition of "the modern Jewish revolution": "This revolution, emerging from the internal responses of Jews to the challenges of history, brought about the total transformation of the Jewish people in the century of 1882–1982. . . . Such responses, implemented by many individuals and in many directions, resulted, on the one hand, in the creation of modern, secular Jewish literature and society and a Jewish state, and on the other hand, in assimilation to other languages and important contributions made by "Jews" and their descendants to general culture and science" (viii).

8. Ken Frieden expresses a similar intent in his *Classic Yiddish Fiction: Abramovitsh, Sholem Aleichem and Peretz* (Albany: State University of New York Press, 1995): "Today, in light of prevailing ignorance of Yiddish culture, the time has come to re-educate the educated" (xi).

9. Donald J. Winslow, *Life-Writing: A Glossary of Terms in Biography, Autobiography and Related Forms* (Honolulu: University of Hawai'i Press, 1995).

10. *Quarterly Review* (London, May 1809): 282, 386. See Annette Wheeler Cafarelli, *Prose in the Age of Poets: Romanticism and Biographical Narrative from Johnson to De Quincy* (Philadelphia: University of Pennsylvania Press, 1990), 204, n.83.

11. The Greek parts of the word autobiography derive from *auto* (combining form of *autos*, self), *bio* (combining form of *bios*, life), and *graphe* (substantive derived from the verb *graphein*, to write). See James Olney, "Autos*Bios*Graphein: The Study of Autobiographical Literature," *South Atlantic Quarterly* 77 (1978): 113–23.

12. See Y. Y. Schwartz, *Yunge yorn: Poeme* (Mexico: Kultur-komisye fun yidishn tsentral-komitet, 1952); Moyshe Kulbak, "Disner tshayld harold" (1933), in *Geklibene verk* (New York: CYCO-Bicher farlag, 1953), 229–68; Menachem Boreisho, *Der geyer. Kapitln fun a lebn* (New York: M. Boreisho, 1943); A. Leyeles, "Kholem tvishn volknkratsers," in *A yid afn yam* (New York: CYCO, 1947), 183–208.

13. See Nokhem Stutshkoff, *Oytser fun der yidisher shprakh* (New York: YIVO Institute for Jewish Research, 1950). Various sub-genres of Yiddish life-writing are listed here: "perzenlekher dokument; biografye; oytobiografye; lebnsgeshikhte; lebnsbashraybung; dos lebn; rayze-bashraybung; zikhroynes; memuarn; togbukh; vide" (personal document; biography; autobiography; life history; life writing; a life; travelogue; memoirs; diary; confession).

14. James Olney, *Memory and Narrative: The Weave of Life-Writing* (Chicago: University of Chicago Press, 1998), xvi.

15. See Paul John Eakin, *Fictions in Autobiography: Studies in the Art of Self-Invention* (Princeton, N.J.: Princeton University Press, 1985) and *Touching the*

World: Reference in Autobiography (Princeton, N.J.: Princeton University Press, 1992); *American Autobiography: Retrospect and Prospect*, ed. Paul John Eakin (Madison: University of Wisconsin Press, 1991); Phillipe Lejeune, *On Autobiography*, ed. Paul J. Eakin (Minneapolis: University of Minnesota Press, 1989); Paula R. Backschneider, *Reflections on Biography* (Oxford: Oxford University Press, 1999); *Mapping Lives: The Uses of Biography*, ed. Peter France and William St Clair (Oxford: Oxford University Press, 2002).

16. Paul John Eakin, "Introduction," in Philippe Lejeune, *On Autobiography*, xx.

17. Paul De Man, "Autobiography as De-Facement," *Modern Language Notes* 94 (1979): 921.

18. Ibid.

19. Karl J. Weintraub, "Autobiography and Historical Consciousness," *Critical Inquiry* 1 (June 1975): 821.

20. Cafarelli, *Prose in the Age of Poets*, 25.

21. See Georg Misch, "Conception and Origin of Autobiography," in his *A History of Autobiography in Antiquity*, vol. 1, trans. by E. W. Dickes (Westport, Conn.: Greenwood Press, 1973), 2.

22. See Karl J. Weintraub, *The Value of the Individual: Self and Circumstance in Autobiography* (Chicago: University of Chicago Press, 1978); Natalie Zemon Davis, "Fame and Secrecy: Leon Modena's Life as an Early Modern Autobiography," in *The Autobiography of a Seventeenth Century Venetian Rabbi: Leon Modena's Life of Judah*, ed. Mark R. Cohen (Princeton, N.J.: Princeton University Press, 1988), 50–70; Natalie Zemon Davis, *Women on the Margin: Three Seventeenth Century Lives* (Cambridge, Mass.: Harvard University Press, 1995), 5–62.

23. Jean-Jacques Rousseau, *The Confessions*, trans. J. M. Cohen (New York: Penguin Books, 1953), 17.

24. See Lejeune, *On Autobiography*, 3–31, 119–41.

25. See Elizabeth Bruss, *Autobiographical Acts: The Changing Situation of a Literary Genre* (Baltimore, Md.: Johns Hopkins University Press, 1976); Lejeune, "Autobiography and Literary History," in *On Autobiography*, 141–63.

26. Eakin, *Fictions in Autobiography*, 5.

27. J. W. Goethe, *Dichtung und Wahrheit. Aus meinem Leben*, ed. Siegfried Scheibe (Berlin: Akademie Verlag, 1970), 11.

28. Olney, *Memory and Narrative*, 406.

29. Ibid., 416.

30. Quoted in Marcus Moseley, "Life, Literature: Autobiographies of Jewish Youth in Interwar Poland," *Jewish Social Studies* 7, no. 3 (Spring/Summer 2001): 22.

31. Benjamin Harshav, *The Meaning of Yiddish* (Berkeley: University of California Press, 1990), 143.

32. Ibid., 155.

33. Misch, *A History of Autobiography in Antiquity*, 4.

34. Bal-Makhshoves, "Undzer memuarn literatur" (1910), in *Geklibene shriftn* 3 (Warsaw 1929), 59.

35. Yankev Shatski, "Yidishe memuarn literatur," *Tsukunft* (April 1925): 483.

36. Nachman Mayzel, "Di yidishe geshikhte un di yidishe literatur" (1940), in *Tsurikblikn un perspektivn* (Tel-Aviv: Peretz farlag, 1962), 92.

37. Yekhezkel Kotik, *Journey to a Nineteenth-Century Shtetl,* 103; *Mayne zikhroynes* (Warsaw: A Gitlin, 1913), 5. See also David Assaf's introduction to *Journey to a Nineteenth Century-Shtetl,* 15–98.

38. See "Doktor yankev shatski vegn zikh aleyn," in *Shatski-bukh* (New York: YIVO Institute for Jewish Research, 1958), 109–38.

39. Bal-Makhshoves, "Undzer memuarn literatur," 69.

40. Mayzel, "Di yidishe geshikhte," 104.

41. *Never Say Die! A Thousand Years of Yiddish in Jewish Life and Letters,* ed. Joshua A. Fishman (The Hague: Mouton, 1981), 33, n.13.

42. *Memuarn, filosofye, forshung,* ed. Shmuel Rozshanski (Buenos Aires: YIVO Institute for Jewish Research, 1984), 8.

43. Yankev Shatski, review of *Memoirs of My People* by Leo W. Schwarz, *YIVO-Bleter* 23 (1944): 389.

44. Two exceptions are included in this study: Jonah Rosenfeld, *Eyner aleyn,* and I. B. Singer, *Love and Exile.* See chapters 3 and 5.

45. Y. L. Peretz, *Ale verk,* vol. 11 (New York: CYCO, 1948), 5. "Before he prays, the pious Jew goes to the ritual bath to wash his sins away. The writer does this spiritually before he writes. Except for the 'modern' writer, who parades his sinfulness, or invents it if he hasn't got as much as the market demands, fleshing out possibilities that didn't have time to develop on their own" (*I. L. Peretz Reader,* ed. Ruth R. Wisse [New York: Schocken Books, 1990], 265).

46. Regionalism and regional differences in Yiddish literature have not been studied in a systematic and comprehensive way. See Seth L. Wolitz and Joseph Sherman, "Bashevis Singer as a Regionalist of Lublin Province," in *The Hidden Isaac Bashevis Singer,* ed. Seth L. Wolitz (Austin: University of Texas Press, 2002), 219–24.

47. The main bibliographical source for Yiddish life-writing is E. Lifschutz, *Bibliography of American and Canadian Jewish Memoirs and Autobiographies* (New York: YIVO Institute for Jewish Research, 1970). The bibliography lists 353 works in Yiddish, English, and Hebrew written by Central and Eastern European Jewish immigrants to the U.S. and Canada. Lifschutz has excluded "Memoirs with a too close relationship to fiction" (3). The most comprehensive bibliography of Yiddish life-writing is the National Yiddish Book Center's list labelled BI, "Biography, Autobiography, Memoirs." It includes literary autobiographies, biographies, reminiscences, diaries, and other kinds of life-writing by professional and non-professional writers (47 pages, approximately 850 titles).

48. *Awakening Lives: Autobiographies of Jewish Youth in Poland before the Holocaust,* ed. Jeffrey Shandler (New Haven, Conn.: Yale University Press,

2002); Moseley, "Life, Literature: Autobiographies of Jewish Youth in Interwar Poland."

49. See Anita Norich, "Jewish Literature and Feminist Criticism," and Kathryn Hellerstein, "Gender Studies and Yiddish Literature," in *Gender and Text in Modern Hebrew and Yiddish Literature,* ed. Naomi B. Sokoloff, Anne Lapidus Lerner, and Anita Norich (New York: Jewish Theological Seminary, 1992), 1–15, 249–56. For a survey of Yiddish life-writing by women: Nachman Shemen, *Batsiung tsu der froy loyt tanakh, talmud, ya'ades un literatur shtudyes* (The Woman's Place in Law, Letter and Lore), vol. 2 (Buenos Aires: YIVO, 1969), 395–425.

50. See Shmuel Niger, "Di yidishe literatur un di lezerin," in *Bleter geshikhte fun der yidisher literatur* (New York: Shmuel Niger bukh-komitet, 1985), 35–108, and Naomi Seidman, *A Marriage Made in Heaven: The Sexual Politics of Hebrew and Yiddish* (Berkeley: University of California Press, 1997), 3–15, 57–66. For recent literary historical analysis of Glikl Hamel's *Memoirs,* Dorothy Bilik, "The Memoirs of Glikl of Hameln: The Archaeology of the Texts," *YIDDISH* 8 (Spring 1992): 1–18; Khave Turniansky, "Vegn di literatur-mekoyrim in glikl hamels zikhroynes," in *Studies in Jewish Culture in Honor of Chone Shmeruk,* ed. Israel Bartal, Ezra Mendelsohn, and Chava Turniansky (Jerusalem: Zalman Shazar Center for Jewish History, 1993), 153–77; Zemon Davis, *Women on the Margin,* 1–61.

51. Maz Erik, *Di geshikhte fun der yidisher literatur fun di eltste tsaytn biz der haskole-tkufe* (New York: Altveltlekhn yidishn kultur kongres, 1979), 406.

52. Israel Zinberg, *A History of Jewish Literature,* vol. 7 (Cincinnati: Hebrew Union College Press, 1975), 246.

53. See Khone Shmeruk, "Medresh Itsik and the Problem of Its literary Traditions," in *Medresh Itsik* (Jerusalem: Magnes Press, 1984), v–xxix. For the influence of Max Weinreich's literary historical work on I. B. Singer see Dovid-Hirsh Roskes, "Maks vaynraykh: oyf di shpurn fun a lebedikn over," *YIVO-bleter* 3 (1997): 308–18.

54. See Chava Weissler, *Voices of the Matriarchs: Listening to the Prayers of Early Modern Jewish Women* (Boston: Beacon Press, 1998), and Jerold Frakes, *The Politics of Interpretation: Alterity and Ideology in Old Yiddish Studies* (Albany: State University of New York Press, 1989).

55. Chava Rosenfarb, "Feminism and Yiddish Literature: A Personal Approach," in Sokoloff, Lerner, and Norich, *Gender and Text in Modern Hebrew and Yiddish Literature,* 226. See Paula Hyman, "Memoirs and Memories: East European Jewish Women Recount Their Lives," *Conference Proceedings: Di froyen* (New York: Jewish Women Resource Center, 1997), 49–52. Hyman examines four Yiddish memoirs by women published after the Holocaust.

56. *I Keep Recalling: The Holocaust Poems of Jacob Glatshteyn,* trans. Barnett Zumoff (New York: KTAV Publishing House, 1993), 2–3; *Selected Poems of Yankev Glatshteyn,* trans. Richard J. Fein (Philadelphia: Jewish Publication Society, 1987), 101–4. I have combined these two translations except for a slight change in the last line.

57. Ruth R. Wisse, "Language as Fate: Reflections on Jewish Literature in America," *Studies in Contemporary Jewry* 12 (1996): 143. See, Wisse's analysis of the poem, 140–43.

58. David G. Roskies, "Yiddish in the Twentieth Century: A Literature of Anger and Homecoming," in *Yiddish Language and Culture: Then and Now,* ed. Leonard Jay Greenspoon (Omaha, Nebr.: Creighton University Press, 1998), 14.

59. Eli Lederhendler, "A Culture of Retrieval," in his *New York Jews and the Decline of Urban Ethnicity* (Syracuse, N.Y.: Syracuse University Press, 2001), 63–78; Sidra Dekoven Ezrahi, *Booking Passage: Exile and Homecoming in the Modern Jewish Imagination* (Berkeley: University of California Press, 2000), 200–220.

60. Joseph Sherman, "A Background Note on the Translation of *Yarme un keyle,*" in Wolitz, *The Hidden Isaac Bashevis Singer,* 188.

Chapter 1. Setting the Stage

1. Doris Lessing, *Under My Skin: Volume One of My Autobiography to 1949* (London: Harper Collins Publishers, 1994), 12.

2. Sh. Y. Abramovitsh, *Shloyme reb khayims, Gezamlte verk,* vols. 3–4, ed. A. Gurshteyn, M. Viner, and Y. Nusinov (Moscow: Emes Farlag, 1935–1940), 74.

3. Isaac Meir Dik, one of the most prolific nineteenth-century Yiddish writers, wrote his autobiography in Hebrew entitled *Mahazeh mul mahazeh* (Warsaw, 1861). The first biographical entries on Yiddish writers appeared in Nahum Sokolov's *Sefer zikaron le-sofrei yisra'el hakhaim itanu kayom* [A Memoir Book of Contemporary Jewish Writers] (Warsaw: Halter, 1889), including Abramovitsh's famous "Reshimot letoldotay" [*Sketches to My Biography*]. Sholem Aleichem presented small biographical entries on Sh. Ettinger, Abramovitsh, Aksenfeld, Goldfaden, and others in *Di yidishe folks-bibliotek* (Kiev, 1888), 250–59. This publication also included a short fictionalized autobiography by Y. Y. Linetski entitled "Der vorem in khreyn" (The Worm in Horseradish), 62–92. In 1909, Linetski published a short autobiographical account entitled *Funem yarid, a fantazye tsu mayn zibetsik-yorikn geburtstog* (*From the Fair: A Fantasy in Honor of My Seventieth Birthday*). In this piece, Linetski argued that "heroysfirn dem naketn 'ikh' farn publikum" (to expose the naked "I" for the audience) contradicted his artistic credo. See also Dan Miron, *A Traveler Disguised* (New York: Schocken, 1973), 86, and Y. Y. Linetski, *Funem yarid* (Odessa, 1909), 2–3.

4. The first part of Linetski's *Dos poylishe yingl* was originally serialized in *Kol mevaser* 16–44 (1867) and later published in book form together with the second part in *Kol mevaser* (Odessa, 1869). Gintsburg (1795–1846) began to write his autobiography *Aviezer* in 1828; it was published posthumously in 1864 in Vilna.

5. See Alan Mintz, *"Banished from Their Father's Table": Loss of Faith and Hebrew Autobiography* (Bloomington: Indiana University Press, 1989), 1–55, and Marcus Moseley, "Jewish Autobiographies in Eastern Europe," 49–108.

6. Maimon's *Lebensgeschichte, von ihm selbst geschrieben* was published in Berlin in 1792. It is available in an excellent Yiddish translation by A. Y. Goldschmidt, *Shloyme maymons lebensgeshikhte, geshribn fun im aleyn* (Vilna: Farlag "Tomor," 1927).

7. Mintz, *"Banished from Their Father's Table,"* 203.

8. Hebrew literature is estimated to have had a reading audience of one hundred thousand readers of a Jewish population in Eastern Europe of five million in 1887. See Dan Miron, "100,000 Readers: Haskalah Literature Ventures Out" [Hebrew] *Etmol* 10 (1985): 6–8. On the mass audience for Yiddish literature in the nineteenth century see Miron, *A Traveler Disguised,* 3, 270, n.7.

9. Miron points out that Sholem Aleichem single-handedly created the myth of a Yiddish literary tradition by naming Sholem Yankev Abramovitsh the *zeyde* (grandfather) and himself *eynikl* (grandchild) of Yiddish literature in his articles from 1888. See *A Traveler Disguised,* 26–33.

10. Ibid., 79. Berditshevski's article entitled "Far dem tararam" (Before the Tumult Began) is included in *Yidishe ksovim fun a vaytn korev,* vol. 2 (New York, 1951), 195–98.

11. In his book on Hebrew autobiography, Alan Mintz includes readings of Mordechai Ze'ev Feierberg's *Le'an* (1899, Wither), M. Berditshevski's *'Urva parah* (1899–1900, A Raven Flies), and Y. Brenner's *Bahoref* (1902–1903, In Winter), in addition to Lilyenblum's and Gintsburg's autobiographies.

12. The first version of William Wordsworth's poetic autobiography *The Prelude* was written 1799–1805 and published in 1850 after the poet's death. J. W. Goethe's *Dichtung und Warheit* was published 1807–1831.

13. See Yekhezkel Kotik, *Mayne zikhroynes* (1913); Abraham Cahan, *Bleter fun mayn lebn* (1926–1931); Y. Y. Singer, *Fun a velt vos iz nishto mer* (1946); Y. Y. Trunk, *Poyln: zikhroynes un bilder* (1944–1953); and literary memoirs such as Avrom Reyzen, *Epizodn fun lebn* (1929–1935) and Melekh Ravitsh, *Dos maysebukh fun mayn lebn* (1962–1975).

14. Sholem Aleichem first mentioned his plan for an autobiography in a letter to the Yiddish writer Mordechai Spektor in 1895. See David G. Roskies, "Unfinished Business: Scholem Aleichem's *From the Fair,*" *Prooftexts* 6 (1986): 65–78.

15. Yitskhok Rontsh similarly noticed the incomplete character of the Yiddish memoir due to the premature death of the writer: "It is a shame that a number of memoir writers start too late and thus do not succeed in finishing their work. The Angel of Death interferes and—the end; or the memoirs remain in manuscript and it is not possible to publish them" (*Amerike in der yidisher literatur,* 188).

16. See Abramovitsh, *Sketches to My Biography:* "To teach the people good taste and science; to include folk life in literary works in order to make the people appreciate it; to develop and be useful—these three things were for me the right goal towards which the writer ought to aim." *Dos mendele bukh,* ed. Nachman Mayzel (New York: Yidisher kultur farband, 1959), 25.

17. David Aberbach, *Realism, Caricature and Bias: The Fiction of Mendele Mocher Sefarim* (London: The Littman Library, 1989), 37. Michael returned to Judaism after the Bolshevik revolution in 1917.

18. See Shmuel Niger, *Mendele moykher-sforim. Zayn lebn, zayne gezelshaft-lekhe un literarishe oyftuungen* (Mendele Moykher-Sforim: His Life, His Social and Literary Achievements) (Chicago: L. M. Stein, 1936; New York, 1970), 164–75.

19. The Hebrew stories published in this period (1886–1896) can be found in *Kol kitvei Mendele Moykher Sforim* (Tel-Aviv: Dvir, 1947), 377–447.

20. Sokolov's book inaugurated the bio-biographical encyclopaedia in Jewish Eastern Europe together with Sholem Aleichem's biographies of Jewish writers in his *Yidishe folks-bibliotek* (Kiev, 1888).

21. Miron, *A Traveler Disguised*, 13.

22. See Ruth Wisse: "Not the '*Pintele Yid*' but the Full-Fledged Jew," *Prooftext* 15, no. 1 (January 1995): 33–63.

23. Steve J. Zipperstein, *Elusive Prophet: Ahad Ha'am and the Origin of Zionism* (Berkeley: University of California Press, 1993), 71. For more information about Abramovitsh's literary circle in Odessa see, Simon Dubnov, "Undzer literarish kreyzl in odes" (Our Literary Circle in Odessa), in *Dos bukh fun mayn lebn* (The Book of My Life), vol. 1 (Buenos Aires: Altveltlekher yidisher kultur kongres, 1962–1963), 231–41.

24. Steve J. Zipperstein, "Remapping Odessa," in his *Imagining Russian Jewry: Memory, History, Identity* (Seattle: University of Washington Press, 1999), 63–87. The quotation is from 81. Zipperstein mentions that only one woman, Maria Saker, belonged to the group.

25. Ibid., 66.

26. Ibid., 83.

27. *Shriftn, ershter band*, ed. Nokhem Shtif (Kiev, 1928), 274. The letter was written in Yiddish.

28. Yiddish literary scholars A. Gurshteyn and Shmuel Niger both mention Abramovitsh's letter to Sholem Aleichem in their analysis of *Shloyme reb khayims*. See A. Gurshteyn, "Vegn Shloyme reb khayims," in *Gezamlte verk fun mendele*, vol. 4 (Moscow: Farlag Emes: 1935), 7–45, and Niger, *Mendele moykher-sforim*, 241.

29. Max Weinreich, "Mendeles eltern un mitkinder," *YIVO-bleter* 6 (1937): 270–86. See the entries about Mendele in *Leksikon fun der nayer yidisher literatur*, 8 vols. (1956–1981), and *Leksikon fun der yidisher literatur, prese un filologye*, 4 vols. (1926–1929).

30. The letter *K* refers to Abramovitsh's home town Kapulie in the province of Minsk, Lithuania. In the English translation of the work in *A Shtetl and Other Yiddish Novellas*, ed. Ruth R. Wisse (Detroit: Wayne State University Press, 1973), the editor decided to use the actual name of the *shtetl:* "The author probably withheld the actual name of his town, in the style of those years, to maintain a

certain discretion and distance, which time and circumstance have now assured" (276). However, the original designation of the town—the anonymous letter *K*—accurately represents the work's focus on the typical social and ethnographic characteristics of the *shtetl*. This is also the case in the Hebrew version of the work in which the *shtetl* is called Dalfona, or Paupersville.

31. For a psychoanalytic reading of Abramovitsh's work, see David Aberbach, *Realism, Caricature, and Bias: The Fiction of Mendele Mocher Sefarim* (London: The Littman Library, 1993), chapter 5. Aberbach mentions that, in addition to the loss of his father, "the formative years from adolescence to early manhood (c. 1848–56)" were marked by two other major tragedies: Abramovitsh's divorce and the loss of his two children. Aberbach argues that, as a result of his wanderings, loneliness, and hardships, Abramovitsh's writing became shaped by a) a strong feeling for and identification with children; b) hatred of authority; and c) empathy with grown-ups in a state of delayed adolescence. See also David Aberbach, *Surviving Trauma: Loss, Literature and Psychoanalysis* (New Haven, Conn.: Yale University Press, 1989).

32. Mayzel, *Dos mendele bukh*, 24.

33. Philippe Lejeune, "Autobiography in the Third Person," *New Literary History* 9 (1977): 42.

34. Ibid., 41.

35. Lejeune, *On Autobiography*, 42.

36. Mendele's role as publisher of Reb Shloyme's account was emphasized when it was first serialized in *Der yid* with the title: *Shloyme reb khayims (in lite), eyn alte mayse: Gedrukt behasdoles mendele moykher sforim* (Shloyme Son of Khayim [in Jewish Lithuania], an Old Story: Printed through the Mediation of Mendele Moykher Sforim).

37. I refer to the Soviet edition of Abramovitsh' work, *Gezamlte verk*, vols. 3–4, ed. A. Gurstheyn, M. Viner, and Y. Nusinov (Moscow: Farlag Emes, 1935–1940).

38. Ibid., 64.

39. For a reading of *Shloyme reb khayims* that examines its gender politics related to Abramovitsh's bilingualism see, Naomi Seidman, *A Marriage Made in Heaven: The Sexual Politics of Hebrew and Yiddish* (Berkeley: University of California Press, 1997), 57–66.

40. Abramovitsh, *Gezamlte verk*, 62.

41. Ibid., 70.

42. Ibid.

43. The title of James Olney's book from 1972, *Metaphors of Self* (Princeton, N.J.: Princeton University Press, 1972).

44. Abramovitsh, *Gezamlte verk*, 71.

45. Marcus Moseley, "Life, Literature: Autobiographies of Jewish Youth in Interwar Poland," *Jewish Social Studies* 7, no. 3 (Spring/Summer 2001): 3. Tolstoy's autobiography of his childhood and youth published in three parts

(1852–1857) was his literary debut. The first part was published when he was only twenty-four.

46. Abramovitsh, *Gezamlte verk*, 77.

47. See also Mendele's comparison of Reb Shloyme with a natural scientist *Gezamlte verk*, 54.

48. Ibid., 77.

49. In 1908, Abramovitsh returned to Odessa (Niger, *Mendele moykher-sforim*, 213–15). For discussion of the causes and character of the Odessa 1905 pogrom, see Patricia Herlihy, *Odessa: A History, 1794–1914* (Cambridge, Mass.: Harvard University Press, 1986), 304–8.

50. The Jewish autobiography as a mode of Rousseauian self-exploration in tension with the autobiographer's concern for his/her community is a recurrent trope in the scholarship on the Jewish autobiography. See Anita Norich, "The Family Singer and the Autobiographical Imagination," *Prooftext* 10 (1990): 92.

51. In a letter to Sholem Aleichem dated June 10, 1888, Abramovitsh characterizes *Dos vintshfingerl* as *a geshikhte funem yidishn lebn* (a history of Jewish life), N. Shtiff, *Shriftn, ershter band* (Kiev, 1928), 251. In *A Traveler Disguised*, Miron mentions that "this novel was to obey historical reality. It was not to be operated by the machinery of entertainment but rather motivated by the dynamics of history" (97).

52. Dan Miron, "Folklore and Antifolklore in the Yiddish Fiction of the Haskalah," in *Studies in Jewish Folklore*, ed. Frank Talmage (Cambridge: Cambridge University Press, 1980), 219–49.

53. Abramovitsh, *Gezamlte verk*, 102.

54. Ibid., 268. Second part.

55. See Richard N. Coe, *When the Grass Was Taller* (New Haven, Conn.: Yale University Press, 1984), 27.

56. Ibid., 7.

57. Ibid.

58. Ibid., 9.

59. See, A. Gurshteyn's introduction to Abramovitsh, *Gezamlte verk*, 34–35.

60. Ibid., 71.

61. Ibid, 64.

62. Ibid., 230. Second part.

63. See chapters 3, 4, and 5 about the life-writing of Yiddish writers Jonah Rosenfeld, Yankev Glatshteyn, and Chaim Grade.

64. See Moseley, "Jewish Autobiographies in Eastern Europe," 526–29. See also Coe, *When the Grass Was Taller*, 139–69.

65. Abramovitsh, *Gezamlte verk*, 220.

Chapter 2. A Whistle of Defiance

1. H. D. Nomberg, *Y. L. Perets* (Buenos Aires: Tsentral-farband fun poylishe yidn in argentine, 1946), 52.

2. Y. Y. Trunk, *Poyln: zikhroynes un bilder,* vol. 5 (New York: Farlag undzer tsayt, 1944–1953), 121.

3. Y. D. Berkovitsh, "A bizl geshikhte tsum bukh 'funem yarid,'" in *Sholem aleichem bukh* (New York: Farlag ikuf, 1926), 8. The full quote can be found in Shmuel Niger, *Sholem Aleichem: Zayne vikhtikste verk, zayn humor un zayn ort in der yidisher literatur* (New York: Yidisher kultur farlag, 1928), 164.

4. The Hebrew introduction to *Shloyme reb khayims,* entitled "Petichta demendele moykher sforim," appears in *Pardes* 2 (1894): 173–88.

5. See, Sholem Aleichem, *Tsu mayn biografye* (To My Biography), vols. 15–16 (New York: Folksfond oysgabe, 1923), 271–81.

6. See Berkovitsh, *Sholem aleichem bukh:* "I remember now how he a few months before his death, after a serious heart attack, asked the old professor Alfred Mayer half in jest, and half in a serious begging voice while gasping for air: 'Herr Professor, I have yet to write ten volumes, ten important volumes—will I be able to accomplish that?'" (12).

7. See Dan Miron, "Journey to the Twilight Zone: On Sholem Aleichem's Railroad Stories," in his *The Image of the Shtetl and Other Studies of Modern Jewish Literary Imagination* (Syracuse, N.Y.: Syracuse University Press, 2000), 256–57.

8. *From the Fair: The Autobiography of Sholom Aleichem,* translated, edited, and with an introduction by Curt Leviant (New York: Viking Penguin 1985). *Funem yarid: Lebensbashraybung, Ale verk,* vol. 15 (New York: Scholem-Aleichem folksfond edition 1925). *From the Fair,* xv.

9. See David Roskies, "Mythologist of the Mundane: Sholem Aleichem," in his *Bridge of Longing: The Lost of Art of Yiddish Storytelling* (Cambridge, Mass.: Harvard University Press, 1995), 147–90, and Ken Frieden, "The Grandson: Trials of a Yiddish Humorist," in *Classic Yiddish Fiction,* 103–35. See also David Roskies, "Unfinished Business."

10. Sholem Aleichem, *From the Fair,* 4; *Funem yarid,* 18.

11. See Sholem Aleichem's introduction to *Menakhem-Mendl, Ale verk,* vol. 10, 10–11. See also the discussion of the Sholem Aleichem figure in Miron, *A Traveler Disguised,* 80–94, and his *Sholem Aleykhem: Person, Persona, Presence* (New York: YIVO Institute for Jewish Research, 1972).

12. My analysis is indebted to Dan Miron's analysis of the Sholem Aleichem figure in *Scholem Aleykhem: Person, Persona, Presence.*

13. Sholem Aleichem, *Funem yarid,* 99; *From the Fair,* 185.

14. See, Dan Miron, "Bouncing Back: Destruction and Recovery in Sholem Aleichem's *Motl peyse dem khazns,*" *YIVO Annual of Jewish Social Studies* 17 (1978): 125–45.

15. Y. Y. Linetski, *Funem yarid: a fantasye af mayn zibetsik yorikn geburtstog* (Odessa, 1909).

16. Ibid., 2.

17. Sholem Aleichem, *Funem yarid,* 17; *From the Fair,* 4.

18. Berkovitsh, *Sholem aleichem bukh,* 10.

19. See, David Assaf's introduction to Kotik's *Journey to a Nineteenth-Century Shtetl*, 37–58. Assaf discusses Sholem Aleichem's letters to Kotik. The book includes translations of two of these letters from January 10 and 11, 1913, originally published in the second edition of Kotik's memoirs (Berlin, 1922).

20. For the text history of *Funem yarid*, see B. Slutsky and Y. Epstein, "On the Variants of Sholem Aleichem's *Funem yarid*," in *Zamlung fun kritishe artikln* (Kiev, 1940), 134–64, and "The Second Variant of Sholem Aleichem's *Funem yarid*," *Sovyetish: Literarisher almanakh* 12 (1941): 360–93. See also, Berkovitsh, "A bisl geshikhte tsum bukh 'Funem yarid,'" in *Sholem aleichem bukh*, 8–14. The most important changes between the *Hatsifirah* version and the handwritten manuscripts are the use of the first person and the omission of most place names. See Roskies, "Unfinished Business," 76–77, n.5.

21. *Briv fun sholem-aleykhem*, ed. Avrom Lis (Tel-Aviv: Y. L. Peretz farlag, 1995), 564.

22. Sholem Aleichem's letters to Shrira, in Lis, *Briv fun sholem-aleykhem*, 564–73.

23. See, Shmuel Niger's introduction "Fun farfaser," 5–17, in *Sholem Aleichem: Zayne vikhtikste verk*.

24. Lis, *Briv fun sholem-aleykhem*, 574. Assaf characterizes Yazkan (1874–1936) as a "controversial figure, mainly because of his arrogance and his businesslike approach to intellectual matters. He promoted the *Shund* literature and crassly interfered in the work of writers and journalist (including Sholem Aleichem) who published in his journals." See Kotik, *Journey to a Nineteenth-Century Shtetl*, 93, n.108, and Assaf's discussion of a letter from Yatzkan to Sholem Aleichem dated 8 June 1913 (57).

25. Mendele Moykher Sforim's "Fun mayn sefer hazikhroynes," *Di yidishe velt: literarish-gezelshaftlekhe monatshrift* 8 (August 1913): 3–11. Sholem Aleichem's "Lekh lekha (a naye mayse fun Tevye dem milkhikn)," *Di yidishe velt*, 3 (March 1914): 367–84. The unfinished second part of *Shloyme reb khayims* was serialized in *Der moment* in 1914. See A. Gurshteyn, "Tsu der tekst-geshikhte fun 'Shloyme reb khayims'," in *Gezamlte verk*, vols. 3–4, 349–54.

26. For a captivating description of Sholem Aleichem's dramatic flight, see Y. D. Berkovitsh, *Undzere rishoynim*, vol. 5 (Tel Aviv: Hamenora Publishing, 1966), 116–45. See also Sholem Aleichem's monologue, "Mayses fun toyznt eyn nakht" (written and published in 1915), based on stories by Jewish refugees from the war zone which Sholem Aleichem collected on board the ship to New York.

27. Berkovitsh, *Undzere rishoynim*, vol. 5, 181–89.

28. See Suzanne Vromen, "The Ambiguity of Nostalgia," in "Going Home," ed. Jack Kugelmass, *YIVO-Annual* 21 (1993): 70. See also Jean Starobinsky, "The History of Nostalgia," *Diogenes* 54 (Summer 1966): 81–103. Using Maurice Halbwachs's seminal work on collective memory, Vromen emphasizes the liberating potential of nostalgia in contrast to the more commonly held view of nostalgia as a sentimental, regressive, and anachronistic perspective on

the past. See Halbwachs, *On Collective Memory* (Chicago: Chicago University Press, 1992). For a discussion of the historical implications of Halbwachs's term "collective memory" for the study of Jewish memory, see Steve Zipperstein, *Imagining Russian Jewry*, 6–8.

29. See Wolf Rabinovitsh's memoir of his brother, Scholem Aleichem, *Mayn bruder sholem aleykhem—zikhroynes* (Kiev: *Melukhe farlag*, 1939), and Dan Miron, *Der imazhsh fun shtetl* (Tel Aviv: Y. L. Peretz farlag, 1981), 21–24. A new and shorter version of this essay was published as "The Literary Image of the Shtetl," *Jewish Social Studies*, n.s. 1, no. 3 (Spring 1995): 1–45.

30. See, Nokhem Oyslender's critical introduction to the Soviet edition of *Funem yarid, Ale verk*, ed. N. Oyslender and A. Frumkin (Moscow: Der emes, 1948), v–xxi.

31. See Berkovitsh, *Sholem aleykhem bukh*, 11.

32. "Scholem Aleichem provides, in ways web-like and plain, the exegetical groundwork for his literary successors: to race along behind his footsteps brings one quickly and intensely into a society an atmosphere, a predicament, and, more than anything else, a *voice*. The voice is monologic, partly out of deepest intimacy, a sense of *tête-à-tête* (with God or the reader), and partly out of verbal ingenuity, comedy, theatricality—even the sweep of aria." Cynthia Ozick, "Scholem Aleichem's Revolution," in *Metaphor and Memory* (New York: Alfred A. Knopf, 1988), 186.

33. See Miron, *A Traveler Disguished*, 82–86, which discusses this famous epitaph as it relates to *Funem yarid*. See Naomi Seidman's discussion of the epitaph in *A Marriage Made in Heaven*, 11–14. For a cultural historical perspective on the epitaph see David Roskies, "A Revolution Set in Stone: The Art of Burial," in his *The Jewish Search for a Usable Past* (Bloomington: Indiana University Press, 1999), 129. My translation of the poem is based on Naomi Seidman's English rendition.

34. Miron, *Der imazsh fun shtetl*, 88.

35. Sholem Aleichem, *Funem yarid*, 135 (book 1); *From the Fair*, 64.

36. Ibid., *Funem yarid*, 67 (book 2); *From the Fair*, 168. See also Shmuel Niger's discussion of this episode, *Sholem Aleykhem: Zayne vikhtikste verk*, 173–74.

37. Sholem Aleichem, *Funem yarid*, 226 (book 2); *From the Fair*, English, 254.

38. Hana Wirth-Nesher, "Facing the Fictions: Henry Roth and Philip Roth's Meta-Memoirs," *Prooftexts* 18, no. 3 (September, 1998): 259.

39. See Niger, *Sholem Aleykhem: Zayne vikhtikste verk*, 159.

40. See Y. Y. Singer's article *"Funem yarid"* (*Literarishe bleter* 23 [Oct. 10 1924]: 1), quoted in Anita Norich, *The Homeless Imagination in the Fiction of Israel Joshua Singer* (Bloomington: Indiana University Press, 1991), 89: "The best autobiographical memoirs, Singer suggested, were those 'through which a world emerged.'"

41. Paul John Eakin, *Touching the World*, 101.

42. See Miron, *A Traveler Disguised*, 83: "Abramovitsh's and Sholem

Aleichem's works are full of theatrical inner dialogues ('dialogues' because in them the consciousness is dramatized as two separate beings engaged in a discussion; 'theatrical' because in spite of being avowedly internal, they are reported as if actually staged, with gesticulations, descriptions of tone of speech, etc.)."

43. See Yankev Glatshteyn's interesting reading of Y. L. Peretz, *Mayne zikhroynes,* in "Peretses yerushe," in *In tokh genumen* (New York: Farlag matones, 1947), 487.

44. There exist only a few critical articles about Peretz's *Mayne zikhroynes.* In their discussions of the work, Yiddish scholars Yankev Shatski and Shmuel Niger primarily mined it as a cultural and historical source. The Yiddish literary scholar Nokhem Oyslender offered a Marxist reading of the work in the Soviet journal *Shtern* in 1935. He emphasized the realist elements of *Mayne zikhroynes* as central to Peretz's work originating in his early "radical" period in the 1890s. David Roskies, "A shlisl tsu peretses zikhroynes," *Di goldene keyt* 99 (1979): 132–59, views the work as an artistic credo that highlights the centrality of Peretz's symbolist works such as *Di goldene keyt, Bay nakht af der alter mark,* and the Hasidic tales written in the first decade of the twentieth century. Roskies's close reading does not discuss the work in the framework of the Yiddish autobiographical genre, except for some general remarks. See also, Yankev Shatski, "Haskole in zamoshtsh," *YIVO-Bleter* 36 (1952): 24–62, and "Perets un der yidisher folklore," *YIVO-Bleter* 18 (1946): 40–77.

45. I quote from *Mayne zikhroynes* in Y. L. Peretz, *Ale verk,* vol. 11, 95.

46. Peretz, *Mayne zikhroynes,* 5.

47. Ibid., 6.

48. Letter to Shmuel Niger, *Briv un redes fun Y. L. Perets,* ed. Nachman Mayzel (New York: IKUF, 1944), 342.

49. In Peretz's letters written in 1913 to Dovid Bergelson, Peretz expresses his admiration for the latter's novel *Nokh alemen* (When Everything Is Said and Done), which had just been published. See also Peretz's letters to Shmuel Niger about *Mayne zikhroynes* from the same time in Mayzel, *Briv un redes fun Y. L. Perets,* 337–42.

50. See Annette Wheeler Cafarelli, *Prose in the Age of Poets: Romanticism and Biographical Narrative from Johnson to De Quincey* (Philadelphia: University of Pennsylvania Press, 1990), 17. Cafarelli mentions Vladimir Nabokov's autobiography *Speak Memory: An Autobiography Revisited* (London: Weidenfeld amd Nicolson, 1967) as essentially expressing a Romantic view of biographical narrative: "thematic designs through one's life should be, I think, the true purpose of autobiography" (27). The primacy of art in shaping "a life" is similarly perceived in Nabokov's and Peretz's autobiographies.

51. Marcus Moseley notes that "From Lilyenblum on, the Haskalah novel becomes the palimpsest that may be discerned—albeit on occasion dimly— beneath the overwhelming majority of Hebrew autobiographical productions

of Jewish Eastern European provenance" ("Jewish Autobiographies in Eastern Europe," 512).

52. In a letter to Y. Tsinberg, Dec. 3, 1911, who had requested "biographical details" for the Jewish Russian Encyclopaedia, Peretz emphasizes his own independence which never had been disrupted by ideological attachment to the Haskalah, Hasidism, or assimilationism. He wanted to appear as the great Jewish intellectual figure following in the steps of the Biblical prophets: "I was never a Hasid and did not become a Maskil . . . but internally I remained a Jew with a Jewish, more or less clear, biblical world view" (Mayzel, *Briv un redes,* 321).

53. See Ruth Wisse, *I. L. Peretz and the Making of Modern Jewish Culture* (Seattle: University of Washington Press, 1991), 71–75. Wisse notices that "the silent exchange between mother and son stands as climax of his autobiography" (73).

54. For an interesting analysis of Peretz's relationship to Lichtenfeld and their collection of poems published in 1877, *Sipurim beshir veshirim shonim,* see Menashe Vakser, "Dos lebn fun a yidishn dikhter," *YIVO-Bleter* 12 (1937): 205–60.

55. Cafarelli, *Prose in the Age of Poets,* 16.

56. See "Vos felt undzer literatur," "Gedanken vegn literatur," and "Vegn der yidisher literatur" from 1910, in Peretz, *Ale verk,* vol. 7.

57. Glatshteyn, "Peretses yerushe," 487.

58. See Miron, *A Traveler Disguised,* 73.

59. Mayzel, *Briv un redes,* 139.

60. Ibid.

61. Ibid., 153–54.

62. Quoted by Khone Shmeruk, *Peretses yiesh vizye* (New York: YIVO, 1971), 200. The article was published on September 16, 1920, in *Forverts.*

63. Glatshteyn, *In tokh genumen,* 497.

64. Ibid., 487.

65. Ruth Wisse notes that this episode "would not have been out of place in rabbinic hagiography" (*I. L. Peretz and the Making of Modern Jewish Culture,* 71).

66. Peretz, *Mayne zikhroynes,* 42.

67. Ibid., 10.

68. Ibid., 37.

69. Peretz, *Di goldene keyt,* in *Ale verk,* vol. 6, 127.

70. Peretz, *Mayne zikhroynes.,* 147.

71. Ibid., 33.

72. Ibid., 96.

73. Reb Zisele (the name indicates the character's sweet, endearing character) in "Vos amol veyniker," a part of Peretz's short story "Yokhanan melameds mayselekh" (1897), is modelled on Rabbi Moshe Wahl (1797–1873). Y. L. Peretz, *Ale verk,* vol. 4 (1947), 66–75.

74. Peretz, *Mayne zikhroynes,* 81.

75. See H. D. Nomberg, *Y. L. Perets* (Buenos Aires: Dos poylishe yidntum, 1946), 65–67.

76. See Peretz's essay "Hofnung un shkrek" (1906), which paints a dark picture of a future socialist state. Y. L. Peretz, *Ale verk,* vol. 9 (1947), 101–4.

77. Yankev Reyman (1818–1894), see Yankev Shatski, "Haskole in zamoshtsh," *YIVO-Bleter* 36 (1952): 42–43.

78. Peretz, *Mayne zikhroynes,* 85, 89.

79. Ibid., 94.

80. The model for the temptress Marie sent by Lilith in Peretz's *poeme Monish* (1888). For a bilingual edition of *Monish,* see *The Penguin Book of Modern Yiddish Verse,* ed. Irving Howe, Ruth R. Wisse, and Khone Shmeruk (New York: Viking 1987), 52–84.

81. M. L. Lilyenblum's *Hat'ot ne'urim* was published in 1876. Bialik's autobiography *Safiah* (1908, Aftergrowth) and Peretz's *Mayne zikhroynes* clearly belong to a fundamentally different autobiographical discourse than the Rousseauian model employed by Hebrew autobiographers such as Lilyenblum and M. A. Gintsburg. This point is made by Alan Mintz, *"Banished from Their Father's Table,"* 19.

82. Four sages enter the mysterious orchard (*pardes*)—Tractate *Hagigah* 15.

83. See Gershom Scholem, "The Meaning of the Torah in Jewish Mysticism," in his *On the Kabbalah and Its Symbolism* (New York, 1965), 56–61.

84. Peretz, *Mayne zikhroynes,* 80.

85. Ibid., 97.

86. Ibid., 99.

87. Nomberg, *Y. L. Perets,* 63.

88. In his analysis of *Bay nakht afn altn mark,* Abraham Novershtern emphasizes Peretz's ambivalent relationship to modernism: "Nomberg limits the extent of the phenomenon by focussing on Peretz's struggle with decadent modernism at the turn of the century, claiming that he later 'freed himself' from its 'damaging influence.' Yet this struggle is evident during much of his life and culminates in *A Night in the Old Marketplace.* Here, in his most modernistic work, Peretz portrayed human existence *in extremis:* the intertwining of Eros and Death, so fervently adored by Romanticism, and Death and Redemption" ("Peretz and the Rise of Yiddish Modernism," *Prooftexts* 12 [1992]: 83).

89. Peretz, *Mayne zikhroynes,* 108.

90. Ibid., 118.

91. Ibid., 120.

92. Patricia Meyer Spacks, "Stages of Self: Notes on Autobiography and the Life Cycle," *Boston University Journal* 25, no. 2 (1977): 7–17.

93. Peretz, *Mayne zikhroynes,* 124.

94. In his analysis of *Mayne zikhroynes,* Mikhail Krutikov mentions that Jewish writers (Martin Buber, Pinhas Sadeh, Scholem Ash, Berditshevski, S. Ansky, and Ilya Ehrenburg) employed the whistle as a "symbolic device" based on modern adaptations of a popular Hasidic tale. Krutikov views the whistle as

a classification that "seeks to establish another closed order that protects the artist's world from disorderly reality." My reading emphasizes the whistle as representing the defiant character of Peretz's self-understanding. Rather than closing the artist's world view, it provides an opening in the neo-romantic epiphany at the end of the book. See Krutikov, *Yiddish Fiction and the Crisis of Modernity, 1905–1914* (Stanford, Calif.: Stanford University Press, 2001), 205–6.

95. Peretz, *Mayne zikhroynes*, ibid., 130.

96. Dan Miron, *Der imazsh fun shtetl*, 106.

Chapter 3. The Trials of a Yiddish Writer

1. Yitskhok Varshavski, "Jonah Rosenfeld and His Way in Our Literature," *Forverts*, 5 July 1964.

2. Yokhanan Tverski, "Yoyne rozenfeld (oyfn frishn keyver)" interview with Jonah Rosenfeld, in *Tsukunft* (September 1944): 553–57.

3. Y. E. Rontsh, *Amerike in der yidisher literatur* (New York: Y. E. Bukh komitet, 1945), 179. The works referred to are: Yankev Milkh, *Oytobiografishe skitsn* (New York: IKUF, 1946); Mordechai Dantsis, *Eygn likht* (New York, 1954); Peretz Hirshbeyn, *In gang fun lebn: zikhroynes* (New York, 1948); Isaac Raboy, *Mayn lebn*, 2 vols. (New York: IKUF, 1945–1947). To this list can be added Abraham Cahan's important five-volume memoir *Bleter fun mayn lebn* (New York: Forverts, 1926–1931) and Y. Y. Singer's *Fun a velt vos iz nishto mer* (New York: Farlag matones, 1946). See E. Lifschutz, *Bibliografye fun amerikaner un kanader yidishe zikhroynes un oytobiografyes af yidish, hebraish un english* (New York: YIVO Institute, 1970).

4. Ruth R. Wisse, "*Di yunge:* Immigrants or Exiles," *Prooftexts* 1 (1981): 58.

5. Moyshe Leyb Halpern, "*Di letste*," *Di goldene pave* (New York: Farlag matones, 1924), 140. The translation is by Nathan Glazer in *A Treasury of Yiddish Poetry*, ed. Irving Howe and Eliezer Greenberg (New York: Holt, Reinhart and Winston, 1969).

6. Nachman Mayzel, *Forgeyer un mittsaytler* (New York: IKUF, 1946), 281.

7. Kalman Marmor, review of *Eyner aleyn*, undated. Jonah Rosenfeld archive, YIVO Institute for Jewish Research.

8. Elizabeth Bruss, *Autobiographical Acts. The Changing Situation of a Literary Genre* (Baltimore, Md.: Johns Hopkins University Press, 1976), 13.

9. Undated, Jonah Rosenfeld archive, YIVO Institute for Jewish Research.

10. Jonah Rosenfeld, *Eyner aleyn, oytobiografisher roman* (New York: Maks N. Mayzel, 1940), 17.

11. For a historical survey of the anti-Semitic sentiments and pogroms in Odessa in this period see Patricia Herlihy, *Odessa: A History, 1794–1914* (Cambridge, Mass.: Harvard University Press, 1986), 299–304.

12. Abramovitsh, *Shloyme reb khayims*, chapter 12, 169.

13. A turner's craft consists of sculpturing wood and stone. Mayzel mentions the similarity between the turner's craft and Rosenfeld's continuous reworking of his stories. See *Forgeyer un mittsaytler*, 286.

14. A typical example is the story *Di konkurentn* (The Competitors) translated by Isaac Rosenfeld in Irving Howe and Eliezer Greenberg's *A Treasury of Yiddish Stories* (New York: Viking, 1953), 386–96. The original Yiddish story was published in Jonah Rosenfeld, *Gezamlte shriftn*, vol. 1 (New York: Jonah Rosenfeld komite, 1924), 235–55.

15. Mayzel, *Forgeyer un mittsaytler*, 275.

16. See Mayzel, ibid., 276, and Shmuel Niger's introduction to Rosenfeld's *Geklibene verk* (New York: CYCO-bikher farlag, 1955), 1–9. On Peretz's attitude toward the Jewish worker, see D. Pinski's autobiographical article, "Dray yor mit Y. L. Perets," *Di goldene keyt* 10 (1951): 5–31.

17. Jonah Rosenfeld, *Gezamlte verk*, vol. 5 (New York: Jonah Rosenfeld komite, 1924), 224. See also my article, "*A bintl briv* to 'The Editor of the Greatest Yiddish Newspaper in the World': Yoyne Rozenfeld's Conflict with Abraham Cahan, 1934–1944," *YIDDISH* 11, no. 1–2 (1998): 152–61.

18. For a similar depiction of the autobiographer's estrangement from both Jews and Gentiles, see Rosenfeld, *Eyner aleyn*, 223–29.

19. Ibid., 224.

20. The correspondence between Rosenfeld and Cahan is located in the Abraham Cahan archive in the YIVO Institute for Jewish Research. The 1937 letter from Rosenfeld to B. Vladek was published in *Epokhe* 35 (1948): 188–91.

21. Apparently, the check was by mistake sent to another Yiddish writer, I. J. Singer. See I. J. Singer's letter in the same issue of *Epokhe*, ibid., 191–92.

22. I have located the following Rosenfeld stories published in *Tsukunft* between 1937 and 1943: "Der nesoyen" (September 1937): 498–506; "Fun droysn" (February 1939): 9–14; "Tsvey veltn" (September 1939) 502–8; "In eynzamkayt" (February 1940): 87–92; "A mentsh trakht un got lakht" (July 1940): 372–77; "Ver iz ver" (April 1942): 215–19; "Dos iz shoyn gor a nayes" (March 1943): 150–56.

23. Unpublished letter in Jonah Rosenfeld archive, YIVO Institute for Jewish Research.

24. The depiction of the first conscious moments as a child typically introduces most Yiddish autobiographies. The following quotations are taken from autobiographies by Yiddish writers in America from the same period as *Eyner aleyn:* "The very first thing I find in my memory is a ripped old couch" (Abraham Cahan, *Bleter fun mayn lebn*, vol. 1, 1926, 12). "My memory leads me to my tender mother when I still spoke to her with my eyes, looking up at her eyes—because words had just started to bloom on my lips" (Peretz Hirshbeyn, *Mayne kinderyorn*, 1937, 7). "During forty eight years, that is, from the day I was two I see a sharp picture in front of my eyes, the first which was engraved in my memory" (Y. Y. Singer, *Fun a velt vos iz nishto mer*, 1946, 15).

25. Rosenfeld, *Eyner aleyn*, 130.

26. Ibid., 388.

27. On *shund*, see Khone Shmeruk, "Letoldot sifrut ha-shund b'yidish," *Tarbiz* 52, no. 2 (Spring 1983): 325–54.

28. In an interesting case of meta-discursive reflection the narrator argues that without the proper explanation of a particular religious ritual question— the rules for wearing *tfiln* (phylacteries) on *khalemoyed peysekh* (the interme- diary weekdays between the first two and last days of Pesach)—"the wider audience does not know what it is all about, [and] my work would have been in vain" (*Eyner aleyn*, 64). This example is only one of many details that char- acterize the book as a religious and cultural catalogue similar to *Shloyme reb khayims*.

29. See Tverski interview in *Tsukunft*, 554. In the few instances in which a Russian phrase is not translated, Rosenfeld sacrificed intelligibility for readers who lack knowledge of Russian in order, most likely, to avoid offending Yid- dish readers with explicit sexual language (see *Eyner aleyn*, 110–11). That this might very well be one of the reasons for Rosenfeld's unwillingness to translate particular Russian sentences into Yiddish is supported by Shmuel Niger's re- view of the book in *Der tog* (undated, Jonah Rosenfeld archive, YIVO Institute): "In some cases (for example, when the professional jargon of a prostitute is de- picted) the writer could have done fine without 'naturalistic' accuracy."

30. Rosenfeld, *Eyner aleyn*, 323.

31. Tverski, "Yoyne rozenfeld (oyfn frishn kever)," 554.

32. Rosenfeld, *Eyner aleyn*, 179.

33. Ibid., 288.

34. For an analysis of *The Mare*, see Ruth R. Wisse, *The Modern Jewish Canon: A Journey through Language and Culture* (New York: The Free Press, 2000), 330– 36. Dan Miron discusses *The Polish Lad* in comparison with Abramovitsh's work in *A Traveler Disguised*, 241–48.

35. See Estelle C. Jelinek, ed., *Women's Autobiography: Essays in Criticism* (Bloomington: Indiana University 1980), and Sidonie Smith and Julia Watson, eds, *Women, Autobiography, Theory* (Madison: Wisconsin University Press, 1998).

36. Tverski, "Yoyne rozenfeld (oyfn frishn kever)," 554.

37. Hillel Rogoff, a staff writer for the *Forverts*, pointed out that it was Rosenfeld's literary style, particularly "his convoluted language," that was the main reason for his exclusion from publication in the *Forverts*: "His style was distorted; his sentences long and confused. Even his admirers had to admit that it was necessary to force oneself to read him. Abraham Cahan, who believed that a writer's most important qualities were clarity and simplicity, and re- quired this from all his colleagues, could not allow the publication in the news- paper of such material, that Jonah Rosenfeld wrote" (Rogoff, *Der gayst fun for- verts* [New York: Forverts, 1954], 73).

38. A letter from Rosenfeld's widow, Khaye Rosenfeld, to the Yiddish critic

Gershon Sapozhnikow dated August 23, 1955, mentions a third part of Rosenfeld's autobiography: "Finally, more about his autobiographical writings: Among them, there is a manuscript of a couple of hundred printed pages, about his early years which has not yet been published. He worked on it during the last years of his life. And although he did not manage to finish it, it is nevertheless a whole, and according to my opinion, a very interesting and talented piece. I intend to publish it in a separate volume, independent of the other volume of Rosenfeld's selected works which wait for a publisher." This manuscript was never published. This typewritten manuscript (101 pages) is located in the Jonah Rosenfeld archive, YIVO Institute for Jewish Research. Khaye Rosenfeld's letter can be found in the same archive. An excerpt from this unpublished work entitled "Fun yoyne rozenfelds literarisher yerushe: Kapitlen funem oytobiografishn verk 'mayn kindhayt'" (From Jonah Rosenfeld's Literary Heritage: Chapters from the Autobiographical work "My childhood") was published in *Yidishe kultur* (November 1944): 14–19.

39. See Shmuel Niger, "Yoyne rozenfeld's oytobiografishe roman," *Der Tog* (undated); Kalman Marmor, "Yoyne rozenfeld's roman fun a lern-yingl" (undated); Hillel Rogoff, "Yoyne rozenfeld shildert tsvey yor fun zayn yugnt in odes," *Forverts,* June 16, 1940; L. Khrunikov, "Yoyne Rozenfeld vegn zikh aleyn" (1941). These reviews can be found in Jonah Rosenfeld Archive at the YIVO Institute for Jewish Research; in several cases without date and newspaper title.

40. Rosenfeld's *Geklibene verk,* edited by Chaim Grade and introduction by Shmuel Niger. A Hebrew translation of *Eyner aleyn* appeared in 1964. As far as I know, no critical articles on Rosenfeld's work have appeared in English except for a note on his life and work in Irving Howe and Eliezer Greenberg's *A Treasury of Yiddish Literature* (New York: Viking, 1953), 85.

41. For Abraham Cahan's conflict with Sholem Ash because of the latter's turn to Christian themes in his novel *The Nazarene,* see Hannah Berliner Fischtal, "Abraham Cahan and Sholem Asch," *YIDDISH* 11, no. 1–2 (1998): 1–17.

42. David G. Roskies, "Yiddish Culture at Century's End," *La Rassegna Mensile* 62, no. 1–2 (1996): 480.

Chapter 4. An American Yiddish Poet Visits Poland, 1934

1. Walter Benjamin, *Illuminations,* ed. Hannah Arendt (New York: Schocken Books 1969), 201.

2. Glatshteyn, *In tokh genumen,* 232.

3. The clearest expression of the new direction in Glatshteyn's artistic and ideological outlook in the late 1930s was the poem "A gute nakht, velt" (Good Night, World), in *Inzikh* 8 (April 1938): 66–67. In the May 1938 issue of *Inzikh,* Glatshteyn presented the ideological underpinnings of the poem in the essay

"Tvishn eygene" (Between One's Own). Glatshteyn acknowledged that, as a journalist with the Yiddish press, he had spent most of his artistic and commercial life in a Jewish cultural ghetto. Polemically he replaced the allures of the outside world (exemplified in the German Jewish assimilation and *kultur*) with the pride of the Jewish ghetto. In 1939 Glatshteyn began to serialize *Ven yash iz gekumen* in the Zionist weekly *Der yidisher kemfer*.

4. "Nokhmen zeygermakher" (Nakhman Watchmaker), a fragment of *Ven yash iz tsurikgeforn*, the unfinished third part of the projected trilogy, was published in *Di goldene keyt* 30 (1958): 256–61.

5. Dov Sadan's introduction to the Hebrew translation of Glatshteyn's poem's *Mikol amali: shirim ufoemot* (Jerusalem, 1964), 19. Janet Hadda divides the critical responses to Glatshteyn's work into two fundamentally different approaches, which she characterizes as "those who perceive a new Glatshteyn emerging after a period of crisis, and others who maintain that the essential Glatshteyn can be traced to his very earliest poems" ("The Early Poetry of Yankev Glatshteyn," unpublished doctoral dissertation, Columbia University, 1975, 1). See also, Y. Rappeport, "Yankev glatshteyns dikhterisher veg: fun zilbekstentrishkeyt tsu groysnatsionaler dikhtung," in *Oysgerisene bleter* (Melbourne 1957), 97–137; B. Alkvit, "Yankev Glatshteyn," *Getseltn* 2 (Oct.–Dec. 1946): 205–18. For a more recent approach, see Avrom Novershtern's "In di videranandn fun yidishn modernism: metapoetishe lider bay dem frien Glatshteyn," *YIVO-Bleter* 1 (1991): 200.

6. Dan Miron's epilogue to his Hebrew translation of *Ven yash iz geforn, Keshe Yash nasa* (Tel Aviv: *Hakkibutz Mameuchad*, 1994) praised the work as one of the greatest Yiddish prose works of the interwar period. Miron also presents an interesting comparison of the Yash books with Agnon's *Oreakh nata lalun* (1939, A Guest for the Night). See also Dov Sadan's introduction to a Hebrew translation of Glatshteyn's poems *Mikol amali: shirim ufoemot*; Leah Garrett, "The Self as Marrano in Jacob Glatstein's Autobiographical Novels," *Prooftexts* 18, no. 3 (September 1998): 207–24; Garrett, *Journeys beyond the Pale: Yiddish Travel Writing in the Modern World* (Madison: University of Wisconsin Press, 2003), 145–65; Ruth R. Wisse, "A Farewell to Poland: Jacob Glatstein and S. Y. Agnon," in *The Modern Jewish Canon*, 163–76.

7. This is a paraphrase of Alfred Kazin's point that the novelist turns "to autobiography out of some creative longing that fiction has not satisfied" (Kazin, "Autobiography as Narrative," *Michigan Quarterly Review* 3 [1964]: 212).

8. Werner Sollors, *Beyond Ethnicity* (New York: Oxford University Press, 1986), 245. See my article "Yankev Glatshteyn's *Ven Yash iz geforn* as a Continuation and a Redefinition of the American Yiddish Novel," *YIDDISH* 10, no. 1 (1995): 62–73.

9. Anita Norich, "*Harbe sugyes*/Puzzling Questions: Yiddish and English Culture in America during the Holocaust," in *Jewish Social Studies* 5, no. 182

(Fall 1998/Winter 1999): 95. This article presents an interesting discussion of the very different responses to the Holocaust during 1939–1945 among Jewish intellectuals writing in Yiddish and in English.

10. This was pioneered by Howe and Greenberg's anthology *A Treasury of Yiddish Literature*.

11. See *Homecoming at Twilight (Ven yash iz gekumen)*, trans. N. Guterman (New York: Thomas Yoseloff, 1962); *Homeward Bound* (abridged translation of *Ven yash iz geforn*), trans. A. Zahaven (New York: Thomas Yoseloff, 1969).

12. See Dovid Bergelson, "Dray tsentern," *In shpan* 1 (1926): 84–96. In Bergelson's analysis the only viable Yiddish literary center was Moscow because of the communist's state sponsorship of Yiddish scholarship and culture. See Joseph Sherman, "Introduction," in Dovid Bergelson, *Descent* (New York: Modern Language Association 1999), xiii–xl.

13. See Ruth Wisse, "Language as Fate: Reflections on Jewish Literature in America," *Studies in Contemporary Jewry* 12 (1996), 126–47.

14. Ewa Morawska, "Changing Images of the Old Country in the Development of Ethnic Identity among East European Immigrants, 1880s–1930s: A Comparison of Jewish and Slavic Representations," in "Going Home," ed. Jack Kugelmass, *YIVO-Annual* 21 (1993): 276.

15. Ibid.

16. Louis Adamic, *The Native's Return: An American Visits Yugoslavia and Discovers His Old Country* (New York: Harper 1934).

17. *Ven yash iz geforn* was serialized in the journal *Inzikh* between November 1934 and December 1937 and published in book form in 1938. The introduction to the Yash books was published in *Inzikh* 6 (October 1934).

18. *Inzikh* 6 (October 1934): 180.

19. Ibid., 179.

20. Ibid.

21. B. Alkvit, "Yankev Glatshteyns nay bukh Ven yash iz geforn," *Inzikh* 5 (May 1938): 100–111.

22. This was based on information by the Polish literary scholar Monika Adamczyk-Garbowska. See, Ruth R. Wisse, *The Modern Jewish Canon*, 168.

23. A. Tabatshnik, "A Conversation with Jacob Glatstein," *YIDDISH* 1 (1973): 52.

24. Ibid., 51.

25. Glatshteyn, *Ven yash iz geforn*, 192–93.

26. Ruth Whitman, "The Man and His Work," in *The Selected Poems of Jacob Glatstein*, trans. Ruth Whitman (New York: October House, 1972), 15.

27. See Dan Miron, *Keshe Yash nasa*, 206. See also Ruth Whitman, "The Man and His Work," 13: "When Glatstein returned to Lublin in 1934 to visit her as she lay dying of cancer, she told her relatives not to let him see her too often because she wanted to spare him the pain of seeing her suffer."

28. Yash refers to his wife and children on 41 and 93. On 173–74, Glatshteyn

describes his sexual development in adolescence as determined by Tolstoy's philosophy of abstinence and sublimation.

29. See Glatshteyn's article "Singer's Literary Reputation" in *Congress Bi-Weekly* (New York) December 27, 1965, 32.

30. According to Leah Garrett, the absence of the actual moment of return to the mother(land) thus expresses Yash's origin among a de-territorialized people. See Garrett, "The Self as Marrano in Jacob Glatstein's Autobiographical Novels," 209.

31. In the introduction to the Yash books (*Inzikh* [October 1934]: 170), Glatshteyn describes the Yash figure as an autobiographical *alter ego:* "Ikh, yash, vel dervayl in mayn araynfir makhn a shveyg iber dem groysn oyfnem, vos ikh hob gekrogn" (I, Yash, will therefore keep silent in this introduction about the big reception I received).

32. Marya Konopnicka, "Mendl Dantsiker," *Di yidishe bibliotek* 3 (1895): 4–34. The story was translated by M. Arenstein.

33. Glatshteyn, *Ven yash iz geforn,* ibid., 234.

34. Ibid., 241–49.

35. Psalms 137.

36. See also, Glatshteyn, *In tokh genumen,* 232.

37. The poet imitates Dovid Eynhorn's poem "Geshtorbn der alter bal-tfile," in *Gezamlte lider 1904–1951* (New York: Farlag arbeter ring, 1952), 18.

38. *The Selected Poems of Jacob Glatstein,* 13.

39. For a discussion of the recent search for Jewish roots in Eastern Europe, see Jack Kugelmass, "Rites of the Tribe: The Meaning of Poland for American Jewish Tourists," in "Going Home," ed. Jack Kugelmass, *YIVO-Annual* 21 (1993): 395–451.

40. "A klezmer toyt," in Y. L. Peretz, *Ale verk,* vol. 2 (1947), 95–99.

41. Richard Fein, "Going Home Again," *YIDDISH* (1990): 9.

42. See Burton Pike, "Time in Autobiography," *Comparative Literature* 28 (1976): 335.

43. See Janet Hadda, "German and Yiddish in the Poetry of Jacob Glatshteyn," *Prooftexts* 1, no. 1 (1981): 192–200.

44. See Meyer Viner, "Di rol fun shprakh-folklor in der yidisher literatur" (The Role of Language Folklore in the Yiddish Literature), *Shriftn* (Kiev, 1928): 128–73.

45. The title of Shmuel Niger's review of *Ven yash iz gekumen,* in *Der tog,* July 12, 1941.

46. In Glatshteyn's reading of Peretz' story "Der kuntsnmakher" (The Magician), he uses a musicological metaphor to describe Peretz's literary style: *"moment muzikal" fun oremkayt* ("moment musical" of poverty) ("Peretses yerushe," in *In tokh genumen,* 485). This designation could just as well be applied to this section of small, impressionistic chapters written in a social realist style.

47. Yitskhok Bashevis recommended the book for "dem besern leser" (the better reader) in his review of *Ven yash iz geforn*. See, Yitskhok Bashevis: "Yankev Glatshteyn: *Ven yash iz geforn*," *Tsukunft* (March 1939): 183.

48. On Peretz's attitude to *shund* theater, see Michael Steinlauf: "Fear of Purim: Y. L. Peretz and the Canonization of Yiddish Theater," *Jewish Social Studies* 1, no. 3 (Spring 1995): 44–64.

49. Glatshteyn later wrote a series of poems based on Nachman of Bratslav. See *Der bratslaver tsum soyfer (1943–1953)* in *Fun mayn gantser mi* (New York: Martin Press, 1956) 159–92.

50. Glatshteyn, "Peretses yerushe," in *In tokh genumen,* 500.

51. The Jew from Bogota refers to the biblical Jacob's deathbed scene in *Ven yash iz geforn,* 194.

52. See Y. L. Peretz, "Vegn der yidisher literatur," in *Ale verk,* vol. 11, 299–305.

53. See Khone Shmeruk, *The Esterke Story in Yiddish and Polish Literature* (Jerusalem: The Hebrew University, 1985).

54. Kuzmir (Kazimierz in Polish) was used as the setting in Sholem Asch's novella *A shtetl* (1904) and Y. L. Peretz' drama *Bay nakht af der alter mark* (1907). See S. L. Schneiderman, *Ven di vaysl hot geredt yidish* (Tel-Aviv: Perets Farlag, 1970).

Chapter 5. Of a World That Is No More

1. Aaron Zeitlin, *Ale lider un poemes: Lider fun khurbn un lider fun gloybn,* vol. 1 (New York: Bergen-Belsen Memorial Press, 1967), 169.

2. Walter Benjamin, "On the Image of Proust," in *Selected Writings, Volume 2, 1927–1934* (Cambridge, Mass.: Harvard University Press, 1999), 245. See also, Malcolm Bowie, *Proust Among the Stars* (London: HarperCollins Publishers 1998), xvii: "If there were no stubborn philosophical problems in the world, and no war, famine, disease or torture in it either, all thinking might resemble a gracious and disinterested Proustian paragraph. In the present sorry state of the world we may find ourselves returning to Proust for a new sense of mental largeness and potentiality."

3. See, Yankev Pat's interview with Abraham Sutzkever in *Shmuesn mit shrayber in yisroel* (London: Der kval, 1960), 166.

4. See David G. Roskies, *A Bridge of Longing,* 312–18.

5. The lecture was held on January 7, 1945, in YIVO Institute for Jewish Research in New York. Stephen J. Zipperstein mentions that the lecture was like a "secular eulogy for the Jews of Eastern Europe . . . before a mostly Yiddishist, secular crowd who stood up at its end and spontaneously recited the Kaddish" (*Imagining Russian Jewry,* 104). The Yiddish text was published as "Di mizrekh-eyropeishe tkufe in der yidisher geshikhte," in *YIVO-Bleter* 25 (1945): 163–83, and in English translation reprinted in *Voices from the Yiddish: Essays, Memoirs,*

Diaries, ed. Irving Howe and Eliezer Greenberg (Madison: University of Wisconsin Press, 1972), 67–87. See also, Abraham Joshua Heschel's *The Earth Is the Lord's: The Inner World of the Jews in Eastern Europe* (1949; New York: Farrar, Straus, Giroux 1978).

6. See *From a Ruined Garden: The Memorial Books of Polish Jewry,* 2nd ed., ed. Jack Kugelmass and Jonathan Boyarin (Bloomington: Indiana University Press, 1998). For memorial books as substitute gravestones, see 34.

7. Howe and Greenberg, *Voices From the Yiddish,* 73.

8. Y. Y. Trunk, *Poyln: Zikhroynes un bilder,* vol. 7 (New York: Farlag Unzer tsayt, 1953), 10.

9. Y. Y. Trunk, *Poyln,* vol. 5 (1949), 121.

10. Y. Y. Trunk, *Idealizm un naturalizm in der yidisher literatur* (Warsaw: Farlag kultur-lige, 1927); *Tvishn viln un onmekhtikayt: H. D. Nomberg* (Warsaw: Farlag kultur-lige, 1930); *Josefus Flavius fun yerushalaim un andere historishe noveln* (Warsaw: Farlag Kultur-lige, 1930).

11. Y. Y. Trunk, *Tevye un menakhem mendl in yidishn velt goyrl* (New York: Central Yiddish Culture Organization, 1944), 5.

12. Y. Y. Trunk, *Sholem-Aleykhem: Zayn vezn un zayne verk* (Warsaw: Farlag kultur-lige, 1937), 1.

13. Trunk, *Poyln,* vol. 7, 253.

14. Yankev Pat, *Shmuesn mit yidishe shrayber* (New York: Martin Press, 1954), 117.

15. A. Glantz-Leyeles, *Velt un vort: Literarishe un andere eseyen* (New York: CYCO, 1958), 104.

16. David G. Roskies, *A Bridge of Longing,* 318 and 403, n.20.

17. *Leksikon fun der nayer yidisher literatur,* "Y. Y. Trunk," 123.

18. Yitkshok Bashevis, "Arum der yidisher literatur in Poyln," *Di tsukunft* (August 1943): 475. The other article was "Problemen fun der yidisher proze in Amerike," *Svive* 2 (March–April 1943): 2–13; "Problems of Yiddish Prose in America," tr. Robert H. Wolf, *Prooftexts* 9 (1989): 5–12.

19. Elie Wiesel, *Un di velt hot geshvign* (Buenos Aires: Dos poylishe yidntum, 1955). Later revised in French as *La nuit* (1958), and translated from the French by Stella Rodway as *Night* (1960).

20. Emmanuel Ringelblum, *Ksovim fun geto* (Ghetto Writings), ed. A. Eisenbach et al. (Warsaw: Jewish Historical Institute, 1963); Yitskhok Rudashevski, *The Diary of the Vilna Ghetto, June 1941–April 1943,* trans. Percy Matenko (Israel: Ghetto Fighters' House and Hakibbutz Hameuchad, 1973); Abraham Sutzkever, *Fun vilner geto* (Moscow: Der emes 1946); Herman Kruk, *Togbukh fun vilner geto* (New York: YIVO, 1961); I. Shpiegl, *Likht funem opgrunt: geto noveln* (New York: CYCO, 1952); Abraham Sutzkever, *Di festung: lider un poemes geshribn in vilner geto un in vald 1941–1944* (New York: IKUF Farlag, 1945); Yitskhok Katzenelson, *Dos lid funem oysgehargetn yidishn folk* (Israel: Ghetto Fighters' House and Hakibbutz Hameuchad, 1964).

21. Aaron Zeitlin, *Lider fun khurbm un lider fun gloybn* (*Poems of the Holocaust and Poems of Faith*), vol. 1 (New York: Bergen-Belsen Memorial Press, 1967); *I Keep Recalling: The Holocaust Poems of Jacob Glatstein,* trans. Barnett Zumoff (New York: Ktav Publishing House 1993); *Paper Bridges: Selected Poems of Kadya Molodowsky,* trans. and ed. Kathryn Hellerstein (Detroit: Wayne State University Press, 1999).

22. Although poetry dominated the Yiddish book market, an increasing number of memoirs, historical works, and chronicles about life before and during the Holocaust were published in the Americas. See, Shmuel Niger, "Tendentsn in der nayster yidisher literatur," *Jewish Book Annual* 13 (1955/1956): 3–8.

23. Irving Howe, *A Margin of Hope: An Intellectual Autobiography* (New York: Harcourt Publishers, 1982), 264. Particularly interesting is Howe's description of the isolation and invisibility of Yiddish writers in America in the early 1950s: "It was hard for me to explain—they [the Yiddish writers] seldom brought it up, but I felt obliged to mention it once in a while—the utter indifference of American literary circles to the presence of a vibrant Yiddish culture that could be found, literally and symbolically, a few blocks away" (265).

24. *Shadows on the Hudson,* trans. by Joseph Sherman (New York: Farrar Straus Giroux, 1998) was originally serialized in Yiddish in the *Forverts,* Jan. 1957–Jan. 1958.

25. See, Judd L. Teller, "Yiddish Litterateurs and American Jews," *Commentary* 18, no. 1 (July 1954): 31–40; Peter Novick, *The Holocaust in American Life* (New York: Houghton Miflin Company, 1999); and Eli Lederhendler, *New York Jews and the Decline of Urban Ethnicity* (Syracuse, N.Y.: Syracuse University Press, 2001), chapter 3, "A Culture of Retrieval."

26. Howe, *A Margin of Hope,* 264.

27. Ruth R. Wisse, "In Praise of Chaim Grade," *Commentary* (April 1977): 71.

28. Lucy S. Dawidowicz, *From That Place and Time: A Memoir 1938–1947* (New York: W. W. Norton, 1989), 127.

29. "Musar Movement, movement for the education of the individual toward strict ethical behavior in the spirit of *halakhah;* it arose in the nineteenth century, continuing into the twentieth, in the Jewish culture of the *mitnaggedim* in Lithuania, in particular becoming a trend in its *yeshivot*" (*Encyclopedia Judaica,* 534).

30. Quoted in Nachman Mayzel, "Khayim grade," in *Forgeyer un mittsaytler,* 418. Grade's speech was published in *Yidishe kultur,* March 1939.

31. See Janet Hadda, *Isaac Bashevis Singer: A Life* (Oxford: Oxford University Press, 1997), 108. She quotes from Singer's memoir *Fun der alter un nayer heym,* March 26, 1965: "During the War, I often comforted my friend Arn Tseytlin, and assured him that his family would return to him, but I knew that my words had no weight. About what had happened to my loved ones, I never spoke to anyone, not even those closest to me. How could anyone help me? Why make someone else sad, even for a minute? Why increase the ocean of suffering? I

was silent and remained silent." For information about the fate of Singer's father, mother and younger brother Moshe, who died after being deported to Siberia, see Maurice Carr, "My Uncle Yitzhak: A Memoir of I. B. Singer," in *Commentary* (December 1992): 31.

32. Hadda, *Isaac Bashevis Singer*, 112.

33. Published in Yiddish in a photo-offset (Jerusalem: Hebrew University, 1969). An abridged translation by Milton Himmelfarb appeared in Howe and Greenberg, *A Treasury of Yiddish Stories*, 624–51. First published in English translation in *Commentary* 16, no. 5 (November 1953): 428–42.

34. Hadda, *Isaac Bashevis Singer*, 147.

35. See Howe and Greenberg's introduction to *A Treasury of Yiddish Stories* and Mark Zborowski and Elizabeth Herzog, *Life Is with People: The Jewish Little-Town of Eastern Europe* (New York: International Universities Press, 1952). On Howe's glorification of Eastern European Yiddish culture, see Theodore Weinberger, "Yiddish Literature as Secular Jewish Scripture: The World of Irving Howe," in Greenspoon, *Yiddish Language and Culture*.

36. Hadda, *Isaac Bashevis Singer: A Life*, 172.

37. Howe, *A Margin of Hope*, 267.

38. Eliezer Greenberg, "Khayim grade—mayster fun proze," *Di goldene keyt* 23 (1955): 259.

39. In her review of *The Yeshiva*, the English translation of *Tsemakh atlas*, Ruth Wisse points out that Grade deliberately restricts "his canvas once again to the internal Jewish world, and within that to the ethical and moral dimensions of its religious culture" ("In Praise of Chaim Grade," 73).

40. See Greenberg's comparison of Abramovitsh and Grade, "Khayim grade—mayster fun proze," 262–64.

41. Rosenfeld, *Geklibene verk*, ed. Chaim Grade.

42. Glatshteyn, *In tokh genumen*, 348.

43. Ibid., 349.

44. Anita Norich, "Mother, Mother Tongue, and Motherland: The Family in Jewish American Fiction," *YIVO Annual* 23 (1996), 160. Grade was inspired by Maxim Gorky's mother figure in his novel *The Mother* (1906), which he stripped of its heroic and revolutionary qualities.

45. See Naomi Seidman, "Elie Wiesel and the Scandal of Jewish Rage," *Jewish Social Studies* 3, no. 1 (Fall 1996): 1–20.

46. Grade, *My Mother's Sabbath Days: A Memoir*, trans. Channa Kleinerman Goldstein and Inna Hecker Grade (New York: Alfred A Knopf, 1986), 123.

47. Ibid., 128.

48. Mayzel, *Forgeyer un mittsaytler*, 415.

49. Abraham Novershtern, "*Yung Vilne*: The Political Dimension of Literature," in *The Jews of Poland between Two World Wars*, ed. Gutman, Mendelsohn, Reinharz, and Shmeruk (Hanover, N.H.: University Press of New England, 1989), 386.

50. Shoshana Felman and Dori Laub, *Testimony: Crises of Witnessing in Literature, Psychoanalysis, and History* (New York: Routledge, 1992), 112.

51. Grade, *My Mother's Sabbath Days*, 362.

52. Ibid., 305.

53. See Robert Alter, *Hebrew and Modernity* (Bloomington: Indiana University Press, 1994), 1–3.

54. Grade, *My Mother's Sabbath Days*, 321.

55. Wisse, "In Praise of Chaim Grade," 73.

56. Ruth R. Wisse, "Singer's Paradoxical Progress," *Commentary* (February 1979): 33–38; Joseph Sherman, "Guilt as Subtext: I. B. Singer's Memoiristic Fictions," in *Studies of American Jewish Literature*, ed. David Walden, vol. 13 (Albany: State University of New York Press, 1994), 106–23; Janet Hadda, "The Double Life of Isaac Bashevis Singer," *Prooftexts* 5 (1985): 165–81.

57. Hadda, "The Double Life of Isaac Bashevis Singer," 175. See also Hadda, *Isaac Bashevis Singer*, 117.

58. The title of Joseph Sherman's article in Walden, *Studies in American Jewish Literature*.

59. Chava Rosenfarb presents a similar view in her article "Yitskhok bashevis un sholem ash. A pruv fun a farglaykh" (Yitskhok Bashevis and Sholem Ash: An attempt at a Comparison), *Di goldene keyt* 133 (1992): 83: "Generally Bashevis is more inclined to depict a human being in abstract, metaphysical terms than to depict the individual in his psychological development. Besides, as we know, he was not interested in social or societal differentiations. He was opposed to political and ideological movements. He disliked them too much to be able to depict them objectively and study their influence on the individual's life; just like Sholem Ash, he was aware that Jewish life in the twentieth century could not be depicted otherwise."

60. See, Yitskhok Bashevis's review of *Ven yash iz geforn*, in *Tsukunft* (March 1939): 182–83.

61. See Yitskhok Bashevis's positive review of *Eyner aleyn*, in *Tsukunft* (June 1940): 364–66; and his review of David Bergelson's autobiographical novel *Bam dnieper* in *Globus* (Warsaw), no. 5 (November 1932): 56–65.

62. Walter Benjamin's distinction between the fundamentally different discourses of the novelist and the storyteller can delineate Singer's uniqueness in modern Yiddish literature: "The 'meaning of life' is really the center about which the novel moves. But the quest for it is no more than the initial expression of perplexity with which its reader sees himself living this written life. Here 'meaning of life'—there 'moral of story': with these slogans novel and story confront each other and from them the totally different historical coordinates of these art forms may be discerned" (*Illuminations*, 99).

63. Singer refers to the Holocaust on 182, 251, and 350.

64. See Z. Zilbertsvayg, *Leksikon funem yidishn teater*, vol. 3, cols. 2186–89. For additional episodes published in *Forverts*, see Khone Shmeruk: "Dray

farshpetikte epizodn fun mayn tatns bezdn shtub" (Three Later Episodes from
My Father's Court), in *Di goldene keyt* 135 (1993): 173–88.

   65. Khone Shmeruk points out that most of the autobiographical material
which Singer published between 1955 and 1980 is accessible only in serialized
form in the *Forverts*. Only the first of these works, the childhood memoir *Mayn
tatns bezdn shtub* was published in book form in Yiddish (1956) and later reprinted (1979). In *Forverts*, Singer serialized the memoirs *Fun der alter un nayer
heym* (1963–65, From the Old and New Home); *Gloybn un tsveyfl oder di filosofye
fun protest* (1974–1976, 1978, Faith and Doubt or the Philosophy of Protest) later
published in book form in English as *A Little Boy in Search of God* (1976), *A Young
Man in Search of Love* (1978), and *Lost in America* (1981), the three parts of his
"spiritual autobiography" *Love and Exile: An Autobiographical Trilogy*; *Figurn un
epizodn fun literatn fareyn* (1979–1980, Figures and Episodes from the Literary
Club); and *Di mishpokhe* (1982, The Family); as well as novels with autobiographical elements such as *Shotns baym hodson* (1957–1958, Shadows on the
Hudson); *Sonim—a geshikhte fun libe* (1966, Enemies—A Love Story); *Vidervuks*
(1969–1970, Aftergrowth); *Der fartribener zun* (1971–1972, The Exiled Son); and
Neshome-ekspeditsyes (1974, Soul Expeditions). The first group of memoirs cover
Singer's life from early childhood until the 1960s; except for *Shotns baym hodson*
and *Sonim—a geshikhte fun libe*, the novels focus on his Warsaw period in the
1920s and 1930s. See Shmeruk, "Bashevis Singer—In Search of His Autobiography," *Jewish Quarterly* 29, no. 4 (1981–1982): 28–36.

   66. Shmeruk mentions that, "For many years he [Singer] wrestled with his
autobiography, to which he regularly returned in various ways. These struggles, which manifest themselves in a large number of his Yiddish writings, de-
serve, no doubt, more detailed and comprehensive research" (*Mayn tatns bezdn
shtub: hemshekhim zamlung* [Jerusalem: The Magnes Press, 1996], xvii).

   67. *Mayn tatns bezdn shtub: hemsheykhim-zamlung*, edited by Khone Shmeruk, has for several reasons not been included in this study. As Shmeruk mentions in his introduction, Singer's autobiographical works serialized in the Yiddish press (primarily in the *Forverts*) between 1935 to 1983 "are buried in old
volumes of Yiddish newspapers that are rather difficult to obtain and are, for
the time being, not recorded in any bibliography" (vii). Singer did not himself
make the selection of episodes for the sequel-collection. Although the book
adds new and interesting material, particular in its third section *Tsurik keyn
varshe*, it must be regarded as belonging to a selected version of Singer's autobiographical writings 1955–1960 rather than to his original, artistic work. Only
a faithful reproduction of the original serialized works in Singer's autobiographical *oeuvre* can do justice to the writer's artistic vision as it developed
over a period of nearly fifty years. Shmeruk's research provides important bibliographical tools for a reconstruction of Singer's multi-faceted autobiographical work. See also Nathan Cohen, "Revealing Bashevis's Earliest Autobiographical Novel, *Varshe 1914–1918*." This work was serialized in *Forverts*

between September 17, 1935, and January 31, 1936. Wolitz, *The Hidden Isaac Bashevis Singer*, 151–61.

68. In an interview with Joel Blocker and Richard Elman in 1963, Singer mentioned that he used the pseudonym Varshavski for his "belletristic journalism": "One of my books, *Mayn tatns bezdn shtub* is a compilation of this kind of work, published under the name of Varshavski. Only later I adopted it, as it were, and signed the name Bashevis . . . after I cleaned it up and worked on it" (*Commentary* 36 [November 1963]: 364–72).

69. Anita Norich points out that Singer rarely leaves the *bezdn shtub*. "Rather than confining him, it will ultimately provide a place for his imagination, a firm grounding in a particular world" ("The Family Singer and the Autobiographical Imagination," *Prooftexts* 10 [1990]: 98).

70. For a psychological reading of this episode, see Hadda, *Isaac Bashevis Singer*, 48.

71. Singer, *In My Father's Court* (New York: Farrar, Straus and Giroux, 1966), 321.

72. In his article "Arum der yidisher literatur in Poyln" (*Tsukunft* [August 1943]: 468–75), Singer generalizes his experience of Bilgoray to that of the Polish-Jewish *shtetl*. He argues that the Polish *shtetl* was enlightened much later and more suddenly than Jewish communities in Russia and Lithuania. According to Singer the change happened "over night" as a result of World War I.

73. See David G. Roskies, "The Demon as Storyteller: Isaac Bashevis Singer," in *A Bridge of Longing*, 266–307.

74. See Janet Hadda's reading of this vignette, *Isaac Bashevis Singer*, 46–47.

75. *The Bakhtin Reader: Selected Writings of Bakhtin, Medvedev and Voloshinov*, ed. Pam Morris (New York: E. Arnold, 1994), 187.

76. Y. Y. Singer, *Fun a velt vos iz nishto mer*; Ester Kreitman, *Der sheydim-tants* (Warsaw, 1936).

77. For interesting biographical information about the complex relationship between Singer and his brother, see Carr, "My Uncle Yitzhak: A Memoir of I. B. Singer"; and Israel Zamir's *Journey to My Father, Isaac Bashevis Singer* (New York: Arcade Publishing, 1995), 50–62.

78. For an interesting psychological analysis of the relationship between the three siblings, see Hadda, *Isaac Bashevis Singer*, 31–45.

79. See the chapter "A tragedye tsulib dem, vos men hot in himl farbitn di yoytsres" (A Tragedy Resulting from the Confusion of One Thing with Another in Heaven) in Y. Y. Singer's *Fun a velt vos iz nishto mer*, 23–42.

80. See my article "'Death Is the Only Messiah': A Comparison of Three Supernatural Stories by Yitskhok Bashevis," in *The Real Bashevis and His Creation: I. B. Singer*, ed. Seth Wolitz (Austin: University of Texas Press, 2001), 107–16.

81. That Singer's success never really went to his head is touchingly disclosed by his son Israel Zamir in *Journey to My Father, Isaac Bashevis Singer*. During the Nobel Prize celebration in which Singer took much pleasure, Zamir told

him that he had donned the mantle of success and behaved like a movie star. After some moments of thought, Singer replied: "No, I'm no movie star. With all the glory and adoration, I'd be far happier if I could go to my father's prayer house on Krochmalna. After all, who am I? An aging Jewish author, who writes about demons and ghosts" (151).

82. The publication of the work in the *Forverts* was advertised with the following notice: "*Faith and Doubt or the Philosophy of Protest* by Yitskhok Bashevis. A private world view seen through the eyes of a Yiddish writer. This new creation by our contributor, the world famous writer, Isaac Bashevis Singer, will begin its publication tomorrow, Friday, in the *Forverts* and will appear twice a week—Thursday and Friday" (*Forverts*, November 13, 1974, 1).

83. For an interesting comparison between the English and Yiddish endings of *Di familye mushkat* see Malka Matsa-Shaked, "Singer and the Family Saga Novel in Jewish Literature," *Prooftexts* 9 (1989): 38–39.

84. Published in *Globus* (Warsaw) 3 (September 1932): 39–49.

85. Joseph Buloff, *Fun altn markplats* (Tel-Aviv: Y. L. Peretz, 1995). Serialized in *Di goldene keyt* 116–25 (1985–1988). Translated as *From the Old Marketplace*, trans. Joseph Singer (Cambridge, Mass.: Harvard University Press, 1991).

86. For an interesting historical account of Jewish Vilna in the interwar period, see Cecile E. Kuznitz, "On the Jewish Street: Yiddish Culture and the Urban Landscape in Interwar Vilna," in Greenspoon, *Yiddish Language and Culture*, 65–92.

87. Buloff, *From the Old Marketplace*, 334.

88. Ruth R. Wisse, "The Survivor's Voice," *The New Republic*, June 24 (1991): 42.

89. Buloff, *From the Old Marketplace*, 335.

90. See Abraham Novershtern, "Between Dust and Dance: Peretz's Drama and the Rise of Yiddish Modernism," *Prooftexts* 12, no. 1 (January 1992): 71–90.

91. Buloff, *From the Old Marketplace*, 320; *lampedusser* is a nonsense word.

92. Buloff later claimed that the origin of the Theater of the Absurd as created by Samuel Beckett and Eugene Ionesco (the latter actually acknowledged his debt to the Yiddish theater in Rumania) was his direction of *Singer of His Sorrow* in the 1920s: "I pioneered Theater of the Absurd back in the Twenties. All across Eastern Europe, I directed and starred in *Singer of His Sorrow*, the story of Yoshke Musicant, an untutored musician who wins a lottery but gives away his winnings so that the girl he loves can wed another. A good old tear jerker, but I directed it as a fantasy seen through the eyes of a child—everything distorted, color enhanced and twice as large as life" (Luba Kadison and Joseph Buloff with Irving Genn, *On Stage, Off Stage: Memories of a Lifetime in the Yiddish Theatre* [Cambridge, Mass.: Harvard University Press, 1992], 54).

93. "They [the Vilna Troupe] were revolutionary in their attention to the literary quality of each play, word by word. And they startled and delighted the intelligentsia with yet another innovation: . . . the Vilna Troupe all spoke in the

same accent and dialect. Most of them were natives of Vilna" (Nahma Sandrow, *A World History of Yiddish Theater: Vagabond Stars* [New York: Harper & Row, 1977], 216).

94. In contrast, Isaac Babel focused on the ambiguities of his identification with the Cossacks in his master piece *Red Cavalry* (1923–1926).

95. A similar metaphor is used in Glatshteyn's *Ven Yash iz gekumen,* 203–4.

96. Buloff, *From the Old Marketplace,* 92–93; *Fun altn markplats,* 107.

97. Buloff, *From the Old Marketplace,* 132; *Fun altn markplats,* 147.

98. Curt Leviant's review was published in *Hadassah* (June/July 1991), 43.

99. Buloff, *From the Old Marketplace,* 327; *Fun altn markplats,* 328.

Conclusion

1. *Roland Barthes by Roland Barthes,* translated by Richard Howard (New York: Hill and Wang, 1977), 120.

2. See "The Semiotics of Yiddish Communication" in Benjamin Harshav, *The Meaning of Yiddish* (Berkeley: University of California Press, 1990), 89–118.

3. Paul John Eakin, *Touching the World,* 98.

4. Sholem Aleichem, *Funem yarid,* book 2, vol. 16, 19; *From the Fair: The Autobiography of Sholom Aleichem,* trans. Curt Leviant, 137.

5. Sholem Aleichem, *Funem yarid,* 11; *From the Fair,* 138. I have revised Leviant's translation slightly by translating the word *biografye* as "biography."

6. Sholem Aleichem, *Funem yarid,* 13; *From the Fair,* 140.

7. Harshav, *The Meaning of Yiddish,* 91.

8. Ibid.

9. Paul John Eakin, *Touching the World,* 136.

10. Kate Simon, *Bronx Primitive: Portraits in a Childhood* (New York: Viking Penguin, 1982) and *Etching in an Hourglass* (New York: Harper Collins Publishers, 1990); Alfred Kazin, *A Walker in the City* (New York: Harcourt Brace Jovanovich, 1951) and *Starting Out in the Thirties* (1965); Irving Howe, *A Margin of Hope* (1982).

11. *Writing Our Lives: Autobiographies of American Jews, 1890–1990,* ed. Steven J. Rubin (Jewish Publication Society, 1991), xxiii.

12. Ibid.

13. See Mintz, *"Banished from Their Father's Table,"* 205. See also Yael Feldman, "Gender In/Difference in Contemporary Hebrew Fictional Autobiographies," *Biography* 11, no. 3 (Summer 1988): 189–209.

14. See Michael Galchinsky, "Scattered Seeds: A Dialogue of Diasporas," in *Insider/Outsider: American Jews and Multiculturalism,* ed. David Biale, Michael Galchinsky and Susannah Heschel (Berkeley: University of California Press, 1998), 202.

Bibliography

Yiddish Life-Writing

Abramovitsh, Sholem Yankev. *Shloyme reb khayims. Gezamlte verk,* vols. 3–4. Eds. A. Gurshteyn, M. Viner, and Y. Nusinov. Moscow: Emes farlag, 1935–1940. Translated as *Of Bygone Days.* In *A Shtetl and Other Yiddish Novellas.* Ed. Ruth R. Wisse. Trans. Raymond P. Sheindlin. Detroit: Wayne State University Press, 1986.

———. *Reshimot letoldotay.* Translated as "Notes for My Literary Biography." In *The Golden Tradition: Jewish Life and Thought in Eastern Europe.* Ed. Lucy S. Dawidowicz, New York: Holt, Rinehart and Winston, 1967.

———. "Ba-yamim ha-hem: petikhta deMendele Moykher Sforim." *Pardes* 2 (1894): 173–88.

Berkovitsh, Y. D. *Undzere rishoynim: zikhroynes-dertseylungen vegn sholem aley-khem un zayn dor,* 5 vols. Tel Aviv: Menorah, 1966.

Bergelson, Dovid. *Bam dnieper.* Moscow: Farlag emes, 1932.

Bergner, Hinde. *In di lange vinternekht.* Montreal, 1946.

Boreisho, Menakhem. *Der geyer. Kapitln fun a lebn.* New York: M. Boraisha, 1943.

Buloff, Joseph. *Fun altn markplats.* Tel Aviv: Perets farlag 1995. Translated as *From the Old Marketplace.* Trans. Joseph Singer. Cambridge, Mass.: Harvard University Press, 1991.

Cahan, Abraham. *Bleter fun mayn lebn,* 5 vols. New York: Forverts, 1926–1931. Translated in part as *The Education of Abraham Cahan.* Trans. Leon Stein. Philadelphia: The Jewish Publication Society of America, 1969.

Chagall, Bella. *Brenendike likht.* New York: Folksfarlag 1945. Translated as *Burning Light.* Trans. Norbert Guterman. New York: Schocken Books, 1946.

———. *Di ershte bagegenish.* New York, 1947. Translated as *First Encounter.* Trans. Barbara Bray. New York: Schocken Books, 1983.

Dubnov, Simon. *Fun "zhargon" tsu yidish un andere artiklen: literarishe zikhroynes.* Vilna: Kletzkin, 1929.

———. *Dos bukh fun mayn lebn,* 3 vols. Trans. Y. Birnbaum. Buenos Aires: YIVO, 1962–1963. Excerpt translated as "Under the Sign of Historicism." In *The Golden Tradition.* Trans. Lucy Dawidowicz. New York: Holt, Rinehart and Winston, 1967.

Glatshteyn, Yankev. *Ven yash iz geforn.* New York: Farlag "Inzikh", 1938. Translated as *Homeward Bound.* Trans. A. Zahaven. New York: Thomas Yoseloff, 1969.

———. *Ven yash iz gekumen.* New York: Farlag M. Shlarski, 1940. Translated as *Homecoming by Twilight.* Trans. N. Guterman. New York: Thomas Yoseloff, 1962.

Glikl Hamel. *Die Memoiren der Glückel von Hameln.* Ed. David Kaufmann. Frankfurt-am-Main: J. Kaufmann, 1896.

———. *Zikhroynes.* Musterverk 26. Trans. Joseph Berenfeld. Buenos Aires: YIVO, 1967. Translated as *The Life of Glückel of Hameln.* Trans. Beth-Zion Abrahams. London: East and West Library, 1962.

Grade, Chaim. *Der mames shabosim. Dertseylungen.* Chicago: L. M. Stein Farlag, 1955. Translated as *My Mother's Sabbath Days.* Trans. Channa Kleinerman Goldstein and Inna Hecker Grade. New York: Alfred A. Knopf, 1986.

———. *Mayn krig mit hersh raseyner.* Jerusalem: Hebrew University, 1969. Translated as *My Quarrel with Hersh Rasseyner.* In *A Treasury of Yiddish Stories.* Ed. Irving Howe and Eliezer Greenberg. Trans. Miton Himmelfarb. New York: Viking, 1989.

Kotik, Yekhezkel. *Mayne zikhroynes.* Warsaw: Farlag A. Gitlin, 1913. Translated as *Journey to a Nineteenth-Century Shtetl: The Memoirs of Yekhezkel Kotik.* Trans. David Assaf. Detroit and Tel Aviv: Wayne State University Press and The Diaspora Research Institute, 2002.

Kreitman, Esther. *Der sheydim-tants* (The Dance of Demons). Warsaw: Farlag Kh. Kzshaza, 1936. Translated as *Deborah.* Trans. Maurice Carr. New York: St. Martin's Press, 1983.

Kulbak, Moshe. "Disner tshayld harold." In *Geklibene verk.* New York: CYCO-Bicher farlag, 1953.

Leyeles, Aaron. "Kholem tvishn volknkratsers." In *A yid afn yam.* New York: CYCO, 1947.

Linetski, Y. Y. *Funem yarid, a fantazye tsu mayn zibetsik yorikn geburtstog.* Odessa, 1909.

———. *Dos poylishe yingl.* Vilne: Der Kval, 1921.

Peretz, Isaac Leib. *Mayne zikhroynes. Ale verk,* vol. 11. New York: CYCO, 1948. Translated as *My Memoirs.* In *I. L. Peretz Reader.* Ed. Ruth R. Wisse. Trans. Seymour Levitan. New York: Schocken Books, 1990.

———. *Bilder fun a provintz rayze.* Translated as *Impressions of a Journey through the Tomaszow Region.* In *I. L. Peretz Reader.* Ed. Ruth R. Wisse. Trans. Seymour Levitan. New York: Schocken Books, 1990.

Ravitsh, Melekh. *Dos mayse-bukh fun mayn lebn,* 3 vols. Montreal: Tsentralfarband fun poylishe yidn, 1962–1975.

Rosenfeld, Jonah. *Gezamlte verk*. New York: Jonah Rosenfeld *komite*, 1924.

———. *Eyner aleyn, oytobiografisher roman*. New York: Maks N. Mayzel, 1940.

Sholem Aleichem. *Funem yarid, lebensbashraybung. Ale verk*, vol. 15. New York: Folksfond edition, 1925. Translated as *From the Fair: The Autobiography of Sholom Aleichem*. Trans. Curt Leviant. New York: Viking Penguin, 1985.

Schwartz, Y. Y. *Yunge yorn: Poeme*. Mexico: Kultur-komisye fun yidishn tsentral-komitet, 1952.

Singer, Isaac Bashevis. *Mayn tatns bezdn shtub*. New York: St. Martin Press, 1956. Translated as *In My Father's Court*. New York: Farrar, Straus and Giroux, 1966.

———. *Gloybn un tsveyfl oder di filozofye fun protest*, 3 vols. Serialized in *Forverts*, 1974–1978. Translated as *Love and Exile: An Autobiographical Trilogy*. Trans. Joseph Singer. New York: Doubleday, 1984.

———. *Shadows on the Hudson*. Trans. Joseph Sherman. New York: Farrar Straus Giroux, 1998.

Singer, Y. Y. *Fun a velt vos iz nishto mer*. New York: Farlag matones, 1946. Translated as *From a World That Is No More*. Trans. Joseph Singer. New York: Vanguard Press, 1970.

Sokolov, Nahum. *Sefer zikaron le-sofrei yisra'el hakhaim itanu kayom*. Warsaw: Halter, 1889.

Trunk, Y. Y. *Poyln: zikhroynes un bilder*. 7 Vols. New York: Farlag medem-klub, 1944–1953. An excerpt translated as "Peretz at Home." In *The Golden Tradition*. Trans. Lucy Dawidowicz. New York: Holt, Rinehart, & Winston, 1967.

Wiesel, Elie. *Un di velt hot geshvign*. Buenos Aires: Dos poylishe yidntum, 1955. Translated as *Night*. Trans. Stella Rodway. New York: Hill and Wang, 1960.

Jewish Life-writing: Works, History and Criticism

Agnon, Shmuel, Y. *A Guest for the Night*. New York: Schocken Books, 1968.

Antin, Mary. *The Promised Land*. 2nd ed. Princeton, N.J.: Princeton University Press, 1985.

Bal-Makhshoves (Isidor Eliashev). "*Memuarn-literatur*." In *Geklibene shriftn*. Vol. 3. Warsaw, 1929.

Bellow, Saul. *To Jerusalem and Back: A Personal Account*. New York: Viking Press, 1976.

Berkovitsh, Y. D. *Sholem aleykhem bukh*. New York: Farlag ikuf, 1926.

Biale, David, Michael Galchinsky, and Susannah Heschel, eds. *Insider/Outsider: American Jews and Multiculturalism*. Berkeley: University of California Press, 1998.

Bilik, Dorothy. "The Memoirs of Glikl of Hameln: The Archaeology of the Texts." *YIDDISH* 8 (Spring, 1992): 1–18.

Boyarin, Jonathan, and Jack Kugelmass, eds. *From a Ruined Garden: The Memorial Books of Polish Jewry*. 2nd ed. Bloomington: Indiana University Press 1998.

Davis, Natalie Zemon. "Fame and Secrecy: Leon Modena's Life as an Early Modern Autobiography." In *The Autobiography of a Seventeenth Century Venetian Rabbi: Leon Modena's Life of Judah.* Trans. and ed. Mark R. Cohen. Princeton, N.J.: Princeton University Press 1988.

Dawidowicz, Lucy S. *The Golden Tradition: Jewish Life and Thought in Eastern Europe.* New York: Holt, Rinehart, & Winston, 1967.

———. *From That Place and Time: A Memoir 1938–1947.* New York: W. W. Norton & Company, 1989.

Ezrahi, Sidra Dekoven. *Booking Passage: Exile and Homecoming in the Modern Jewish Imagination.* Berkeley: University of California Press, 2000.

Feldman, Yael. "Gender In/Difference in Contemporary Hebrew Fictional Autobiographies." *Biography* 11 (1988): 189–209.

Felman, Shoshana, and Dori Laub. *Testimony: Crises of Witnessing in Literature, Psycho-analysis, and History.* New York: Routledge, 1992.

Fishman, Joshua A., ed. *Never Say Die! A Thousand Years of Yiddish in Jewish Life and Letters.* The Hague: Mouton, 1981.

Frieden, Ken. *Classic Yiddish Fiction: Abramovitsh, Sholem Aleichem and Peretz.* Albany: State University of New York Press, 1995.

Garrett, Leah. "The Self as Marrano in Jacob Glatstein's Autobiographical Novels." *Prooftexts.* 18, no. 3 (September 1998): 207–24.

———. *Journeys beyond the Pale: Yiddish Travel Writing in the Modern World.* Madison: University of Wisconsin Press, 2003.

Green, Arthur. *Tormented Master: A Life of Rabbi Nahman of Bratslav.* New York: Schocken Books, 1981.

Greenberg, Eliezer, and Howe, Irving, eds. *Voices from the Yiddish; Essays, Memoirs, Diaries.* Madison: University of Wisconsin Press, 1972.

Greenspon, Leonard Jay, ed. *Yiddish Language and Culture: Then and Now.* Omaha, Nebr.: Creighton University Press, 1998.

Hadda, Janet. *Yankev Glatshteyn.* Boston: Twayne Publishers, 1980.

———. *Isaac Bashevis Singer: A Life.* Oxford: Oxford University Press, 1997.

Hadda, Janet, and Hana Wirth-Nesher, eds. "American Jewish Autobiography." *Prooftexts* 18, no. 3 (September 1998) and 19, no. 1 (January 1999).

Harshav, Benjamin. *Language in Times of Revolution.* Berkeley: University of California Press, 1993.

———. *The Meaning of Yiddish.* Berkeley: University of California Press, 1990.

Hoffman, Eva. *Lost in Translation: A Life in a New Language.* New York: E. P. Dutton, 1989.

Howe, Irving. *A Margin of Hope: An Intellectual Autobiography.* New York: Harcourt Publishers, 1982.

Hyman, Paula. "Memoirs and Memories: East European Jewish Women Recount Their Lives." In *Conference Proceedings: Di froyen.* New York: Jewish Women Resource Center, 1997.

Kazin, Alfred. "Autobiography as Narrative." *Michigan Quarterly Review* 3 (1964): 210–16.

————. *A Walker in the City*. New York: Harcourt, Brace, 1951.

Kligsberg, Moshe. *Child and Adolescent Behavior Under Stress*. New York, 1965.

————. "Sotsial-psikologishe problemen arum dem YIVO konkurs oyf oytobiografien." *YIVO-Bleter* 21 (1943): 262–75.

Kronfeld, Chane. *On the Margins of Modernism: Decentering Literary Dynamics*. Berkeley: University of California Press, 1996.

Krutikov, Mikhail. *Yiddish Fiction and the Crisis of Modernity, 1905–1914*. Stanford, Calif.: Stanford University Press, 2001.

Lederhendler, Eli. *New York Jews and the Decline of Urban Ethnicity*. Syracuse, N.Y.: Syracuse University Press, 2001.

Lerner, Anne L., Anita Norich, and Naomi B. Sokoloff, eds. *Gender and Text in Modern Hebrew and Yiddish Literature*. New York: Jewish Theological Seminary, 1992.

Lifschutz, Ephraim E. *Bibliography of American and Canadian Jewish Memoirs and Autobiographies*. New York: YIVO Institute for Jewish Research, 1970.

Lisitzky, Ephraim. *In the Grip of Cross-Currents*. Trans. Moshe Kohn and Jacob Sloan. New York: Bloch Publishing Co., 1959.

Maimon, Solomon. *Lebensgeschichte, von ihm selbst geschrieben*. Berlin, 1792.

————. *Shloyme maymons lebensgeshikhte, geshribn fun im aleyn*. Trans. A. Y. Goldschmidt. Vilna: Farlag "Tomor," 1927. Translated as *The Autobiography of Solomon Maimon*. Trans. J. Clark Murray. Oxford: East and West Library, 1954.

Mayzel, Nachman. "Di yidishe geshikhte un di yidishe literatur." In *Tsurikblikn un perspektivn*. Tel Aviv: Y. L. Peretz, 1962.

Mintz, Alan. *"Banished from Their Father's Table": Loss of Faith and Hebrew Autobiography*. Bloomington: Indiana University Press, 1989.

Miron, Dan. *A Traveler Disguised: The Rise of Modern Yiddish Fiction in the Nineteenth Century*. New York: Schocken Books, 1973.

————. *Der imazsh fun shtetl*. Tel Aviv: Perets farlag, 1981.

————. *The Image of the Shtetl and Other Studies of Modern Jewish Literary Imagination*. Syracuse, N.Y.: Syracuse University Press, 2000.

Moseley, Marcus. "Jewish Autobiographies in Eastern Europe. The Prehistory of a Literary Genre." D. Phil. Trinity College, Oxford University, 1990.

————. "Life, Literature: Autobiographies of Jewish Youth in Interwar Poland." *Jewish Social Studies* 7, no. 3 (Spring/Summer 2001): 1–51.

Norich, Anita. "The Family Singer and the Autobiographical Imagination." *Prooftexts* 10, no. 1 (1990): 91–109.

Pat, Yankev. *Shmuesn mit yidishe shrayber*. New York: Aroysg. durkhn mehaber; hoypt-farkoyf, Tsiko un Arbeter-ring bikher-lager, 1954.

————. *Shmuesn mit shrayber in yisroel*. London: Der kval, 1960.

Rontsh, Yitskhok. "Amerike in der memuarn-literatur." In *Amerike in der yidisher literatur*. New York: Rontsh bukh-komitet, 1945.

Rosenfeld, Alvin. "Inventing the Jew: Notes on Jewish Autobiography." *Midstream* 21 (April 1975): 54–67.

Roskies, David G. "A shlisl tsu peretses zikhroynes." *Di goldene keyt* 99 (1979): 132–59.

———. "Unfinished Business: Scholem Aleichem's *From the Fair.*" *Prooftexts* 6 (1986): 65–78.

———. "The Forms of Jewish Autobiography." Unpublished paper, 1987.

———. *A Bridge of Longing: The Lost Art of Yiddish Storytelling.* Cambridge, Mass.: Harvard University Press, 1995.

———. *The Jewish Search for a Usable Past.* Bloomington: Indiana University Press, 1999.

Roth, Henry. *Mercy of a Rude Stream.* New York: St. Martin's Press, 1994.

Roth, Philip. *The Facts: A Novelist's Autobiography.* New York: Farrar, Straus & Giroux, 1988.

———. *Patrimony: A True Story.* New York: Simon & Schuster, 1991.

Rozhanski, Shmuel, ed. *Memuarn, filosofye, forshung.* Musterverk 97. Buenos Aires: YIVO Institute for Jewish Research, 1984.

Ruben, Steven J., ed. *Writing Our Lives: Autobiographies of American Jews, 1890–1990.* Philadelphia: Jewish Publication Society, 1991.

Sadeh, Pinchas. *Life as a Parable.* Trans. Richard Flantz. London: Anthony Blond, 1966.

Schwarz, Leo W., ed. *Memoirs of My People through a Thousand Years.* New York: Farrar & Rinehart, 1963.

———. "The Role of Autobiographical Literature in Jewish Historiography." Unpublished paper in Isaiah Trunk collection, YIVO Institute for Jewish Research.

Seidman, Naomi. *A Marriage Made in Heaven: The Sexual Politics of Hebrew and Yiddish.* Berkeley: University of California Press, 1997.

———. "Elie Wiesel and the Scandal of Jewish Rage." *Jewish Social Studies* 3, no. 1 (Fall 1996): 1–20.

Shandler, Jeffrey, ed. *Awakening Lives: Autobiographies of Jewish Youth in Poland before the Holocaust.* New Haven, Conn.: Yale University Press, 2002.

Shatsky, Jacob. "Yidishe memuarn literatur." *Tsukunft* 30 (August 1925): 483–88.

———. "Yidishe memuarn literatur fun der velt milkhome un der rusisher revolutsye." *Tsukunft* 31 (April and July 1926): 241–43, 428–30.

———. Review of Leo W. Schwarz's *Memoirs of My People.* *YIVO-Bleter* 23 (1944): 389–95.

Sherman, Joseph. "Guilt as Subtext: I. B. Singer's Memoiristic Fictions." *Studies in American Jewish Literature* 13 (1994): 106–23.

Shmeruk, Khone. "Bashevis Singer—In Search of His Autobiography." *Jewish Quarterly* 29, no. 4 (1981–1982).

Singer, Isaac Bashevis. "Tsu der frage vegn dikhtung un politik." *Globus* 3 (September 1932).

———. Review of Dovid Bergelson's *Bam dnieper.* *Globus* 5 (November 1932).

———. "Yankev glatshteyns ven yash iz geforn." *Tsukunft* (March 1939): 182–83.

———. "Problems of Yiddish Prose in America." Trans. Robert Wolf. *Prooftexts* 9, no. 1 (1989): 5–12.

Turniansky, Chava. "Vegn di literatur-mekoyrim in glikl hamels zikhroynes." In *Studies in Jewish Culture in Honor of Chone Shmeruk*. Ed. Bartal Israel, Ezra Mendelsohn, and Chave Turniansky. Jerusalem: Zalman Shazar Center for Jewish History, 1993.

Wengeroff, Pauline. *Rememberings: The World of a Russian-Jewish Woman in the Nineteenth Century*. Trans. Henny Wenkart. Ed. Bernard Cooperman. Potomac: University Press of Maryland, 2000.

Wisse, Ruth R. "Language as Fate: Reflections on Jewish Literature in America." *Studies in Contemporary Jewry* 12 (1996).

———. *The Modern Jewish Canon: A Journey through Language and Culture*. New York: The Free Press, 2000.

Yerushalmi, Y. Zakhor: *Jewish History and Jewish Memory*. Seattle: University of Washington Press, 1982.

Zipperstein, Steve J. *Imagining Russian Jewry: Memory, History, Identity*. Seattle: University of Washington Press, 1999.

General Life-Writing: Works, History and Criticism

Adamic, Louis. *The Native's Return: An American Visits Yugoslavia and Discovers His Old Country*. New York: Harper 1934.

Aries, Philip. *Centuries of Childhood*. Trans. Robert Baldick. New York: Knopf, 1962.

Augustinus, St. The *Confessions of St. Augustine*. Trans. Rex Warner. New York: Penguin, 1963.

Babel, Isaac. *The Complete Works*. Ed. Nathalie Babel. Trans. Peter Constantine. New York: Norton, 2002.

Backscheider, Paula R. *Reflections on Biography*. New York: Oxford University Press, 1999.

Barthes, Roland. *Roland Barthes by Roland Barthes*. Trans. Richard Howard. New York: Hill and Wang, 1977.

Bruss, Elizabeth. *Autobiographical Acts: The Changing Situation of a Literary Genre*. Baltimore, Md.: Johns Hopkins University Press, 1976.

Buckley, Jerome. *The Turning Key: Autobiography and the Subjective Impulse since 1800*. Cambridge, Mass.: Harvard University Press, 1984.

Cafarelli, Annette Wheeler. *Prose in the Age of Poets: Romanticism and Biographical Narrative from Johnson to De Quincey*. Philadelphia: University of Pennsylvania Press, 1990.

Coe, Richard N. *When the Grass Was Taller: Autobiography and the Experience of Childhood*. New Haven, Conn.: Yale University Press, 1984.

Conway, Jill K. *When Memory Speaks: Reflections on Autobiography*. New York: Alfred A. Knopf, 1998.

Davis, Natalie Zemon. *Women on the Margin: Three Seventeenth Century Lives*. Cambridge, Mass.: Harvard University Press, 1995.

De Man, Paul. "Autobiography as De-Facement." *Modern Language Notes* 94 (1979): 919–30.

Eakin, Paul J. *Fictions in Autobiography: Studies in the Art of Self-Invention*. Princeton, N.J.: Princeton University Press, 1985.

———, ed. *American Autobiography: Retrospect and Prospect*. Madison: University of Wisconsin Press, 1991.

———. *Touching the World: Reference in Autobiography*. Princeton, N.J.: Princeton University Press, 1992.

Erikson, Erik H. *Life History and the Historical Moment*. New York: Norton, 1975.

———. "Reflection on Dr. Borg's Life Cycle." In *Aging, Death and the Completion of Being*. Ed. David D. Van Tassel. Philadelphia: University of Pennsylvania Press, 1979.

———. *The Life Cycle Completed*. New York: Norton, 1982.

France, Peter, and William St. Clair, eds. *Mapping Lives: The Uses of Biography*. Oxford: Oxford University Press, 2002.

Franklin, Benjamin. *The Autobiography of Benjamin Franklin*. Knoxville: University of Tennessee Press, 1981.

Freud, Sigmund. *An Autobiographical Study*. Trans. James Strachey. New York: Norton, 1927.

Goethe, Johann Wolfgang von. *Dichtung und Wahrheit. Aus meinem leben*. Ed. Siegfried Scheibe. Berlin: Akademie Verlag, 1970.

Gunn, Janet V. *Autobiography: Towards a Poetics of Experience*. Philadelphia: University of Pennsylvania Press, 1982.

Gusdorf, Georges. "Conditions and Limits of Autobiography." In *Essays Theoretical and Critical*. Ed. James Olney. Princeton, N.J.: Princeton University Press, 1980.

Jelinek, E., ed. *Women's Autobiography: Essays in Criticism*. Bloomington: Indiana University Press, 1980.

Jensen, Johan Fjord. *Livsbuen. Voksenpsykologi og livsaldre*. København: Gyldendal, 1993.

Joyce, James. *A Portrait of the Artist as a Young Man*. New York: Vintage Books, 1992.

Kondrup, Johnny. *Levned og tolkninger. Studier i nordisk selvbiografi*. Odense: Odense universitetsforlag, 1980.

———. *Erindringens udveje. Studier i moderne dansk selvbiografi*. København: Amadeus, 1994.

Lejeune, Philippe. *On Autobiography*. Ed. Paul John Eakin. Minneapolis: University of Minnesota Press, 1989.

———. "Autobiography in the Third Person." *New Literary History* 9 (1977): 27–50.

Lessing, Doris. *Under My Skin: Volume One of My Autobiography to 1949*. London: HarperCollins, 1994.

Misch, Georg. *The History of Autobiography in Antiquity*. 2 vols. Trans. F. W. Dickes. New Haven, Conn.: Greenwood Press, 1973.

Nabokov, Vladimir. *Speak Memory: An Autobiography Revisited*. London: Weidenfeld & Nicolson, 1966.

Olney, James. *Metaphors of Self*. Princeton, N.J.: Princeton University Press, 1972.

———. "Autos*Bios*Graphein: The Study of Autobiographical Literature." *South Atlantic Quarterly* 77 (1978): 113–23.

———. *Autobiography: Essays Theoretical and Critical*. Princeton, N.J.: Princeton University Press, 1980.

———. *Memory and Narrative: The Weave of Life-Writing*. Chicago: University of Chicago Press, 1998.

Pascal, Roy. *Design and Truth in Autobiography*. Cambridge, Mass.: Harvard University Press, 1960.

Pike, Burton. "Time in Autobiography." *Comparative Literature* 28 (1976): 326–42.

Rousseau, Jean-Jacques. *The Confessions*. Trans. J. M. Cohen. New York: Penguin Books, 1953.

Schafer, Roy. *Retelling a Life: Narration and Dialogue in Psychoanalysis*. New York: Basic Books, 1992.

Scholem, Gershom. *From Berlin to Jerusalem: Memoirs of My Youth*. Trans. Harry Zohn. New York: Schocken Books, 1980.

Smith, Sidonie. *A Poetics of Women's Autobiography*. Bloomington: Indiana University Press, 1987.

Spacks, Patricia M. "Stages of Life: Notes on Autobiography and the Life Cycle." *Boston University Journal* 25, no. 2 (1977): 44–60.

Spengeman, William C. *The Forms of Autobiography*. New Haven, Conn.: Yale University Press, 1980.

Watts, Ian. *The Rise of the Novel: Studies in Defoe, Richardson and Fielding*. Berkeley: University of California Press 2001.

Weintraub, Karl. J. *The Value of the Individual: Self and Circumstance in Autobiography*. Chicago: University of Chicago Press, 1978.

Winslow, Donald J. *Life-Writing: A Glossary of Terms in Biography, Autobiography and Related Forms*. Honolulu: University of Hawai'i Press 1995.

Index

Aberbach, David, 30, 33, 197n31

Abramovitsh, Sholem Yankev: Ahad Ha'am and, 31; childhood and, 29–30, 34, 43–45, 197n31; depression of, 29–30; *Fishke der krumer*, 32; forced migration of, 39–40; Hebrew writing of, 29–30, 31, 34; *Dos kleyne mentshele*, 13, 25, 33, 83; *Di kliatshe*, 33, 93; literature as vehicle for enlightenment, 29, 195n16; as Mendele, 26–27, 34, 36; monologues of, 60, 95, 201n42; myth of a Yiddish literary tradition, 195n9; Odessa circle of Jewish writers, 31; pogroms (1881–1882), 15; on Russian gentry autobiography, 38–39, 197n45; serializations in Yiddish press, 13; Sholem Aleichem and, 32, 33, 54, 196n28; *Sketches to My Biography*, 29, 30, 195n16; son's conversion to Christianity and, 29–30; *Di takse*, 30, 32, 168; third-person narrative, 27, 35; *Dos vintshfingerl*, 27, 33, 198n51; Yiddish as literary medium, 30. *See also Shloyme reb khayims*

Adamic, Louis, 100

Agnon, Shmuel Yosef, 164, 209n6

Di agune (Grade), 135, 172

Ahad Ha'am, 31

Aksenfeld, I., 40

Aleichem, Sholem. *See* Sholem Aleichem

Alkvit, B., 101

America: as center of Yiddish literature, 17; English as language of Jewish writing in, 17, 100, 135, 181, 182; estrangement as allegory, 104, 111; isolation of Yiddish writers in, 63, 133–34, 163, 214n23; Jewish identity in, 100, 163; literary autobiography in, 18, 99; reverse migration from, 21, 100–101, 103, 108, 124, 138–39; Yiddish popular theater in, 121. *See also* dislocation; exile; Grade, Chaim; Singer, Isaac Bashevis

"And When the King Went to War" (Konopnicka), 101, 106

Anski, Sh., 155

Antin, Mary, 99, 163

anti-Semitism: Esterke legend and, 122–23, 212; Glatshteyn on, 20, 98, 107; medicine and, 124; in Odessa, 83; pogroms, 15, 37, 39–40, 109, 156, 198n49; Polish-Jewish coexistence, 106–7, 123, 124; socialism and, 105

Arbeter tsaytung, 174

Asch, Sholem, 212n54, 216n59

assimilation. *See* America; anti-Semitism; Jewish identity

autobiography. *See* confession; life-writing; Yiddish life-writing

Aviezer (Gintsburg), 26

Bal-Makhshoves, 11, 12, 16, 54

Baron, Salo W., 13

Barthes, Roland, 160

Bayamim ha-hem. See A bild fun yidishn lebn in der lite